Beyond
The Chinese Connection

Beyond
The Chinese Connection
CONTEMPORARY AFRO-ASIAN CULTURAL PRODUCTION

CRYSTAL S. ANDERSON

University Press of Mississippi / Jackson

www.upress.state.ms.us

The University Press of Mississippi is a member
of the Association of American University Presses.

First printing 2013

∞

Library of Congress Cataloging-in-Publication Data

Anderson, Crystal S.
Beyond the Chinese connection : contemporary
Afro-Asian cultural production / Crystal S. Anderson.
pages cm
Includes bibliographical references and index.
ISBN 978-1-61703-755-9 (cloth : alk. paper) — ISBN 978-1-61703-756-6
(ebook) 1. Asian Americans in literature. 2. Asian Americans in
motion pictures. 3. Asian Americans in popular culture. 4. African
Americans in literature. 5. African Americans in motion pictures.
6. African Americans in popular culture. 7. Asians in mass media.
8. African Americans—Relations with Asian Americans. I. Title.
E184.A75A53 2013
305.895′073—dc23   2012044349

British Library Cataloging-in-Publication Data available

Contents

Acknowledgments

Books do not write themselves, and as an author, I am indebted to a number of individuals and institutions without whose help this volume would remain a vague idea in my head. Many thanks to my mentors in this process who thoughtfully read pieces of the project, especially Thomas Scanlan, Sherrie Tucker, and Gary Okihiro, and scholars whose encouragement as well as insight were invaluable, including Robin Kelly, Bill Mullen, Mark Anthony Neal, Vijay Prashad, Amritjit Singh, and William Tsutsui. Special thanks to Bertram Ashe, who was the first person to encourage me to pursue "that Afro-Asian thing."

I am indebted to Ohio University, University of Kansas, and Elon University for providing the time that a scholar needs to work in the form of sabbaticals and leaves, as well as colleagues at those institutions who shaped the project in innumerable ways. I am particularly indebted to Ronald Richardson and Chris Loken-Kim for organizing three conferences on blacks and Asians at Boston University that were invaluable as this project evolved.

Last but not least, I must thank my family, especially my parents, Mary and Perry Boyd, as well as my siblings, Terry Peace, Jeffrey Boyd, and Perry L. Boyd, whose frequent inquiries about "the book" served as motivation. I also must thank friends who are family, especially Anne Soon Choi, Traci Currie, Mara Holt, Jackie Modeste, and Renee B. Nick, who, in addition to offering emotional support, read parts of the manuscript almost as many times as I did. Of this group, special thanks goes to Eric Ashley Hairston.

Beyond
The Chinese Connection

Introduction

Like many black people growing up in the United States during the 1970s and 1980s, I always seemed to have Asian culture in my house. From kung fu and samurai movies to anime, Asian culture wove itself into the fabric of my cultural imagination. Looking back as an academic, I realize that my early exposure to Chinese and Japanese cultures marked the beginning of my interest in the complex intersections among African American, Asian, and Asian American cultures. A one-size-fits-all approach cannot address such complexity, especially when one factors in the impact of global flows of culture in both directions. Using the legacy of Bruce Lee, *Beyond "The Chinese Connection": Contemporary Afro-Asian Cultural Production* interrogates cross-cultural dynamics in a variety of cultural productions within a transnational context. Such cultural production includes novels such as Frank Chin's *Gunga Din Highway* (1999), Ishmael Reed's *Japanese by Spring* (1992), and Paul Beatty's *White Boy Shuffle* (1996); films such as *Rush Hour 2* (2001), *Unleashed* (2005), and *The Matrix* trilogy (*The Matrix* [1999], *The Matrix Reloaded* [2003], *The Matrix Revolutions* [2003]) and the Japanese anime series *Samurai Champloo* (2004).

This study interrogates cross-cultural dynamics in two major ways. First, it examines Lee's emergence as a cross-cultural hero and global cultural icon through his films and explores how he resonated with the experiences of African American, Asian American, and Hong Kong youth affected by the rise of a global economy in the 1970s. Second, it uses Lee's films, which prefigure themes that reflect cross-cultural negotiations with global culture, to interrogate post-1990 Afro-Asian novels, films, and anime. Recurrent themes of interethnic male friendship, ethnic imperialism, and ethnic conflict reflect cross-cultural negotiations with global culture for post-1990 Afro-Asian cultural production.

Such negotiations reveal a continuum of intercultural interactions. At one end, Afro-Asian cultural production may engage in what I call cultural emulsion, when cultures come together but do not mix, in response to pressures to reinforce ethnic or national boundaries. At the other end, cultural production may engage in cultural translation, where one ethnic culture is used to interpret another ethnic culture, in order

3

to explore situations that range from prioritizing national identifications over ethnic ones to privileging cultural identifications over ethnically based ones. Drawing on theories of cosmopolitanism and hybridity, my study reveals that post-1990 Afro-Asian cultural production that relies on monolithic perceptions of ethnic culture or national identity result in distance between African American and various Asian and Asian American cultures. Novels and visual culture that rely on hybridized perceptions of ethnic culture or national identity result in exchange between African American and various Asian and Asian American cultures.

Lee's films are few, but remain significant because they simultaneously highlight engagements with global culture and hold meaning for various ethnic cultures during the 1970s. Focusing on Lee's legacy in this fashion represents a significant development in Afro-Asian cultural studies. Other approaches focus on the social and political dimensions of Lee's impact. Such approaches view Lee primarily as a metaphor for anti-colonial and anti-capitalist stances. As a result, such investigations focus on instances where African Americans and various Asian and Asian American groups find common political ground. Conversely, my study locates Lee's legacy along a continuum to account for various collaborations and contestations involving African American, Asian, and Asian American cultures. My use of the concepts of cultural emulsion and cultural translation expands beyond more generalized sociological and political modes of inquiry into difference and grapples with the multiple ways that Afro-Asian cultures engage one another.

My examination of Lee's dual legacy begins in chapter 1, "Afro-Asian Cultural Production and the Rise of the Global Culture," which examines one of Lee's most iconic films as a model for interpreting representations of contemporary Afro-Asian cultural interaction. Using Lee's 1972 film *Way of the Dragon*, this chapter establishes Lee as a cross-cultural icon within a transnational context in the 1970s. It shows the successful navigation of a racialized urban landscape shaped by an emerging global economy, thus providing a cross-cultural model that resonated with African Americans. They flocked to Lee's film in metropolitan metroplexes to see a man of color successfully challenge overwhelming odds that mirrored their own situations, contextualized by dwindling economic opportunities and serious rollbacks of civil rights gains of the 1960s. *Way of the Dragon* also resonated with youth emigrating from China to Hong Kong in the 1960s and 1970s who sought to maintain ties to a national identity in a strange and bustling metropolis. The film creates a transnational imaginary that places ethnicity at its center, resonating with Asian Americans during a time when they were being conflated with an Asian enemy of the United States during and after the Vietnam War. Compared to other films of the time, Lee's film represented a cinematic intervention into stereotypical depictions of people of color by featuring an icon with an ethnic consciousness and awareness of a global context.

Lee's legacy functions as a framework to interrogate the contemporary landscape because the post-1990 era experienced similar shifts in globalization. These shifts engendered cultural production that engages a transnational context, just like cultural production in the 1970s. While more than twenty years separated the eras, the 1990s also witnessed the transfer of economic capital out of the United States to overseas locations, resulting in unprecedented proliferation of free trade. Immigration brought global economic shifts into play in the 1990s for Asian Americans, just as global politics did in the 1970s. Along with such economic globalization came a simultaneous rise in transnational culture in the form of transnational corporations that profit from the construction, transmission, and consumption of images as markers of culture. It became even more important what people thought and said about others, for the circulation of these images across national boundaries replaced actual contact. While Afro-Asian cultural production of the post-1990 era echoes the way cross-cultural dynamics are contextualized by global culture in Lee's films, it also contends with lingering reductive dynamics that gloss over the impact of transnational context on cross-cultural dynamics.

In order to read such dynamics within a global context, I utilize the concepts of cultural emulsion and cultural translation in the form of a continuum. At one end, cultural emulsion results in cultural distance that is maintained when ethnic cultures come together. Like oil and vinegar, each culture maintains its respective identity even as it engages the other ethnic culture. Cultural emulsion draws on the concept of hybridity, in which cultures remain intact and distinct. At the other end, cultural translation uses one ethnic culture to interpret another. It is not merely the exchange of cultural matters; it is a cultural interaction contextualized by the traversal of national boundaries. Such traversals not only make one aware of multiple nationalisms, they also bring up the histories of those nationalisms and how they shift over time. As a result, cultural translation relies on the concept of cosmopolitanism, which can be used to highlight the deployment of difference outside the United States. American culture looks different when the context changes to global locales. The result is an awareness of particular histories and unpredictable blendings that go beyond consensus and conflict. With this awareness of multiple factors in play in Afro-Asian cultural interaction, the backdrop of a global culture becomes significant, as many instances of cultural translation involve the appropriation of cultures across national boundaries.

Subsequent chapters explore how Lee's other films generate recurrent themes of interracial male friendship, ethnic imperialism, and ethnic conflict that are adopted and adapted by post-1990 Afro-Asian cultural production in a variety of ways. Overall, the study demonstrates that Afro-Asian cultural production that relies on monolithic perceptions of ethnic culture or national identity results in distance between African American and various Asian and Asian American cultures. Novels and visual culture that rely on hybridized perceptions of ethnic culture or national identity result in exchange between African American and various Asian and Asian American cultures.

Chapter 2, "You Can Stay At My Crib, I Will Show You My 'Hood: Interethnic Male Friendship," uses Lee's 1973 film *Enter the Dragon* to interrogate the theme of interethnic male friendship between African American and Chinese men in Chin's novel, *Gunga Din Highway*, and two films released since 2000, *Rush Hour 2* and *Unleashed*. *Enter the Dragon* engages an Afro-Chinese male friendship within the context of an international martial arts tournament in Hong Kong, providing a transnational backdrop that brings ethnic identity and national association into sharp relief.

Contemporary Afro-Asian cultural production picks up on this theme, sometimes diverging from and sometimes expanding upon it as responses to developments in global culture in the 1990s. Chin's *Gunga Din Highway* initially embraces interracial male friendships. Through actual interethnic friendships and Afro-Asian theatre based on masculinity, the novel recognizes the marginalization shared by African American and Chinese American men in American society. It also reflects the protagonist's reliance on a masculinist perspective that blends 1960s Black Aesthetic and Chinese American masculinity. Ultimately, *Gunga Din Highway* rejects interethnic camaraderie initiated in Lee's *Enter the Dragon* by having the protagonist develop a sense of detachment from African Americans and their culture and outright hostility toward black radical politics. Instead, the novel embraces an individualism derived from Chinese myth that places Asians and Asian Americans within a common diaspora grounded in China, effectively choosing a national mode over an interethnic one. In doing so, the novel ultimately reinforces distance between the cultures. Chin's novel diverges from the Afro-Chinese camaraderie of *Enter the Dragon* by advocating a Chinese identity at odds with African American culture in a global age.

While Chin's *Gunga Din Highway* ultimately rejects the theme of interethnic male camaraderie established by *Enter the Dragon*, films like *Rush Hour 2* and *Unleashed* build on Lee's legacy and Chin's intervention within a global context. Both feature full-fledged friendships between African American and Chinese leads in locales outside the United States. *Rush Hour 2* embraces an interethnic male friendship based on a reductive notion of national identity, which ultimately reinforces distance between the African American and Chinese leads. As a result, their dynamics embody cultural emulsion. The setting of Hong Kong allows the national differences of African American and Chinese protagonists to be distinct, while racial differences fall to the background. *Rush Hour 2* provides a fuller representation of Afro-Chinese male friendship, but ultimately retreats into familiar stereotypes.

By contrast, *Unleashed* suggests an interethnic male camaraderie where African American and Chinese men share experiences based on both national association and ethnic identity, resulting in cultural exchange. Just as in *Enter the Dragon*, a transnational location has a huge impact on the types of interethnic dynamics that occur between these men. In Glasgow, the African American and Chinese protagonists are both outsiders, but share a legacy of subjugation. The film uses elements of a discourse of transatlantic slavery to underscore a modern-day Chinese coolie experience; both rely upon ethnic identity and national association. In *Unleashed*, the interethnic friendship builds on the similarities between the African American and Chinese protagonists.

While *Enter the Dragon* prefigures a theme of Afro-Chinese male friendship, *The Chinese Connection* (1972) (also known as *Fist of Fury*) features an interrogation of Japanese imperialism from a Chinese perspective. Chapter 3, "'Scheming, Treacherous and Out For Revenge': Ethnic Imperialism," uses Lee's *The Chinese Connection* to interrogate the theme of ethnic imperialism involving Japanese and African American cultures in Ishmael Reed's *Japanese by Spring* and the Japanese anime series *Samurai Champloo*. Set against the backdrop of Shanghai in 1908, tensions resulting from Japanese encroachment on Chinese sovereignty and resources drive the action. In this way, *The Chinese Connection* prefigures the theme of ethnic imperialism, with the Japanese as antagonists who represent a colonizing power bent on erasing Chinese culture and imposing Japanese culture upon the citizens.

Contemporary Afro-Asian cultural production reproduces and challenges this ethnic imperialism in post-1990 novels and anime. In *Japanese by Spring*, Reed uses Japanese economic imperialism that ultimately relies on national association and maintains distance between African American and Japanese cultures. Initially, the novel recognizes a largely unfamiliar history of Afro-Japanese solidarity from the early twentieth century. By citing this history, it highlights parallels in American perceptions of African Americans and Japanese as common threats to the social fabric. Ultimately, the novel reinforces the World War II characterization of the Japanese as enemy within a late-twentieth-century context, where economic success underscores an image of the Japanese as a conquering horde. This is residual from the 1980s, where media and film described the Japanese as faceless figures who seek to take over the United States through businesses and corporations. Rather than the promise of transnational cooperation, an American nationalism emerges in the wake of this characterization, which shuts down the potential for further Afro-Japanese cultural exchange in the novel. Cultural distance results from this reliance on national association rather than ethnic culture.

While Reed's novel echoes *The Chinese Connection*'s characterization of ethnic imperialism, *Samurai Champloo* presents a more cosmopolitan and globally engaged Japan, positioning it as an imagined site where multiple cultures meet and participate in exchange. The series uses African American hip-hop to re-envision eighteenth-century Japan as a site where youth have more opportunities for individual expression. The anime series shows how African American hip-hop aesthetics complement Japanese cultural expression. It also uses hip-hop to privilege a contemporary Japanese individualism that counters a more traditional discourse of conformity. Because the series addresses both ethnic and national dynamics, it reinforces the synergy between the two cultures, resulting in cultural exchange.

While Lee's *The Chinese Connection* deals with ethnic imperialism where one culture seeks to overcome another, *The Big Boss* (1971) examines both intra-and inter-ethnic conflict as well as solidarity. Chapter Four, "'Some Things Never Change, and Some Things Do:' Inter-ethnic Conflict and Solidarity," uses *The Big Boss* to examine the theme of ethnic conflict and solidarity within and between ethnic groups in Paul Beatty's novel, *White Boy Shuffle* and *The Matrix* film trilogy. The film pits Chinese immigrants against the Thai criminal underworld. It reveals inter-ethnic conflict between Chinese immigrant workers with less power and henchmen of the Thai criminal underworld who control their fate. Yet, *The Big Boss* also features intra-ethnic solidarity when the Chinese immigrants band together against the Thai henchmen.

The Big Boss prefigures post-1990 representations of conflict involving ethnic groups. The 1992 Los Angeles riots emerge as a metaphor for urban ethnic conflict, as it is routinely described as the climax of tensions between African American and Korean residents. This ethnic conflict metaphor figures prominently in post-1990 cultural production. Just as *The Big Boss* explores inter- and intra-ethnic conflict, Beatty's *The White Boy Shuffle* interrogates both ethnicity and national identity against the backdrop of the 1992 Los Angeles riots. Beatty's novel uses Japanese puppet plays and post-war nihilism to explain contemporary African American despair brought on by the riots. It also employs the Japanese American internment experience to provide unexpected role models for young black men, models that act as bulwarks against the turmoil represented by the riots. Not confined by a unilateral consideration of cross-cultural dynamics, the novel also uses African American culture to envision alternative modes of acculturation for Korean and Japanese immigrants, modes that diverge from the assimilation model implied by the ethnic conflict metaphor that emerges in the wake of the Los Angeles uprisings. By interrogating both ethnicity and national identity, Beatty's novel engages in cultural translation that results in cultural exchange and rejects the reductive notions represented by the ethnic conflict metaphor.

While Beatty's novel echoes the complex examination of dynamics between ethnic groups found in *The Big Boss*, *The Matrix* trilogy adds the element of gender cooperation to the consideration of interethnic conflict. While the narratives surrounding the Los Angeles riots construct tensions between African Americans and Korean immigrants in an urban area, *The Matrix* trilogy presents inter-ethnic and inter-gender cooperation against forces represented as white and male. The trilogy revolves around a revolution that pits blacks and Asians against forces characterized as white, a revolution that resembles the power dynamics of the Los Angeles riots. It employs an ethnic discourse, womanism, to enact Afro Asian cooperation that crosses gender lines against white authority. In doing so, this African American discourse interprets the dynamics between African American and pan-Asian cultures in ways that make gender central. Traditional power relations that grant authority to white males are inverted, as both men and women of color are imbued with authority as they work together to reach a common goal. Featuring multiple Afro Asian pairings between men and women, *The Matrix* trilogy invests transgressive power in the relationship between Asian male characters and African American female characters. The relationships between Asian men and African American women conform to a pattern of mutual respect and duty to the larger cause. The films resolve ethnic conflict by positing the solidarity between Asian men and African American women, again expanding the parameters of *The Big Boss*.

In centralizing cross-cultural dynamics within a global context, *Beyond "The Chinese Connection"* expands how we view the interactions among ethnic cultures. No longer tied to one-dimensional approaches to multiple cultures that intersect across the globe, audiences and readers come away with a more adept ability to read complex intersections of African American, Asian and Asian American cultures.

1

Afro-Asian Cultural Production and the Rise of the Global Culture

In 2003, The Studio Museum of Harlem sponsored the *Black Belt* exhibition and produced a catalog whose front cover featured a bright yellow background surrounding a grainy picture of Jim Kelley, the African American martial artist who appeared in Bruce Lee's 1973 film, *Enter the Dragon* and later starred in *Black Belt Jones* (1974). The back cover featured a representation of a lighted sign with lettering, "Bruce Leroy's Kung-Fu Theater," emblazoned over a graphic rising sun in black and red. Literally bookending the catalog, these visuals testify to a recurrent theme of Afro-Asian cultural interaction in the exhibit. Assistant Curator Christine Kim describes the exhibition as a collection of "over forty works of art by nineteen living American artists whose work has been influenced by African- and Asian-American intersections, specifically in relation to popular culture, martial arts and spirituality from the 1970s."[1]

While the artists examine various interpretations of the Afro-Asian cultural dynamics in a roundtable featured in the exhibition catalog, several works feature the image of Bruce Lee. Patty Chang's *Death of Game* (2000) centers Bruce Lee's image in the frame facing the observer, with his arms in a defensive position in the iconic yellow jumpsuit worn in his final film, *Game of Death* (1978). Chang balances the power of Lee's martial arts by using pastels and undefined lines associated with impressionism to soften his face and body and render the climactic battle between Lee and Kareem Abdul-Jabbar from the film in a more esoteric light. The figures, frozen in the frame, are less noted for the skill of their martial art and more for the impression of movement they give: Jabbar in an aggressive position and Lee in a defensive one. Chang observes that the scene creates a "quizzical awe": "The watercolors bring the video stills back into a tactile, low-tech, nostalgia form."[2]

While Chang's watercolors act as an echo to Lee's performance, David Diao's *Hiding* (2000) uses actual stills from another Lee film, *Enter the Dragon* (1973), in a more ambivalent way. Kim notes that Diao's use of a smiley face over Lee's face in the still "emphasizes masking and minstrelsy. . . . a sort of futility in seeking originality within the social reliance on reproduction for cultural understanding."[3] Lee's image questions notions of authenticity, the ability to know, through the consumption of the image. Rico Gaston takes an overtly political stance in his installation, *The Art of Battle* (2003). Here, he features what appears to be at first glance a celebration of racially-charged violence in the use of an image of a burning cross. This image is interspersed with images from Bruce Lee's film poster for *Game of Death* and rapper LL Cool J. Taken together, these images "speak to Gaston's belief in non-violence as the first form of resistance, based on Bruce Lee's perpetual semi-autobiographical film character's vow of non-violence."[4] Gaston brings up the social relevance that Lee's image can bring by juxtaposing it among references of racial injustice.

The recurrent use of Bruce Lee's image in an exhibition devoted to Afro-Asian cultural dynamics demonstrates its resonance not just with multiple ethnic groups in general, but with African American, Asian American and Asian groups in particular. The catalog features several African American and Asian American artists sharing childhood recollections of the kung fu icon. Kim reminisces: "I too grew up idolizing both Muhammad Ali and Bruce Lee. It is fascinating that these two men of color, icons of masculinity, heroes of the (not so) free world, alive and kicking (ass), had such polyethnic and transcultural transcendence."[5] Deborah Grant links Lee to her urban experience: "Our neighborhood was poor, poor black, poor black and poor white, poor Asian. . . . There was a sort of camaraderie, especially when *Return of the Dragon* came out. . . . Bruce Lee's showdown with world-champion karate artist Chuck Norris in the Roman Colosseum littered with paper, detritus and rubble, witnessed only by a cat, represented possibilities to numerous young blacks and Hispanics in these neighborhoods."[6] These comments and the work produced by the artists reveal a specific cross-cultural appeal among blacks and Asians. The catalogue features Lee in relation to African American figures of masculinity, such as Jabbar in Chang's work and LL Cool J in Gaston's installation. Asian American artists like Diao also see Lee's image as a site to interrogate the formation and perpetuation of images of Asian American men in American culture.

While the exhibition reveals Lee's continued resonance with Afro-Asian cultural dynamics within the United States, other recent examples of popular culture underscore his function as a transnational icon. While Lee attained legions of fans within the United States during his brief career in the 1970s, he did so by starring in several Hong Kong films, which brought him fame throughout Asia. In Hong Kong entertainment, Lee has never lost his influence. Several remakes of Lee's films have been made starring some of Hong Kong's biggest stars, including *The New Fist of Fury* (1976) with Jackie Chan and *Fist of Legend* (1995) with Jet Li. That year also produced the television series *Fist of Fury* starring Donnie Yen. Other films, like *Fearless* (2006), play on Lee's appeal by providing more backstory on significant figures from Lee's films. This film revolves around Huo Yuan Jia, the off-screen teacher of Lee's character Chen Zhen in *Fist of Fury*. Li's performance provides more biography and historical context for this founder of wushu, a form of Chinese martial arts. Echoes of Lee's work can be found in numerous contemporary kung fu films as well. One of the most referenced scenes from *Fist of Fury* involves a sign that reads "Sick Man of Asia," which the rival Japanese judo school presents to the Chinese martial arts school. In *House of Fury* (1995), a fight in an herbal medicine shop breaks the shop's sign so that it reads "Fist of Fury" in Chinese. In *Dragon Tiger Gate* (2006), the villain shows up at the dojo of the heroes and breaks the sign of their school to indicate his disrespect, much like Lee does when he returns the sign to the Japanese judo school in *Fist of Fury*. Lee's appeal is not limited to Hong Kong. Although all the characters in the Korean cartoon *Pucca* are practitioners of martial arts, Abyo, son of the town's police chief, sports Lee's haircut, and has an extraordinary passion for kung fu and *nanuchukus*. He frequently reads *Hi-Ya* magazine, a publication devoted to martial arts. Most eager to show off his fighting skills, he occasionally even dons a yellow jumpsuit for adventures, like the one Lee sports in *Game of Death*.

Given his personal journey, it is no wonder that Lee came to have a lasting impact as a cross-cultural and transnational icon. Born as Lee Jun Fan in San Francisco on November 27, 1940, he soon returned with his family to Hong Kong. There, he became a child actor in Cantonese movies and studied martial arts. He returned to the United States to go to college, but after spending three years as a philosophy major at the University of Washington, he quit to pursue martial arts full-time, teaching others in his own martial arts school. Eventually, Lee pursued a career in entertainment in the United States, landing a high-profile role as Kato, the adept sidekick in *The Green Hornet* (1966–67) television series. However, pickings were slim in a racially-conscious country that was not ready for an Asian male lead in films or television. While Lee experienced moderate success as Kato, he was denied the opportunity to star as the lead in the television series *Kung Fu* (1972). When the series ultimately cast David Carradine as a Eurasian hero, Lee headed back to Hong Kong to try his fortunes. There, he encountered a film industry with global aspirations. David Bordwell notes that by the 1960s, the kung fu film craze allowed the Shaw Brothers studio to penetrate Western box offices with such critically praised films as King Hu's *Come Drink With Me* (1966) and Chang Cheh's *The One-Armed Swordsman* (1966). Lee found a home at Golden Harvest, the Hong Kong studio created by former Shaw Brothers' managers Raymond Chow and Leonard Ho, where he gained fame both in Asian countries and the United States in the four complete films that make up his body of work.

Lee's rejection by the American entertainment industry for reasons related to ethnic stereotypes particularly resonated for Asians and Asian Americans. Hollywood designated Lee as too "Oriental," which had implications for ethnic and national identities. Robert G. Lee notes: "Yellowface exaggerates 'racial' features that have been designated 'Oriental,' such as slanted eyes, overbite, and mustard-yellow skin color." At the same time, "Oriental" alludes to national associations, for Lee represents "the 'common understanding' of the Oriental as racialized alien [that] originates in the realm of popular culture, where struggles over who is or who can become a 'real American' take place."[7] Such issues factored into casting decisions involving Lee in the United States. Vijay Prashad quotes journalist Pierre Berton's opinion about Lee's casting in *The Green Hornet*: "I mean it's always the pigtail and the bouncing around, chop-chop, you know, with the eyes slanted and all that."[8]

Ironically, Lee's appeal also relied on the ethnic and national associations that made majority audiences and power brokers so uncomfortable. When he found success in the Hong Kong film industry, Asian audiences readily identified him using national associations. Kwai-Cheung Lo argues that Lee "was generally viewed as a Chinese hero who used the power and philosophy of kung fu to defeat the Westerner and the Japanese, arousing a Chinese nationalistic fantasy within the Hong Kong audience more strongly than any particular local identification."[9] At the same time, Lee's appeal to African American and Latino audiences in the United States attested to his appeal to ethnic groups, for Bordwell notes, "many a black or Hispanic youth was inspired by Lee's fearless confrontations with white power."[10] Such audiences saw Lee as a marginalized figure that took center stage and addressed oppressive forces.

The *Black Belt* exhibition at the Studio Museum of Harlem and the global appropriations of Lee's image remind us of the ways that Lee resides in the collective cultural consciousness of people of color both within and outside the United States. His films function as a lens through which we can consider Afro-Asian dynamics in a global context, both during the 1970s as well as in the post-1990 era.

Transnational Popular Culture and the Rise of Globalization

Lee's 1972 film *Way of the Dragon* (also known as *Return of the Dragon*) provided a model for engaging cross-cultural dynamics within a global context for African American, Hong Kong, and Asian American youth as they encountered an increasingly global culture in the 1970s. *Way of the Dragon* shows the successful navigation of a racialized urban landscape shaped by an emerging global economy, which resonates with the experiences of many African Americans. The film reveals the maintenance of a distinct national identity within a transnational context, which resonates with Hong Kong youth. For Asian Americans, the film creates a transnational imaginary that places ethnicity at its center. In appealing to these experiences affected by cross-cultural and transnational contexts, the film presents an alternative to stereotypical representations of people of color on a global stage in the popular culture of the time.

Rome, the setting for *Way of the Dragon*, seems an unlikely backdrop for a meditation on cross-cultural dynamics that resonated with African American, Asian Americans, and Asian experiences in the 1970s. It is not the United States or Hong Kong, locations that might make more sense in a film about the experiences of a man of Chinese descent for multi-ethnic audiences. However, Rome's function as a metaphor for Western civilization is key to the film. In the ancient world, Rome represented the heart of the Roman Empire, the cradle of Western civilization, and a cosmopolitan space. Elzbieta Foeller-Pituch characterizes Rome as "the Eternal City, meeting place of paganism and Christianity, where classical ruins and sculptures mingle with the art and architecture of the Renaissance, and the majesty of the Catholic Church, embodied by the Vatican and St. Peter's Basilica, is superimposed on the splendors of the ancient Roman Empire. A classical locus of imperial conquest and aesthetic pleasure, it is a cosmopolis."[11]

Such associations continued into the twentieth century and underscored Rome as a transnational backdrop in *Way of the Dragon*. The film tells the story of Lee's character Tang Lung, a rural Chinese man who travels to Rome at the request of a friend to help his niece, Chen Ching-hua. Chen owns a restaurant and faces extortion from a local gangster, who wants her to sign over her business. He repeatedly sends thugs to terrorize Chen and her workers. With Tang Lung's arrival, the restaurant employees hope that they will retain control of the restaurant. With each defeat of the thugs, the gangster becomes more incensed. After a failed assassination attempt on Tang Lung, he finally sends to America for their best fighter, Colt, portrayed by Chuck Norris. In an iconic fight with Tang Lung, Colt meets defeat with his life against the backdrop of the Roman Colosseum. After taking out the rest of the gang, Tang Lung moves on to help someone else in distress.

The film reveals Tang Lung's successful negotiation of a racialized urban landscape shaped in part by an emerging global economy. The film establishes Rome as a dangerous space. In defending Chen's restaurant, Tang Lung repeatedly encounters the muscle for a criminal organization in Rome. The gangster uses any and all means to secure Chen's restaurant, including destroying her property, assaulting her workers, and attempting to assassinate Tang Lung. While the danger is initially characterized as Asian through the figure of the gangster, it is also significantly character-ized as white in other ways. As he waits for his ride at the airport, Tang Lung encounters a white woman who stares at him unapologetically. She does not speak to him, but the expression on her face suggests that she does not think he belongs there. Jachinson Chan notes, "This short scene encapsulates how racially marked minorities are treated by Europeans/ Americans: Asians are mysterious, exotic, and fascinating as texts to be read and analyzed."[12]

Tang Lung himself senses that the racial differences in Rome's urban environment could result in harm. In a park, Chen lectures Tang Lung about being more friendly and open to others. As she drones on, he catches the eye of a white woman. She walks up to him and invites him back to her apartment, and he obliges. However, when he arrives and she enters into the living room topless, Tang Lung immediately leaves the premises. Given the history of men of color and white women on many continents, he instinctively knows that this situation may not end well for him. Sucheng Chan reminds us that since the nineteenth century, Asian immigrants have been aware of the serious consequences for non-com-pliance with prohibitions against intimate interracial encounters: "Elabo-rate 'scientific' explanations of nonwhite 'inferiority' and the belief that minorities should be kept in their place were widely accepted by the late nineteenth century. . . . To preserve Anglo-Saxon purity, it was argued, no interracial mixing should be allowed. The outbreaks of violence, therefore, served . . . [as] intimidation tactics to drive out Asians."[13] Since Lee had more input into *Way of the Dragon* as director, he may have drawn on his own experiences with white attitudes toward people of Chinese descent. Jachinson Chan points to how Lee's own interracial marriage caused an uproar in his wife's family, who were "against miscegenation" to the extent that "Linda's uncle even quoted parts of the Bible that discouraged inter-racial marriages."[14]

In spite of these brief brushes with danger, Tang Lung consistently avoids the pitfalls of the racialized city. He is able to flee the woman's apartment unscathed. Throughout the film, he routinely defeats the underworld thugs who threaten Chen's restaurant in ways that demonstrate his understanding of power dynamics. Teo points to his confrontation with the lead gangster this way: "His lack of English means that he cannot verbally warn the boss to lay off. He mimes it all out, with clenched fists, body movements, grunts and scowls, overcoming his verbal shortcomings and conveying a clear message to the enemy."[15] Tang Lung's successes in the urban environment reach their height in the battle with Colt, portrayed by Chuck Norris, who is brought from the United States by the gangster to eliminate Tang Lung. A brief explication of this battle shows how martial arts choreography uses a vocabulary of action to establish Lee as the clear winner in this fight, a victory that has racial implications. Ho, one of the gangster's thugs, lures Tang Lung to the Colosseum, a huge, decayed structure that brings to mind brutal and ancient combat. Knowing he is walking into a trap, Tang Lung enters cautiously. As he enters, he hears the disembodied voice of Ho echo throughout the arena, taunting him with statements about his eminent failure. Colt emerges, framed by a stone opening. He exhibits his confidence by giving Tang Lung the Roman sign for disapproval and defeat: the down-turned thumb. After beckoning him to come down, Tang Lung meets Colt, not on the floor of the arena, but in an interior hallway.

Here, they prepare for battle, each showing their potential prowess for the fight. The ensuing action clearly shows Tang Lung to be the superior warrior. While Colt practices punching the air, Tang Lung does a series of stretches, foreshadowing his ability to adapt and change. The referee, a lone kitten, signals the start of the fight with a meow. Initially, Colt has the upper hand. He makes first contact with a kick to Tang Lung's face, which knocks him to the ground. He stands over him with a slight smile and a sense of satisfaction, perhaps thinking that others have grossly overestimated Tang Lung's abilities and sensing a quick victory. Tang Lung quickly disabuses him of that notion. A flip by Colt brings him to the ground, giving him the opportunity to grab his chest hair and blow it away as he gets up. Colt knocks Tang Lung to the ground again, this time signaling that he should remain there by wagging his finger back and forth. Tang Lung sighs, and, without taking his eyes off of Colt, gets up.

Midway through the fight, Tang Lung changes his approach, demonstrating his ability to adapt as a fighter. As the music crescendos, he begins alternating from one foot to another, much like a boxer. This puts him into constant motion, and at an advantage against Colt. Colt appears unfazed. The following slow-motion sequence demonstrates the effectiveness of Tang Lung's new strategy: Colt fails to land a sequence of kicks due to Tang Lung's constant movement. When the film returns to regular speed, Colt finally looks down at Tang Lung's constantly moving feet. Despite this realization, Colt does not change tactics, and continues to lose ground in the fight. Tang Lung lands a series of kicks, and Colt falls to the ground, stunned. Tang Lung blocks several punches and lands his first blows and Colt falls to the ground again. Even when Colt begins to do the boxer bob himself, he cannot adjust and is punched to the ground again. This time, his vision is blurred and when he gets up, he is clearly unsteady. In the next series of blows, Tang Lung lands several punches that break bones in Colt's arm and lower leg. At this point, Tang Lung stops the boxer bob, waiting for Colt's next move. Colt pulls himself up, using the wall for leverage, and finds that he cannot put weight on his leg; he winces in pain and falls to the ground. Tang Lung looks down at his leg and back at Colt and shakes his head to indicate that it would not be a good idea for him to attempt to continue the fight. However, Colt makes one last lunge, which results in Tang Lung putting him in a headlock that results in Colt's broken neck. After the fight is over, Tang Lung shows respect for his fallen opponent by covering his body with his clothes.

Overall, Tang Lung's behavior depicts him as an honorable and superior fighter using a style associated with a different culture. Bordwell notes that his encounter with Colt represents "a clash between a free-limbed, resourceful warrior (Lee) and a master (Chuck Norris) who cannot adjust to mercurial changes in attack."[16] However, we can never forget the setting for this clash. While it takes place in the ancient proving ground of the Colosseum, we can still see the bustle of modern Rome in the background.

The audience is constantly reminded that this battle is part of Tang Lung's encounter with a hostile urban environment. So, when he wins the fight against Colt, he also implicitly triumphs in his encounter with a dangerous urban zone.

Many scholars view *Way of the Dragon* as one of Lee's inferior films because of the way it handles the tensions with Western civilization. Stephen Teo declares it "a flawed and transitional work which must now remain as Lee's testament, a reminder of themes which could have developed further and with more assurance and confidence had he lived."[17] He argues that the comedy takes over the film to the detriment of the dignified image Lee establishes in other films: "The character is really part bumpkin, part martial arts master-philosopher. We see more of the former while the latter is relatively undeveloped. . . . Lee becomes a cult figure more at home in a cartoon comic."[18] Teo assumes that such a portrayal "does not stand him in good stead with Western critics who will be put off by the grossness and crass naivety of his character. . . . This bumpkin easily reminds Westerners of the infamously rude Chinese waiters in Chinese restaurants all over Europe. On top of this negative image is Tang Lung's buffoonery."[19] Measuring Lee's performance in relation to more serious portrayals, Teo's commentary reduces Lee's performance to a binary: "No other figure in Hong Kong cinema has done as much to bring East and West together in a common sharing of culture as Bruce Lee in his short lifetime."[20]

However, Tang Lung's identity can be read multiple ways by different audiences. Teo notes that Lee's characters represent "Chinese nationalism as a way of feeling pride in one's identity."[21] Such associations with Chinese culture inform his use of martial arts. Teo notes that Tang Lung projects an image "as a super fighting specimen of manhood who derives his status from 'traditional' skills. . . . [Audiences] know from versions and legend of Chinese history that this skill is achievable, a result of fitness and rigorous training."[22] Bordwell looks to the incorporation of Lee's fighting style, one informed by an awareness of antagonistic subject positions that exist between Tang Lung and Colt: "For unworthy opponents he shows undisguised contempt, cocking his head, strolling around them, rolling his eyes."[23] When Tang Lung defeats Colt in the climatic fight scene, it represents a clash not just between martial arts adepts, but also between cultures. Bordwell suggests that Tang Lung "turns the West's emblem of combat, the Coliseum, into an arena for Eastern gladiators."[24] Yet, Teo correctly points out that this is a victory not just for the Chinese but for anyone who identifies with their position as subject to the whims of an urban environment, suggesting that "his international appeal does not appear to contradict his forthright insistence on his Chineseness."[25] I carry this premise even further, arguing that Lee addresses both transnational and cross-cultural concerns. Elements of the film resonate differently for different groups.

Tang Lung's encounter with ethnic danger in the city resonates with the urban experiences of African Americans in the late 1960s and early 1970s who migrated to Northern cities. Like Tang Lung, these black migrants emerged from rural towns to face the bustling metropolises in the United States from the 1940s up to the 1970s. Part of the Great Migration, this movement of blacks from the South by the 1970s significantly shifted the numbers of blacks living outside the South, in particular the rural South. Farah Griffin notes that by the late 1960s, "the arrival of Southern blacks is marked by an immediate confrontation with a foreign place and time, with technology and urban capitalism, with the crowd and the stranger."[26] Many black migrants encountered an urban world with which they were completely unfamiliar. Upon arrival, they did not know the geography, and their ignorance of urban ways was apparent.

African American migrants encountered a specifically racialized danger similar to that alluded to by *Way of the Dragon*. According to John Hope Franklin, the material life of African Americans in cities was directly tied to racial discrimination, sometimes accompanied by violence. Despite legislation designed to ensure fairness in housing, "If Negroes attempted to move into neighborhoods where they were not wanted, they often met stern resistance, hostility, and even violence." Incidents involved mobs who "broke windows, mutilated the exterior, and shouted vile epithets."[27] Racial violence reached an all-time high in the late 1960s with race riots, such as the Newark riot in 1967: "With the nation's highest rates of black joblessness, condemned housing, crime, new cases of tuberculosis, and maternal mortality, Newark verged on the brink of a race war between its despairing majority black population and a callous, corrupt, almost all-white city administration. The arrest of a black taxi driver and rumors that he had been beaten to death triggered the bloodbath on July 12."[28]

The racialized dangers of the city for African Americans were also reflected in the popular culture of the time. Songs such as Stevie Wonder's 1973 single, "Living for the City," document one Southern migrant's encounter with the urban. After describing a rough life in Mississippi, the song traces the persona's migration to New York.[29] During a narrative interlude, a naïve migrant is dragged unwittingly into a criminal enterprise, arrested and unfairly sentenced to twenty years, which the song suggests far exceeds the nature of the crime. The song goes on to reveal the persona's post-incarceration life, a life lacking personal and political hope. The persona feels the ill effects of environmental pollution as well as disenfranchisement from the political process. The song poignantly displays how African Americans encountered a city where being black was a liability.

These urban conditions were, in part, caused by the emergence of a global economy in the 1970s that caused economic shifts prompted by the transnational exchange of capital. In addition to a recession and urban unrest in the form of riots in major cities in the 1960s, David Wilson recognizes another economic reality, "structural changes in local, regional and national economies" that could be characterized as "a shift from 'Fordist-Keynesianism' to a 'post-Fordist' regime of accumulation," and manifests in "the closure or out-migration of manufacturing from cities."[30] Prior to the 1970s, cities like Cleveland were bustling hubs of manufacturing that attracted migrants to appealing jobs. However, the impact of foreign competition created a major economic shift:

> Deindustrialization, numerous plant closures, and rising unemployment led to enormous socioeconomic dislocations. . . . Many large multi-establishment firms in mature industries, increasingly mobile in a competitive world economy and hampered by high-cost, unionized labor of the Midwest evacuated the decaying cities of the Great Lakes and Northeastern United States to find greener pastures—and higher profits—in the Sunbelt or overseas.[31]

Tang Lung's successful encounter with such urban dangers resonated with the experiences of urban blacks who faced a similar urban terrain affected by global economic shifts.

Such an emphasis on the cultural resonance of Lee for African Americans diverges from other readings that focus on his political significance. Fred Ho contextualizes Lee within Third World realities that bring together culture and politics: "Obvious political 'readings' can be made of the 'nonwhite' Third World beating, defeating the 'white' First World as a statement of anti-imperialist and nationalist pride. . . . powerful whites are defeated by nonwhites, the same nonwhites who, for the most part, have been disparaged, underestimated, and treated as outcasts in media portrayals and in U.S. society."[32] In this interpretation, African Americans would find parallels between their relationship to the international power structure and Lee's conflict with Colt. Ho argues that films like *Way of the Dragon* "offered for the first time a heroic world not populated by whites but by a Third World people, specifically the Chinese. The Chinese were seen by black and brown youth as a people with a long and glorious history that extended further back than the historical greatness of Europe, including knowledge and ways not monopolized or dominated by white Europeans such as the martial arts."[33] Ho connects African Americans to the emergence of a "Third World consciousness," "an anti-imperialist solidarity among 'peoples of color' that identified with their brothers and sisters in their ancestral homelands who were often fighting for national liberation or independence against the Western powers, but that also represented a solidarity across national, racial, and ethnic lines."[34] Ho does an excellent job delineating the transnational appeal of Lee for African Americans, but does not take into consideration the ways the film resonates with the urban experiences of American blacks at the dawn of the global economy.

While Tang Lung's experiences resonate with an ethnic urban reality in the United States for African Americans, it also speaks to a transnational reality outside of the United States for Asian immigrants, particularly Chinese immigrants to Hong Kong. His status as an immigrant with a distinctly Chinese identity shapes his encounter with Rome. His journey from the airport is told visually by a series of wide shots showing Chen's car traveling to her apartment through busy traffic. The first is a wide shot from above the Piazza del Popolo, which historically is a traveler's first view of Rome. Next they pass the Monument of Vittorio Emanuele, a monument erected to commemorate the first king of a unified Italy. Such well-known Roman landmarks reinforce the foreign nature of Tang Lung's new environment. It is clearly not Chinese.

Against this distinctly Italian backdrop, Tang Lung maintains his rural Chinese identity. When he arrives in bustling Rome, he is wary of strangers, from the staring white woman whom he refuses to speak to at the airport to the banker who tries to exchange his money. Bordwell describes the character as "a good natured bumpkin scorned by the West."[35] Yet, he maintains a distinct Chinese identity in a way that deflects assimilation into Roman society. He does not express any sense of awe when faced with the cradle of Western civilization. Instead, the film reinforces Tang Lung as a rural Chinese immigrant proud of his identity. He arrives in Rome dressed in a black peasant jacket and pants. He only exchanges this outfit for another Chinese traditional gown he wears for Chinese New Year. He also expresses pride in living in the Hong Kong New Territories on a farm, where he practices his martial arts. Even his martial arts is characterized in nationalist terms, repeatedly described as "Chinese boxing" throughout the film. It proves to be superior to karate, knives, handguns, and rifles. Tang Lung does not learn the language and mostly speaks Chinese. This is in contrast to the other Chinese immigrants who have made a home for themselves in Rome by downplaying their Chinese connections. Chen has not been back to Hong Kong for twelve years, and constantly rolls her eyes when Tang Lung waxes poetic about his superior life on the farm. The other Chinese immigrants who work in the restaurant, most of whom have taken English names, initially look down on Tang and his "weak" Chinese boxing. Tang Lung's experiences deal with "the theme of the Chinese immigrant who must face discrimination and oppression: double blows to the pride and dignity of the Chinese character as they put roots in foreign lands."[36]

Like Tang Lung, youth immigrating to Hong Kong from China in the 1960s and 1970s experienced a bustling metropolis. Hong Kong's distance from Communist China and colonial history as port city gave it the ability to develop into a cosmopolitan area. R. H. Hughes notes that since 1949, "The sea routes leading to the Pearl River inlet to South China . . . have become, in the post-war world of shipping, sea routes to Hong Kong itself."[37] Irene Taeuber observes that in the early 1950s, Hong Kong became a destination for Chinese migrants: "Migrants had become net additions to a resident population rather than portions of a fluid labor supply or refugees who would return. Major exits from Hong Kong were closed as Southeast Asian and other countries barred almost all movements of Chinese. Thus the migrant population of Hong Kong was subject to increase by further in-flows from China but not to compensatory outflows, whether to China or elsewhere."[38] Moreover, the linguistic diversity among Hong Kongers reflected the exotic nature of the city: "The areas from which the migrants came were linguistic mosaics, and there were major linguistic diversities among the indigenous or long-established peoples of the New Territories."[39] Compared to China, Hong Kong developed into a more cosmopolitan city, functioning much like the foreign setting that Rome does for Tang Lung. Siu-lun Wong argues: "The inherent eclecticism of their cosmology should enable the Chinese to become adept borrowers of foreign practices. . . . In Hong Kong at least, this incorporative attitude has apparently facilitated a flexible adoption of foreign ways."[40]

As Tang Lung maintains ties to his national identity, so too did youth immigrating to Hong Kong from China in the 1960s and 1970s. Teo suggests they participated in an "abstract nationalism," "an emotional wish among Chinese people living outside China to identify with China and things Chinese, even though they may not have been born there or speak its national language or dialects. They wish to affirm themselves and fulfill their cultural aspirations by identifying with the 'mother culture,' producing a rather abstract and apolitical type of nationalism."[41] This may seem inconsistent, but Lo says such inconsistency is key:

> The China portrayed in Lee's films is a remote space emptied of social
> and political reality, an imaginary and void China with which Hong Kong
> inhabitants and many other diasporic Chinese can associate. The national-
> istic feeling stimulated by Lee's kung fu exercised its influence through this
> alienation and distance. As such, Hong Kong identity or the cultural identity
> of overseas Chinese could be said to have derived from an ambivalent emo-
> tional attachment to a fictional China.[42]

For Hong Kongers in particular, Lee's Chinese pride also provided a form through which they could identify with a generic Chinese nationalism. Kwai-Cheung Lo argues that Lee reflected a distinct lack of localism, and as a result, "gives new symbolic meaning to the community even though— or because—he is not an integral part of it. . . . This hole becomes the new symbolic center for identity construction."[43] Bordwell suggests this kind of Chinese identity revolved around the individuality Lee created in his films. This identity alludes to a Chinese identity in an environment that may not embrace it. It is this type of nationalism that appealed to Hong Kong youth in the 1970s: "Nothing shows Lee's nonconformity—and his address to Hong Kong's 1970s youth culture—more starkly than his insistence that the young warrior must often unseat the older man whom society has venerated."[44]

This particularly had an impact on youth, whose attitudes differed greatly from those of their parents' generation. They desired to be different and distinct from their forbears, partly because they faced more global prospects. Gordon Mathews, Eric Kit-wai Ma, and Tai-lok Lui argue that economic shifts, coupled with civil unrest in the form of riots in 1966 and 1967, contributed to a youth-oriented mindset, which "symbolized the emergence of a new local generation ready to express their hopes and

frustrations, as their immigrant elders had not."[45] Ensuing protests generally emanated from challenging the thinking of the generation before them:

> The pessimism was connected with the downward social mobility expe-
> rienced by a significant proportion of the population. . . . Young people's
> search for identity and their growing social activism in the years imme-
> diately following the riots have to be seen in light of their perception of
> inequalities under colonialism and structural constrains on their personal
> career development. Unlike their parents, these young people were no lon-
> ger content with the status quo. If they were to stay in Hong Kong after the
> 1967 riots, at a point at which many people believed that the colonial regime
> would fall or become submissive to China, the problems in front of them
> had to be dealt with.[46]

Tang Lung speaks to this youth-oriented transnationalism. For immigrating youth, Hong Kong represented a different imaginative space from
mainland China. Hong Kong represented the land of opportunity in sharp
contrast to the repressive shadow cast by China. Matthews et al. note: "[It]
was a sense of Hong Kong as a home based not in any deep loyalty to Hong
Kong as a place, but rather a recognition that Hong Kong offered better
prospects for the attainment of an affluent life than anywhere else."[47] A
burgeoning global economy fueled such affluence:

> Economic restructuring from the 1970s onward diminished the importance
> of manufacturing in Hong Kong, especially as cheaper factories grew in
> China (often with Hong Kong connections). Hong Kong became a ter-
> tiary center where tourism, finance, trade, real estate, and information all
> expanded, including managerial and intermediary roles vis-à-vis China,
> reinforcing to some extent the "Westernness" of the colony.[48]

For Hong Kong youth, Tang Lung represents a way to negotiate this new
space by hearkening back to generalized Chinese identity. Hong Kong's
position as a global city, with a colonial relationship with England as well as
a historical link to China, placed Hong Kong youth in a transnational swirl
of influence. Hong Kong's history as a port city factored into its international growth and development. As early as the 1950s, R. H. Hughes notes:
"The story of Hong Kong is largely a story of its port and the associated
financial and commercial undertakings. Even though it is now becoming

to some extent a manufacturing centre, it is likely that most of its inhabitants will continue to be employed in commerce and distribution; this is the more likely now that the emphasis is on far eastern trade in general rather than on trade with South China."[49] Ironically, one of the industries that reflected Hong Kong's emerging global economy was the film industry, an industry populated by emerging multinational corporations like the Shaw Brothers studio, whose products were popular within and outside East Asia. While African Americans found parallels with Lee's experience with a dangerous city, Hong Kong youth saw his character maintain a general national identity distinct from their parents' generation, within a transnational context.

As his resonance with African American and Hong Kong youth demonstrates, Tang Lung represents a figure that simultaneously speaks to cross-cultural and transnational realities. In addition, Tang Lung resonates with Asian Americans in the 1960s and 1970s, who experienced different cross-cultural dynamics that occurred against a transnational backdrop. His story unfolds in the cosmopolitan city of Rome, but has ramifications for other global locations. In *Everybody Was Kung Fu Fighting*, Vijay Prashad argues that Lee represented the transnational concerns of Asian Americans against the backdrop of the Vietnam War in ways that did not forgo ethnicity. Prashad argues: "To speak out against the Vietnam War, to kick it against international corruption—this is what it took to be a worthy non-white icon. And Bruce did it without guns, with bare feet and fists, dressed in the black outfits associated with the North Vietnamese army. For U.S. radicals, the Vietnamese became a symbol of barefoot resistance."[50] Lee represented a subject of agency for Asian Americans during a time when they were being conflated with an Asian enemy of the United States. William Wei notes that the term gook, initially a "panracial epithet" that since the Korean War "has been used mainly by U.S. soldiers to denigrate Asian people," was expanded to refer to Asian Americans: "'Gookism' made no distinctions between the Vietnamese, Laotians and Cambodians (among other Asians) encountered overseas and Asian Americans at home. . . . As far as European American soldiers were concerned, Asians and Asian Americans not only looked alike but were one and the same."[51] Not only did Asian American activists see the impact of transnational characterizations on themselves, they linked themselves to the liberation struggles of other Asian groups:

> They further drew parallels between their incipient Asian American Movement and the national liberation movements in Asia, particularly in Vietnam

and China. They readily identified with Asians struggling to free themselves from Western colonizers, especially American imperialists. . . . Although scholars have found the "internal colony" paradigm wanting as an analytic tool, Asian American activists at the time appreciated it, for it placed racial conflicts within an international context.[52]

As an icon connected with conflicts associated with Asian liberation struggles, Lee spoke to the way Asian Americans related to their Asian identity on the global stage.

This kind of transnational imaginary, one that contextualizes ethnic associations within transnationalism, differs radically from other representations of people of color in popular culture at the time. Films like those in the James Bond franchise in the 1960s and 1970s reinforce limiting stereotypes of people of color in order to highlight the exploits of the white male hero. *Dr. No* (1962), first in the franchise, sets a racial model followed by other Bond films, which consistently feature villains of color that pale in comparison to Bond. While Bond is a secret agent and womanizer, James Chapman cites Raymond Durgnat's argument that he also literally acts as an agent for British imperialism:

> Bond isn't just an Organization Man, but a rigid jingoist. . . . [In *Dr. No*], Bond glides along the Establishment's Old Boy Net. The British Raj, reduced to its Caribbean enclave, lords it benevolently over jovial and trusting West Indians and faithful coloured police sergeants, the Uncle Toms of Dock Green. . . . Meanwhile out on Crab Key lurks Dr. No, last of the warlords, whose "chigro" minions . . . [representing a] blend of the Yellow Peril and the Mau-Mau, battle it out with his English co-anachronism.[53]

Goldfinger (1964) features one of Bond's most well-known adversaries, the Korean bodyguard Odd Job, portrayed by Harold Sakata. Rather than a fully fleshed out character, Odd Job represents a racialized objectification of evil. He first appears in the film as a disembodied hand that incapacitates Bond, then as an ominous shadow in profile that reveals his iconic hat. When we see Odd Job completely, Goldfinger describes him as an "admirable manservant, but mute," robbing him of any individual agency and motives.[54] His name marks him as a tool to be used by others. He has no voice with which to counter Goldfinger; he serves in all capacities to do his bidding. Odd Job is not just Goldfinger's right-hand man. He represents a particular brand of savagery. While he initially demonstrates the destructive power of his hat on a marble statue at the golf club, he later kills a woman with it. In fact, Simon Winder notes that the film actually softens Odd Job's savage character from the novel, which contains a scene where Odd Job destroys Goldfinger's dining room: "What is unleashed is clearly a demon rather than a human being, doing impossible violence (and Goldfinger rewards him with a cat to eat: no reader searching for racial stereotypes goes unrewarded)."[55] He certainly retains his dehumanized demeanor in the film, and by taking away his voice and replacing it with a characterization based on sinister savagery and brute strength calls to mind racial stereotypes of Asians such as Fu Manchu.

Robert Lee describes Fu Manchu as "the archetype of the sado-masochistic Asian male character in American popular culture narratives of the twentieth century" and "the very definition of the alien, an agent of a distant threat who resides among us."[56] *Goldfinger* ups the ante by placing this racial characterization within a global context. Goldfinger's plot to upset the world's gold market by making the gold in Fort Knox radioactive and unusable is complemented by his use of Communist Chinese agents. He plans to use a Chinese bomb to create economic chaos in the West and allies himself with the Red Chinese agent Ling, which accounts for the unusual number of Asian henchmen populating the film. Goldfinger's alliance with Communist Chinese agents "reflects growing fears in the West over the growth of Chinese military strength."[57] It racializes national threats from without.

Lee's portrayal of Tang Lung represents a stark contrast to such representations on the global stage. Unlike the Asian villains of the Bond franchise, Tang Lung speaks to multiple realities, across cultural lines, within and outside the United States. His figure brings together cross-cultural association within a transnational context in a way that challenges other popular constructions of the day. Because films like *Way of the Dragon* engage in cross-cultural dynamics within a transnational context in the 1970s, they provide a lens through which we can understand post-1990 Afro-Asian cultural production.

Afro-Asian Dynamics and Contemporary Global Culture

Like the films of Bruce Lee, post-1990 Afro-Asian cultural production emphasizes cross-cultural interaction within a transnational context. The 1990s witnessed a more interconnected global economy, providing conduits that allowed for the traversal of cultures across national boundaries.

Such an economy created circumstances that allowed African Americans, Asians, and Asian Americans to explore an imaginary within a global context.

While twenty years separated the 1970s and the 1990s, economic developments and cultural production linked these eras. The initial transfer of economic capital out of the United States to overseas locations in the 1970s developed into an unprecedented proliferation of free trade. Lane Crothers argues that "with the end of the Cold War in 1991, new areas of trade emerged, financial markets were deregulated, and it became possible to invest—and compete for capital—around the world. . . . New institutions rose to exploit the economic opportunities afforded on a worldwide stage: this was the emergence of the transnational corporations."[58] Robin Kelley makes a convincing observation that post-1990 America looked a lot like the dawn of the post–civil rights era for African Americans. Just as the rise of the global economy resulted in economic changes in cities that made employment hard to secure for African American residents in the 1970s, "the decade of hope [the 1990s] was marked by the disappearance of heavy industry, the flight of American corporations to foreign lands and the suburbs, and the displacement of millions of workers across the country." The result was "a greater concentration of wealth while the living conditions of working people deteriorate—textbook laissez-faire capitalism."[59]

Immigration shifts brought global economic shifts into play in the 1990s for Asian Americans, just as did global politics in the 1970s. Lisa Lowe notes that changes in immigration rules in the late 1960s changed the makeup of incoming Asian immigrants into "low-wage, service-sector workers as well as 'proletarianized' white-collar professionals, a group which supplies laborers for services and manufacturing and which furnishes a technically trained labor force that serves as one form of 'variable capital' investment in the U.S. economy."[60] In other words, labor received an influx of foreign workers, bringing a global aspect to the United States economy.

What began as small ethnic enclaves in the 1970s grew into internal sites that negotiated the globalization of the 1990s. David Palumbo-Liu notes that increased immigration translated into successful Chinatown businesses, using an infusion of Asian foreign capital:

> From being a small business community whose owners, workers, and
> customers were largely part of that community, Chinatown became a space
> of speculation and foreign investment, with more and more of its economy

given over to a small economic elite with few ties to the community. The narrative of the ethnic minority achieving the "American Dream" was subverted as the benefits of that dream were diverted into the hands of big real estate and foreign capital.[61]

This shift in foreign economic capital in the 1990s mirrored the rise of the global economy in the 1970s.

Along with such economic globalization came a simultaneous rise in transnational culture. In addition to the rise of transnational corporations that profited from the consumption of such images, the emphasis on the construction and transmission of images as markers of the global culture increased. It became even more important what people thought and said about others, for the circulation of these images across national boundaries replaced actual contact. Crothers puts it this way: "Most people around the world will never visit the United States or meet an American in person. They will never have a Peace Corps volunteer work in their town, village or city. . . . Accordingly, what people are likely to see of America and what they are likely to know about America will be filtered through the lens of American popular culture."[62] Even within the United States, images and representations in popular culture carried much weight. Despite the increased diversity of the country as a result of immigration and expansion of Asian communities, demographics showed the United States becoming even more segregated, decreasing the amount of actual contact these communities had with one another. Representations and images also replaced actual contact for African Americans and Asian Americans within the United States as well.

Yet, these representations in Afro-Asian cultural production depend on knowledge of multiple ethnic cultures both inside and outside the United States. As a result, understanding the global context is key. For example, the impact of African American hip-hop in Japan demonstrated how such shifts in the global economy resulted in the traversal of cultures across national boundaries and their integration into other cultures, producing a more transnational mindset. Moves used in hip-hop, like the spinning windmill where dancers spin on their backs, bear striking resemblance to martial arts moves found in kung fu films of the 1970s. Yet, hip-hop dance also draws heavily from African American expressive traditions. Katrina Hazzard-Donald observes that "competitive one-upmanship" is central to breakdancing, analogous to "the cutting contests of Harlem rent-party musicians" and "the verbal arts of toasting, signifying, burnin' or 'cutting his mouth out,' usually performed with rhyming dexterity, articulation, and style."⁶³ These dance styles also speak to cultural realities, for "hip hop dance permits and encourages a public (and private) male bonding that simultaneously protects the participants from and presents a challenge to the racist society that marginalized them."⁶⁴

According to Ian Condry, hip-hop fans in Japan embraced breakdancing as a space for a similar masculine expression. He cites a member of a Japanese breakdance crew, who "believes that the appeal of breakdancing is its combination of aggressive showmanship without the violence of fighting. It is a dance form where one competes in a very masculine way."⁶⁵ At the same time, African American cultures like hip-hop dance get transformed to reflect the cultures they encounter as they traverse national boundaries. Condry also points out that purveyors of Japanese hip-hop adapt the form to local realities: "In its lyrics there are no guns, no misogyny, and little violence. . . . the language is Japanese, as are the images of schools, television and daily life that pepper the songs."⁶⁶ Such cultural translations suggest that global culture can also provide more complex representations of cultures because, as Condry puts it, while "popular music styles travel on the winds of global capitalism, they ultimately burn or die out on local fuel."⁶⁷

Afro-Asian cultural production of the post-1990 era echoes the way cross-cultural dynamics are contextualized by global culture in Bruce Lee films, but it also contends with lingering reductive dynamics that gloss the impact of transnational context on cross-cultural dynamics. The characterization of the Japanese in the 1990s shows how national association and ethnicity become conflated in reductive stereotypes. Mimi Thi Nguyen and Thuy Linh Nguyen point to an orientalism that emerges in Hollywood films as "the spectre of Japanese financial dominance figured by the electronic billboard of a geisha drinking Coca-Cola" in Ridley Scott's *Blade Runner* (1982).⁶⁸

While *Blade Runner* may abstract the issues of cross-cultural dynamics and transnationalism onto a science fiction futuristic landscape, a film like *Rising Sun* (1993) demonstrates how cross-cultural dynamics pit the Japanese against Americans within a transnational context. Based on the novel by Michael Crichton, the film casts Japanese businessmen as villains in ways reminiscent of Sax Rohmer and Fu Manchu. Robert Lee calls the film "a jeremiad against an economic and cultural threat from Japan": "In the Fu Manchu stories . . . a single Oriental man bent on world domination embodies Asiatic evil. In *Rising Sun*, it is Japanese culture, with its interchangeable minions, that is the villain."[69] Ostensibly about a murder that takes place at the headquarters of a Japanese business in Los Angeles, the film is rife with stereotypes of "sneaky" Japanese who seek to take down the United States through underhanded business practices. Here, transnationalism results not in better cooperation and cultural exchange but in the beginnings of an intercontinental battle. Post-1990 economic shifts had cultural ramifications, including the reinforcement of reductive notions of difference.

Not only does *Rising Sun* pit Americans against Japanese, it also places African Americans in the mix in a way that reinforces reductive Japanese stereotypes and denies the possibility of solidarity based on ethnicity rather than nationality. While Japanese youth were consuming African American hip hop in ways that retain the essence of the form while adapting it to local situations, Japan was being figured as an alien horde hostile to blacks in *Rising Sun*. African American actor Wesley Snipes plays Sean Connery's streetwise sidekick who helps him take down the Japanese businessmen. Robert Lee notes that this casting decision was made "in response to criticism that the novel's polemics trade in racist stereotypes," but such a decision completely overlooks "the obvious stereotype that marries black brawn and hip style with white brains and control."[70] Michael Omi and Howard Winant describe it as a new version of racism that "defends white racial privilege. It employs a particular interpretative schema, a particular logic of racial representation, to justify a hierarchical racial order in which, albeit more imperfectly than in the past, dark skin still correlates with subordination, and subordinate status often, though not always, is still represented in racial terms."[71] Moreover, such a pairing suggests "the crisis of race between white and black can be resolved in a new alliance that restores national unity against the alien."[72] This reinforces yet another set of reductive stereotypes, where the impact of the African American experience in the United States (and blacks' potentially ambivalent position toward their home country) is subsumed by national politics. American blacks conveniently become American. Just like the Bond film franchise, films like *Rising Sun* flatten dynamics between ethnic groups in favor of a cultural discourse that relegates people of color to flunkies.

This kind of convergence of ethnic cultures across national boundaries hearkens back to the dawn of the global age and the emergence of Lee's films. Like the Bond franchise before it, *Rising Sun* does not engage the impact of transnational realities on the interaction among the Japanese businessmen, a black detective, and a white advisor. Because post-1990

Afro-Asian cultural production continues to engage the same kinds of issues that emerge at the dawn on the global age, Lee's films become key to the way they prefigure themes that recur in contemporary Afro-Asian novels and visual culture. However, theoretical tools that can gauge cross-cultural dynamics within a transnational context are crucial to understanding the complex cultural forms that Lee's films and contemporary Afro-Asian cultural production represent.

Interpreting Afro-Asian Cultural Production

Post-1990 Afro-Asian novels, films, and other visual culture reflect a range of cross-cultural responses to global culture. Drawing on theories of hybridity and cosmopolitanism, I identify two poles between which these manifestations fall, poles that I refer to as cultural emulsion and cultural translation. Cultural emulsion describes a scenario where cultures come together but do not mix. Afro-Asian cultural production that features monolithic perceptions of ethnic culture or national identity results in distance between constituent cultures. Cultural translation uses one ethnic culture to interpret another ethnic culture. Novels and films that rely on more hybridized perceptions of ethnic culture or national identity result in exchange between cultures. I use these concepts to expand the exploration of intercultural interaction beyond more generalized modes of inquiry into difference that do not take into consideration how specific ethnic cultures interact.

Many theoretical tools applied to Afro-Asian cultural production either focus on the cross-cultural dynamic or zero in on the transnational. Because contemporary Afro-Asian cultural production includes both, I use critical concepts capable of interrogating both elements. These concepts reveal how contemporary Afro-Asian cultural production combines ethnic and national associations in ways that both challenge and reinforce homogenizing stereotypes within a global context. With cultural emulsion, each maintains its respective identity even as it engages the other ethnic culture. The concept draws from Homi Bhabha's notion of hybridity, which describes a messy rather than a neat process of cultural interaction: "The problem is not of an ontological cast, where differences are effects of some more totalizing, transcendent identity to be found in the past or the future. Hybrid hyphenations emphasize the incommensurable elements—the stubborn chunks—as the basis of cultural identifications."[73]

By allowing for the existence of incomplete cultural interactions, hybridity enacts "the move away from the singularities of 'class' or 'gender' as primary conceptual and organizational categories." The resulting "articulation of cultural differences culminate in 'in-between spaces' that provide the terrain for elaborating strategies of selfhood—singular or communal—that initiate new signs of identity, and innovative sites of collaboration, and contestation, in the act of defining the idea of society itself."[74] Cultural emulsion results in cultural distance when ethnic cultures come together. Hybridity does not mean a seamless coming together of cultures; parts of each remain intact. In this vein, cultural emulsion recognizes that cultures interact but ultimately remain distinct.

The maintenance of cultural distance is particularly salient for the interaction between two ethnic cultures. Rather than assuming that the two cultures form a dominant/subordinate relationship, cultural emulsion allows for the coming together of two ethnic cultures, both of which may be marginalized by larger, more dominant cultures. Bhabha posits difference as central to hybridity, where the "minority position" represents "an encounter with the ambivalent process of splitting."[75] Cultural emulsion allows us to consider more complex interactions when two cultures, both of which result from such splitting, come together. Stuart Hall similarly emphasizes the need to recognize that difference in cultural identity, "critical points of deep and significant *difference* which constitute 'what we really are,' operates according to a "*positioning*, which makes meaning possible" and functions as "an arbitrary and contingent 'ending' which is 'strategic.'"[76] Hall opens up the possibility of considering the ramifications of kinds of difference rather than only one that emerges in clashes between cultures. Similarly, cultural emulsion places cultures in a conversation with one another. The cultural difference that remains between them is important because it reinforces the reality that not all cultural interactions result in some kind of mixture, or the absorption of one culture into another. Ethnic cultures can interact with one another while maintaining their respective distinctiveness.

Moreover, hybridity is particularly salient when looking at representations of ethnic cultures in cultural production, as Bhabha identifies a performative quality to the hybridity that underscores cultural emulsion: "What is at issue is the performative nature of differential identities: the regulation and negotiation of those spaces that are continually, contingently, 'opening out,' remaking the boundaries, exposing the limits of any claim to a singular or autonomous sign of difference—be it class, gender or race."[77] Hybridity can function because it is not based on immutable differences that define ethnic cultures, but on the premise that identities are performed. Such identities, and I argue by extension their ethnic cultures, are flexible enough to engage other ethnic cultures. In the case of cultural emulsion, such flexibility allows ethnic cultures to encounter one another within a transnational space rather than being contained in expected contexts.

In contrast, cultural translation uses one ethnic culture to interpret another ethnic culture. Extending the idea of the "stubborn chunks" of hybridity, Bhabha argues for the benefits of "a space of translation":

> [Translation] acknowledges the historical connectedness between the subject and object of critique so that there can be no simplistic, essentialist opposition between the ideological miscognition and revolutionary truth. . . . If one is aware of this heterogeneous emergence (not origin) of radical critique, then . . . it makes us aware that our political referents and priorities— the people, the community, class struggle, anti-racism, gender difference, the assertion of an anti-imperialist, black or third perspective—are not there in some primordial, naturalist sense.[78]

Rather than maintaining cultural distance, translation wards off simple explanations and recognizes more complex combinations of cultures. It forces us to recognize multiple factors at play in cultural exchange, such as national association, in addition to ethnic and cultural associations and the different results of intercultural interaction. For example, cultural translation can interrogate those instances that prioritize national associations over ethnic ones. Cultural translation often emerges to make intercultural dynamics consider the impact of national association when cultures traverse national boundaries.

With this awareness of multiple factors in play in Afro-Asian cultural interaction, the backdrop of a global culture becomes significant, as many instances of cultural translation involve the appropriation of cultures across national boundaries. Deployment of difference in a context defined by American culture looks different when the context changes to locales outside the United States. "American" becomes one of several national identities in play; identities and cultures get shaped by various historical circumstances. To respond to the impact of transnational context, I employ the concept of cosmopolitanism as articulated by Inderpal Grewal. She stresses that the traversal of cultures globally produces relationships between cultures in what she describes as "transnational connectivities," which "enabled communication across boundaries and borders through articulations and translations of discourses that circulated within networks. . . . Comprising histories of various kinds, of new and old forms of globalization, transnational connectivities enabled multiple nationalisms and identities to coexist as well as to shift from one to the other."[79] Thus, cultural translation is not merely the exchange of cultural matters; it is a cultural interaction contextualized by an awareness of the traversal of national boundaries. Such traversals not only make one aware of multiple nationalisms, but also bring up the histories of those nationalisms and how they shift over time. These result in an awareness of particular histories and unpredictable blendings that go beyond consensus and conflict.

Rather than focusing on the movement of peoples in a diasporic sense, cultural translation follows the cultures, therefore not only interrogating how cultures move across boundaries but also how they are appropriated and used by other cultures. Such interactions, then, are expressed discursively, particularly in the 1990s era, which brought together multiculturalism and cosmopolitanism in discursive practices that "produced specific raced, gendered and sexualized subjects able to negotiate transnational contexts in cosmopolitan terms."[80] The "cosmopolitan knowledges" that emerge from such discursive activity are tied to a consumer culture: "It is only by examining the production and circulation of consumer culture and consumer goods within the context of biopolitics and geopolitics that we can see how identity politics operate at the complex nexus of political economy, national imaginaries, and related mobilizations of desire and individuality within liberal and neoliberal politics."[81] Thus, cultural translation focuses on how ethnic cultures get translated in a context that encourages the exchange of cultural production involving multiple factors.

Cultural emulsion and translation represent two poles between which various collaborations and contestations involving African American, Asian, and Asian American cultures emerge. I use these concepts to expand the consideration of intercultural interaction beyond more generalized modes of inquiry into difference, modes that attempt to grapple with these multiple factors, but fail to focus on the multiple ways that Afro-Asian cultures can engage one another. Vijay Prashad cites the motivation "to work across the lines that divide us in the fabric of the social injustice movements" in his investigation of Afro-Asia. Yet, he falls into the conflict/consensus dyad.[82] He acknowledges that people of African and Asian descent "have long been pitted against each other as the model versus the undesirable."[83] To counter this tendency, Prashad relies on "the polycultural, a provisional concept grounded in an antiracism rather than in diversity. Polyculturalism, unlike multiculturalism, assumes that people live coherent lives that are made up of a host of lineages."[84] He recognizes a discourse of conflict, and addresses it with a discourse of consensus that is grounded in politics: "Polyculturalism is a ferocious engagement with the political world of culture, a painful embrace of the skin and all its contradictions."[85] Yet, Prashad uses broad brushstrokes. He does not get into specific Afro-Asian dynamics, and overlooks how varied they may be. He does not take into consideration the way the histories of individual ethnic groups may impact their interaction with one another.

For example, the dynamics between American blacks and the Japanese is vastly different from the interaction between American blacks and the Chinese. American blacks have a documented history with the Japanese in the United States. During World War II, several Japanese internees left property in the hands of their African American neighbors, while black civil rights organizations like the NAACP debated the justice of internment within a larger civil rights context. In the wake of World War II, black servicemen were stationed in Japan. Conversely, American blacks have a different experience with Chinese immigrants in the United States. Dating back to the Reconstruction era, Chinese immigrants were attracted to the South by plantation owners wanting to supplant blacks as a cheap labor source. On one hand, southern blacks viewed the Chinese as economic competition. At the same time, they saw them subject to the same racial polices that they endured themselves. While polyculturalism recognizes a history of dynamics among a generalized grouping of diverse cultures, it fails to interrogate how particular groups interact with one another in different time periods under different circumstances.

Other approaches to Afro-Asian cultural studies avoid the complexity of such cultural interactions by viewing such dynamics primarily in political terms. Despite his transnational and cross-cultural resonance, Lee's importance has largely been interpreted in political terms in academic studies of Afro-Asia. Prashad notes that Lee's presence "provided young people with the sense that we, like the Vietnamese guerrillas, could be victorious against the virulence of international capitalism."[86] In doing so, Prashad places Lee in a larger context of Afro-Asian political discourse, a discourse that has a long history. In fact, much scholarship on Afro-Asian cultural interaction focuses on its political dimension. Bill Mullen grounds his framework of Afro-Orientalism in a political frame guided by an anti-capitalist theme. Mullen argues that Afro-Orientalism "accords primacy to an attack on Western Orientalism(s) as byproducts of Western capitalism. It foregrounds the relationship between peoples of African and Asian descent as a dialectical synecdoche of Western capitalist modernity."[87] Orientalism appropriates a revision of the Marxist view of capitalism that has ramifications for people of African and Asian descent: "Asia, in Marx and Engel's enlightened view, was the unhappy inheritor of absence. Just as Hegel, their dialectical master, declared that Africa had 'no history,' so Marx and Engels perceived that only when European capitalism had created the conditions for proletarian revolution in Asia could it enter the evolutionary narrative of history."[88] Given that African and Asian peoples provide resources for capitalism with their bodies, Afro-Orientalism appropriates Marxism's critique, where "colored people themselves particularly peoples of African and Asian descent, would often come to supplant the international (i.e. European) working class," thereby centralizing "not identity or hybridity movements . . . but a movement to reimaging black and Asian people as hand-holding grave diggers of Western capitalist modernity."[89] Mullen use this politically inflected lens to read cultural production ranging from Richard Wright's poetry to Fred Ho's music. In doing so, he overlooks other meanings of the cultural production, certainly impacted by socioeconomic factors, but not completely determined by them. While such cultural production engages the political to varying degrees, it is not the only dimension to the work.

Focusing on the political aspects of Afro-Asian interaction also results in a myopic view of periodization. The recent anthology, *Afro-Asian Encounters: Culture, History, Politics*, edited by Heike–Raphael Hernandez and Shannon Steen, establishes 1955, the year of the Bandung conference, as the starting point for the political alignment and struggles of African and Asian peoples. Organizing the essays around the theme of "Bandung's sense of struggle," the collection seeks to "capture Bandung's attempt to forge cross-racial political alliances, analyze the tensions that can make those coalitions difficult, and trace the way those alliances are co-opted with monotonous regularity within mainstream cultural venues."[90] Using Bandung as a point of origin, the collection establishes a continuous Afro-Asian era from the 1950s to the present and ignores subsequent historical developments, such as the rise of a global economy in the 1970s.

By focusing on political rather than cultural paradigms, these approaches overlook various models of interculturality, ways that cultures interact and are appropriated and adapted in ways that traverse cultural and national boundaries. Considering a cultural approach to Lee as a significant icon in Afro-Asian studies introduces the post-1965 era as a significant period in the trajectory of Afro-Asian cultural relations, one in which the rise of a global economy has significant impact on the meaning of Afro-Asian cultural production of the 1970s. Distinguishing a post-1990 era also highlights changes in the engagement of global culture with cultural production. As a result, I view Lee's films as generators of themes that recur in several Afro-Asian novels, films, and other visual culture. Some subsequent Afro-Asian cultural production extends these themes in ways that reflect the post-1990 era, while other examples explicitly reject them. Afro-Asian cultural production that relies on monolithic perceptions of ethnic cultures or national identity results in distance between African American and various Asian and Asian American cultures. Novels and films that rely on hybridized perceptions of ethnic culture or national identity tend to emphasize cultural exchange between African American and various Asian and Asian American cultures. As the subsequent chapters will show, cross-cultural interactions read with the transnational in view enhances our understanding of complex cultural production.

"You Can Stay at My Crib, I Will Show You My 'Hood"

Interethnic Male Friendship

Bruce Lee's 1973 film *Enter the Dragon* reflects a cross-cultural dynamic against the backdrop of the transnational, even in its conception and production. Michael Allin, the film's screenwriter, remembers that he was conscious of "creating an international movie that would present Bruce properly," especially after the lack of enthusiasm in the United States over his potential role as leading man in the television series *Kung Fu*.[1] Having secured a degree of stardom in Asia with cinematic successes such as *The Big Boss* and *Fist of Fury*, Lee agreed to star in *Enter the Dragon* to cement his success on a global stage. The film represents a co-production between American producers Paul Heller and Fred Weintraub of Warner Brothers and Raymond Chow of Hong Kong–based studio Golden Harvest. American filmmaker Robert Clouse directed the movie, which was shot primarily in Hong Kong. David Desser reminds us that this collaboration also inaugurated links between Hong Kong martial arts films and blaxploitation movies during the mid-1970s. Seeking to cash in on the popularity of both, Warner Brothers double-billed martial arts films with blaxploitation films in locations frequented by urban black youth. After *Enter the Dragon*, Clouse went on to direct *Black Belt Jones* (1974). Martial arts themes begin to emerge in other blaxploitation films like *Cleopatra Jones* (1973). The sequel, *Cleopatra Jones and the Casino of Gold* (1975), sees Cleopatra to go to Hong Kong.

The plot of *Enter the Dragon* also reflects cross-cultural interaction positioned within the global. Williams, portrayed by African American actor Jim Kelly, Lee (Lee's character is also named Lee), and Roper, a white American martial artist portrayed by John Saxon, all attend an underground martial arts tournament held by Han, a rogue Shaolin temple monk. Prior to the tournament, Braithwaite, a British agent, recruits Lee to infiltrate the tournament to gather evidence for the prosecution of Han for his illegal opium trade and traffic in women. The Shaolin monks also want Lee to confront Han in order to restore Shaolin's honor. However, Lee ultimately accepts the assignment in order to avenge the death of his sister caused by one of Han's henchmen. While bouts take place during the day at the tournament, Lee snoops around at night to learn more about Han's operation. One of his late-night reconnaissance missions results in Lee's discovery as a spy among the martial artists. Williams's refusal to expose Lee leads to his death, while Roper becomes the target of recruitment for Han's illegal operations. Han's exposure of Lee as the spy sparks a free-for-all fight. Lee and Han clash in the spectacular climax of the film, a fight in a mirrored room, where Lee defeats Han.

The transnational setting of Han's island functions as a transnational backdrop for the Afro-Chinese dynamics of the film. Before beginning his mission, Braithwaite shows Lee a map featuring Hong Kong, clearly under the administration of Great Britain, as well as other unidentified islands. Han's island lacks a national designation as a result of a dispute over ownership between the British and Chinese governments. Neither of the countries owns the island, which places it in national limbo. It represents a space where only Han's individual will holds sway. It is this reality that prompts Braithwaite to send Lee in as an undercover agent, for neither the British nor the Chinese seem to have jurisdiction. Han's island also brings together an international array of participants, underscoring it as a transnational space. Participants hail from the United States, China, and Australia. More than merely the site of a kung fu tournament, Han's island functions as a hub in the global economy. His organization represents an illegal profit-making venture with international connections. Braithwaite explains that Han attracts girls from all over the world, hooks them on drugs, and sells them on an international black market. Han tells Roper, "We are investing in corruption. . . . The business of corruption is like any other."[2] Han also seeks to expand his enterprise, inviting Roper to represent his organization in the United States.

This transnational enterprise brings the Afro-Chinese male friendship in sharp relief. *Enter the Dragon* is the one film completed during Lee's lifetime that features a major African American character, Williams. The bond between Lee and Williams is partially based on their shared marginalization from the global capitalist culture in which Han participates. Jachinson Chan observes, "Lee is not a product of a Western capitalist social system" but associated with "the Shaolin Temple, a monastery that rejects external social orders." Similarly, Williams reflects "the desire to escape America's capitalistic and racist social structure."[3] Lee and Williams's brief friendship brings together ethnic identity and national association within the transnational context of the island.

Williams appears as a raced body with international aspirations. His larger-than-life Afro, use of black slang, and familiarity with black culture and African American economic realities in the 1970s mark his blackness. Yet, he also has a transnational mindset. This comes in part from his participation in black radical politics. Prior to his trip to Hong Kong, Williams stops by his local American dojo to bid farewell to its black managers, who also sport Afros. The art on the walls of the dojo and flags featuring the African color palette of red, green, and black combine with Asian iconography, including snakes and Chinese characters. His radical attitude fits right in with the black militant images that cover the walls of the dojo. These scenes establish Williams as the kind of African American willing to participate in Asian martial arts, and highlight the links between African American self-determination and decolonization movements underfoot in African countries.

Accepting Han's invitation also allows Williams to escape American racial realities in the 1970s by leaving the country. His departure is punctuated by a racial incident involving two white cops. During his detention by the cops on the road at night, one cop marvels that "this jig's got a passport" and the other queries, "Where you going, jig?"[4] He responds, not by turning the other cheek, but by meeting their police brutality with brutality. He retaliates, renders the cops unconscious, and steals the police car. This scene recalls countless clashes between African Americans and white cops in the 1970s, and demonstrates how his motives to leave the country are based on American racial realities. Williams's racial identity continues to be underscored with a transnational perspective even after he leaves the United States. A frequent traveler who knows Roper from a previous martial arts tournament in Vietnam, Williams notes the similar impact of poverty in both the United States and Hong Kong when he notices the Chinese poor in the harbor who live on boats in less than stellar conditions after his arrival in Hong Kong. This prompts him to observe, "They don't live too big over there. Ghettos are the same all over the world. They stink."[5]

While Williams suggests an ethnic identity, national association defines Lee in the same transnational location. His successful infiltration of Han's island demonstrates Chinese prowess in relation to British ineffectualness. Braithwaite's request for Lee's services is not really a request, but an expectation that Lee will cooperate based on the colonial relationship between Hong Kong and Britain. He explains to Lee, "We'd very much like you to attend this tournament." When Lee tries to get him to elaborate on the "we," Braithwaite fails to reply and leaves. Later, Braithwaite hints that he represents certain governmental interests when he explains his own inability to deal with Han: "We aren't an agency of enforcement. We function as gatherers of information, evidence, upon which interested governments can act."[6] Such exchanges allude to the colonial relationship between Britain and Hong Kong, with Britain using Hong Kong as a colony as circumstances arise. The end of the film under- scores such Western ineffectualness, when the military arrives after Lee, the Chinese agent, defeats Han.

While national identity defines Lee, the theme of Afro-Chinese male friendship links Lee and Williams in a global setting. The friendship is based in part on their identities as strong men of color who defy white authority. Lee embodies a specific Chinese masculinity geared toward challenging the stereotype of Asian men as weak. Screenwriter Allin insisted that the film "needed Lee to be the coolest of the three."[7] Chan argues that Lee's masculinity conforms to a "hegemonic masculinity": "Lee's characters are strong, physically superior to other male characters, regardless of race and he is a hero who dominates his opponents by using excessive violence. This model of masculinity counters, in a dramatic way, the cultural inheritance of previous images of the Chinese male, such as Dr. Fu Manchu and Charlie Chan."[8] The film also defines Williams in ways that highlight a particular brand of masculinity. His defiant attitude and personal style may be read as a performance that Richard Major and Janet Mancini Billson identify as the "cool pose," which they define as "a ritual- ized form of masculinity that entails behaviors, scripts, physical posturing, impression management, and carefully crafted performances that deliver a single, critical message: pride, strength, and control."[9] Key to such a per- formance is a style that "is highly individualized and is expressed through variations in walk, talk, choice of clothes (threads) and natural or pro- cessed hair ('do')."[10] It is precisely Williams's Afro, black leather jacket, rev- olutionary black turtleneck, and defiant speech that mark him as a defiant black man in a transnational space.

Such characterizations operate as double-edged swords, for they flirt with common stereotypes that seek to undermine the strength of the char- acters. A hypermasculinized image of Lee can also serve to dehumanize him to a certain extent. Allin envisions Lee's character as a "force of nature" rather than a fully realized character.[11] William Wei describes Bruce Lee as a "one-man wave of death and destruction" that develops into a stereotype that robs Asian Americans of their humanity: "[His] exaggerated attributes are narrowly focused and are achieved at the expense of other qualities," rendering him inhuman.[12] Williams also exhibits behaviors based on assumptions about the sexual prowess of black men that mark him as a black male stereotype. When offered the "companionship" of a woman by Han, Williams chooses four. This plays on the stereotype of the unbridled sexual appetite of black men, which can be traced back to the antebellum era, and reflects the ways that dominant society justifies its subjugation of black men as it protects white womanhood. This sexual prowess also becomes a mark of pride in blaxploitation films of the 1970s as a misguided way to retain a mode of black masculinity with agency. As a result, women, like the Asian women in this scene, often function as sexually available objects.

Despite the forays into these stereotypical images, Williams and Lee make important gestures toward an Afro-Chinese male friendship. They share certain sentiments related to justice, equality, and fairness. Williams flees to the tournament to escape two racist American cops. Lee takes the assignment to avenge the death of his sister at the hands of a white male. Williams clearly sees Lee roaming the grounds of Han's estate at night, but refuses to reveal his secret, a decision that costs him his life. The film subtly puts Williams and Lee together in ways that imply a bond. Chan suggests that "the homosocial community is celebrated."[13] This dynamic opposes the traditional interracial buddy paradigm. Melvin Donalson argues that "men of color in Hollywood features . . . have been juxtaposed with white male characters to accentuate and enhance the latter; in short, the characters of color have been rendered to make white males appear more courageous, tolerant, heroic, intelligent, etc. in the narrative."[14] Donalson suggests that an unequal power dynamic emerges when men of color are paired with white men in film. Yet, this is downplayed in the camaraderie between Williams and Lee.

Ultimately, *Enter the Dragon* introduces a discourse of interethnic male friendship within the context of a global culture. Hong Kong provides an international backdrop against which ethnic identity and national association are brought into sharp relief. Contemporary Afro-Asian cultural production picks up on this theme, sometimes diverging from it, and sometimes expanding upon it in response to developments in global culture in the 1990s. Frank Chin's *Gunga Din Highway* (1999) rejects interethnic male friendships built on Afro-Chinese dynamics in favor of an individualism based on Chinese culture, thereby reinforcing distance between African American and Chinese American cultures. Films move cross-cultural dynamics outside the United States. *Rush Hour 2* (2001) embraces interethnic male friendship, but only on the basis of a reductive notion of national identity, which reinforces distance between the African American and Chinese leads. *Unleashed* (2005) uses an interethnic male friendship based on cultural sympathies to counteract psychological damage with national overtones, which results in cultural exchange.

Chinatown Black Tigers: Black Cultural Ambivalence in Frank Chin's *Gunga Din Highway*

Ulysses, the protagonist in Frank Chin's *Gunga Din Highway*, waxes poetic about his skepticism about Afro-Asian politics throughout the novel. Invoking black radical leaders like Huey Newton, co-founder and leader of the Black Panthers, he characterizes the mission of the Chinatown Black Tigers, a fictitious Chinese American radical political group, as misguided and exploitative. While the Chinatown Black Tigers couch their activities using the language of self-determination, Ulysses believes its members actually seek a measure of fame by engaging in the radical rhetoric of the day. He implies that the language of black radicalism remains foreign to the lives of Chinese Americans in Chinatown and suggests that societal change is the furthest thing from his mind. In criticizing Asian American politics, Ulysses also implicitly critiques the black radical tradition that partially informs it, indicating a distance between African American and Chinese American cultures and distorting the legacy of Afro-Asian politics.

Instead of using such radical groups as a jumping-off point to explore Afro-Chinese cultural interactions, *Gunga Din Highway* rejects interethnic camaraderie initiated in Lee's *Enter the Dragon* in favor of a Chinese individualism that reinforces the distance between African American and Chinese American cultures. Using interracial male friendships as a lens, the novel initially recognizes the shared marginalization of African American and Chinese American men by American society. It also reflects Ulysses's reliance on 1960s Black Aesthetic in his attitude and writing about Chinese Americans. However, the novel ultimately reinforces distance between the cultures by rejecting interethnic camaraderie. Ulysses develops a sense of detachment toward African Americans and their culture, and outright hostility toward black radical politics. Instead, he embraces an individualism derived from Chinese myth that places Asians and Asian Americans within a common diaspora grounded in China. Chin's novel diverges from the Afro-Chinese camaraderie of *Enter the Dragon* by advocating a Chinese identity at odds with African American culture in a global age.

Gunga Din Highway reflects a complex view of the dynamics between Chinese American and African American cultures. The novel is a coming-of-age story expressed in a nonlinear narrative related through recollections, stories, and references to fiction, newspaper articles, and films. It begins not with its chief protagonist, Ulysses S. Kwan, but with his father, Longman Kwan Sr., a Chinese American actor who gains fame playing stock Asian characters in war movies and portraying one of Charlie Chan's sons. Longman goes to Hawaii to convince Anlauf Lorraine, the last white man to portray Charlie Chan in cinema, to make an appearance at a music festival. Their encounter reveals Longman's desires to assimilate into American culture by being tapped as the first Chinese American to portray the Chinese detective.

The novel then abruptly switches to Ulysses's recollection of his early childhood. A retired white vaudeville couple raises him until his Chinese family retrieves him at around age six. When Ulysses enrolls in Chinese after-school as a youngster, he meets Benedict Han and Diego Chang, two Chinese American boys who become his lifelong friends. Born in China to opera star parents, Ben Han aspires to assimilate into American culture and leave his Chinese heritage behind. Diego Chang lives in a black neighborhood and identifies strongly with black culture as a youth, and as he matures, chooses to remain on the margins of society.

The novel alternately traces the adventures of these three friends. Ulysses's path is the most convoluted. Caught between pressures to emulate Longman Jr., his older brother who serves in the military, and neglect from his father, Ulysses apprentices himself to an eccentric Chinese poet. While participating in extracurricular activities in high school, he befriends Jason Peach, a young black man who seeks to take advantage of the status quo whenever he can. From then on, Ulysses explores various avenues: attending Berkeley, working on the railroad, reporting on a demonstration in a black neighborhood, participating in the Chinese American radical organizations, writing plays. When he becomes disillusioned with the state of Chinese American drama, he gives up on cultural reform and becomes a writer of Hollywood zombie movies.

Ulysses's two childhood friends follow divergent paths. Ben Han, desperate to shed any connection to Chinese culture, becomes a writer of politically correct plays and a conservative Asian American professor. He marries Pandora Toy, an Asian American feminist who promotes assimilation for Asian American men in her columns and novels. Diego Chang becomes a musician and continues to live on the fringes of society in communes in Hawaii and on the mainland. The paths of all characters converge at several points throughout the novel, but it is the death of Ulysses's father that sparks the final reunion of the childhood friends. With Ulysses completely alienated from his family, Ben Han estranged from his wife, and Diego divorced and retired from the stage, the novel ends with these childhood friends barreling toward the hospital in Ulysses's mother's car, along with Diego's pregnant housekeeper.

Rather than simply pitting one ethnic group against another, *Gunga Din Highway* initially reflects how African American and Chinese American men respond similarly to dominant white American society. Ulysses remarks that he and Jason Peach, his African American friend, share "the same comic books, the same movies," which reflects the shared sense of marginalization of African American and Chinese American cultures from American society. Ulysses gleans strategies from African American radical organizations and activist theater, both of which use ethnic masculinity to respond to such marginalization.

Ulysses provides a unique perspective through which the reader perceives Afro-Chinese cultural interactions. Because such interactions take a variety of forms, he develops an imagination capable of envisioning multiple perspectives. A performer able to interact with multiple cultural spheres, Ulysses transforms his surrounding reality as a result of having spent his formative years with actors. Initially adopted by "the childless retired vaudeville acrobat and his retired silent screen bit player wife," he returns to his Chinese family, which also has a history of performance.[15] Before the family's Hollywood aspirations, they perform in Chinese theater: "Ma says Pa used to play Lowe Bay, Kwang Kung's blood brother, in Cantonese opera, because he was so handsome."[16] Such aspirations continue in California. During one of his childhood recollections, Ulysses remembers a banquet where Longman introduces Ulysses's elder brother: "Pa calls his first son 'Hollywood Junior' and dreams out loud over the food of my first Chinese banquet about the Kwan family becoming the 'Chinese Barrymores' of Hollywood."[17] Under these circumstances, Ulysses comes to see himself as a performer capable of assuming multiple roles. He admits, "Wherever I am, I don't *live* the part. I'm on location, *playing* the part."[18] He possesses a malleable personality that allows him to traverse African American, Chinese, and Chinese American cultures.

Ulysses's dramatic background also informs his imagination. Chin uses a narrative strategy whereby Ulysses's daydreams present alternative possibilities for the reality he knows. Ulysses describes such narrative excursions as "The Movie About Me" and often inserts his persona in arenas devoid of Chinese Americans. For example, he creates a presence for himself in his fantasies about the railroad:

> My job isn't much more than writing or rubber-stamping railroad initials on baggage tags, handing the stubs over to the passengers, tagging the bags, loading the bags on the carts, wheeling the carts out to the baggage car, and loading the bags off the carts onto the train. . . . some nights I ride the Zephyr though the washer and am on my way to Chicago in The Movie About Me. In the movie about my years as a fearless Saturday baggage man, a passenger comes into the baggage room expecting a counter and a scale, but sees, instead, me—in a smoking jacket, puffing on a pipe, seated in an overstuffed chair, with my feet wallowing in the fur of a polar bear rug. My fingers laze over a large globe. I offer the passenger a sherry, a cigar and a seat. We talk of baggage through the ages, and the greater meaning of the railroads they will ride out of town.[19]

In Ulysses's fantasy, he goes from lowly baggage handler to sophisticated connoisseur of the railway. He exchanges the baggage room for an environment of opulence and leisure. He calmly sits and chats with the passenger, and shares his wisdom about the trains and their lines. It is significant that Ulysses places himself in this position of luxury and authority, given the history of Asian Americans and the railroad. Ronald Takaki notes that Chinese immigrants contributed their labor to the endeavor in the 1860s: "Not only did they perform the physical labor required to clear trees and lay tracks; they also provided important technical labor by operating power drills and handling explosives for boring tunnels."[20] However, their contribution to such work did not create a legacy of legend, like John Henry, who shows that human drive can beat a steam engine at the expense of his life. Despite their crucial contribution to the completion of the railroads, Sucheng Chan notes that many Chinese immigrants were dismissed, and "were not even allowed to ride the trains free of charge back to California."[21] While labor was valued, Chinese labor was not:

"Chinese labor was not Free Labor in the republican sense, because it had been decided that the Chinese were not capable of transcending their status as wage labor to become independent producers (notwithstanding the widespread existence of Chinese laundry operators, shopkeepers, masons, carpenters, tailors, etc), and therefore participants in civic life."[22] Rising anti-Chinese sentiment based on this belief obscured their heroic work on the railroad, and reinforced an image of Chinese railroad workers as "coolie labor." Ulysses reimagines the Chinese American relationship with the railway in his fantasy.

This active imagination contributes to the way Ulysses goes through his life. He recognizes that the world often does not have a place for him. He always feels out of place, but his imagination allows him to construct bonds with unlikely allies. The friendship between Ulysses and Jason Peach, his African American friend, echoes the theme of interracial friendship initiated by Lee's *Enter the Dragon* by acknowledging the shared marginalization of African American and Chinese men. Both Ulysses and Jason resort to trickster strategies of subversion at a youth conference in response to their shared marginalization. When they first meet each other, they immediately establish a bond: "The instant Jason locks eyes with me and pushes and I push back, we smile and see now, if we didn't see before, that we are both here for mischief. We both know at heart that we don't belong here. Being here is part of using everything we learned to make high school work for us. The look and the smile are as good as a blood oath."[23] This unspoken camaraderie acts as proof of their joint decision to subvert the conference and use it to their advantage, a mischievous side that they both use in response to their common alienation among whites. They find solace in each other's common experiences: "We talk of how we make high school work for us. He's been playing blues and old-timey music on the guitar and singing at Pepe's Pizza up the street two nights a week for twenty-five dollars. I've been selling my paintings and pen-and-ink drawings to a Spanish teacher and a social studies teacher after school for five dollars each. Other stuff. Yeah. The same comic books. The same movies."[24] They both turn to creative expression as a response to marginalization and as a means for profit.

Their bond is based not only on a shared subject position, but also on their shared gender: "Now I know we have seen the same comic books and movies as boys, and we are allies defending the essentials of civilization: *King Kong, The Thing, Shane*."[25] *King Kong* is a classic film where men demonstrate their prowess against a primitive, oversized ape. *The Thing* pits male explorers against an unknown entity from outer space. *Shane* features a classic western male hero. Ulysses and Jason bond over entertainment that appeal to young males: heroic narratives with a traditional sense of masculinity that revolve around a male protagonist. Their friendship provides the ground for an interracial male camaraderie that also works to ward off the alienation they face.

While Ulysses and Jason are drawn to such traditional narratives of heroic masculinity, they are also marginalized from them. Traditional masculinity is linked to the hegemony of whiteness, and constructed in ways that exclude men of color. Ruth Frankenberg uses a kind of shorthand that encapsulates common tropes that involve white men and men of color: "White Man is strong, dominant, arbiter of truth, and self-designated protector of white womankind, defender of the nation/territory (and here defense of the nation and its honor often also entails defending White Woman's racial chastity." While such a trope is not designed to describe all white men, Frankenberg notes that it reveals the interplay of race and masculinity, for white privilege "is precisely the leverage white men have sought to use in their efforts to manufacture a sense of inclusion (to varying degrees illusory) in the dominant, to claim and seek to enforce ownership of nation or neighborhood."²⁶ Occupying the margins is Man of Color, which includes African American and Asian American men to varying degrees, and "is sexually rapacious, sometimes seductive, usually predatory, especially towards White Woman; it is he, in fact, from whom White Woman must be protected by White Man."²⁷ The trope constructs men of color as a threat to the norm. In addition to the threat, however, more contemporary constructions of ethnic masculinity build on earlier stereotypes to constrain Asian American men. Frankenberg notes a schizophrenic basis to the Man of Color trope for some Asian American men: "Asian men have at times been positioned in the trope-ical family in the classic Man of Color category, a sexual threat to white women. At other times, however, Asian men have been feminized in the racist imagination of the United States. And at still other times, they have been promised partial and conditional access to some of the benefits enjoyed by white men."²⁸ Asian American men face a more diverse set of stereotypes, some diametrically opposed to one another, but all of which marginalize them from normative notions of traditional masculinity.

While such stereotypes often use violence or sexuality to define Asian American and African American men, both Ulysses and Jason Peach are marginalized as a result of a new deployment of the stereotype of men of color within the education arena. Hazel Carby suggests: "If the spectacle of the lynched black body haunts the modern age, then the slow disintegration of black bodies and souls in jail, urban ghettos and beleaguered schools haunts our postmodern times."[29] Carby draws parallels between incarceration and education, suggesting that both construct black men in limiting ways. As a result, the scholastic arena where Jason and Ulysses meet gains new significance as a site of shared marginalization. Jason knows that African Americans may be constructed as raceless in such circles, and he pushes against that in a speech directed toward a "handsome, soft-voiced Negro in a white sweater" who has spoken against the creation of a Fair Employment Practices Commission at the high school student senate meeting:

> The truth is, brother, you got here to these exalted chambers with these, the brightest and most hip high school hustlers in the bountifully hustling state of California, the same way I got here. You know what I mean, brother. Hard work. Making your mama work extra hard to put up the money for this trip. And also by kissing a lot of Caucasian ass. . . . I wish we were both here because of our talent, man. I really do. We should not have to kiss behinds to play high school legislature just because of the color of our skin. I shouldn't have to shame my people to be here.[30]

High school is the new frontier of stereotypes. Jason recognizes the power relationships that mark people of color and force them to conform that are in play. In this instance, high school legislature effects the same kind of exclusion as the larger society, and as a result, Jason must resort to trickster strategies to participate.

So must Ulysses. If his relationship with Jason marks his participation in an Afro-Chinese male friendship in his youth, his reliance upon the style and substance of the 1960s Black Aesthetic represents an extension of interracial male camaraderie into his adult life. While in his early twenties, Ulysses espouses ideas about racial pride that echo those of the Black Power Movement. At one point, he complains about Asian Americans who are afraid to embrace their ethnicity:

> Fame and money are the only truths American yellows respect. They don't want to act. They want to be stars. They don't want to write. They want to be stars. They don't want Asian-American plays. They want stardom. No swearing in front of whites. No criticism of white racism. No railroad stories

or Japanese-American concentration camp stories that do not confirm the stereotype and reassure whites. Yellows are a pathological victim people. They don't want Asian-American theater. They want the secret of the stereotype.[31]

Ulysses criticizes Asian Americans who prefer to play into the societal expectations he believes are designed to keep them silent and marginalized. He chastises actors who fail to embrace significant elements of the Asian American experience, such as the Chinese American railroad legacy or Japanese American internment.

This focus on racial pride and self-determination echoes the Black Power Movement's focus on racial pride and self-empowerment. The mid-1960s witnessed the passage of the Civil Rights Act and Voting Rights Act, but many young activists did not see such legislation translate into change at the grass roots level. Harvard Sitkoff argues, "Continued school and residential segregation convinced the disenchanted blacks that [Martin Luther] King's goals of an integrated society was an impossible dream." They shifted their goals to focus on self-determination and "would engage in grass-roots organizing that built the power of black communities and enabled African-Americans to control their own destinies." They linked this self-determination to racial pride. Stokely Carmichael coined the term "Black Power" following his release from jail in 1966, and Sitkoff notes the psychological power of the phrase: "The major thrust of Black Power was to make blacks proud to be blacks, a psychological precondition for equality. It fostered a new sense of racial pride and self-confidence that helped revolutionize the black perspective, confining to the dustbin of the African-American past the belief born out of centuries of oppression that what was white was good and what was black was inferior."[32] Asian American activists emulated such racial pride. William Wei explains that they "expressed admiration for the Black Power movement, with its emphasis on ethnic identity and pride."[33] The centrality of racial pride in the Black Power movement motivated Asian Americans "to assert themselves as a people of color" rather than succumb to complete assimilation.[34]

In emulating such sentiments of the Black Power movement, Ulysses also embraces the problematic gender discourse that accompanied such calls for racial pride. He criticizes the work of Pandora Toy, Ben Han's girlfriend, because it caters to feminist expectations that exclude male agency in favor of ethnic authenticity. Ulysses criticizes her erroneous presentation of Chinese foot binding: "Were your mother's feet bound?

Did Pandora's mother have bound feet? It was never a popular or common practice. Nothing in Chinese folk tales praise women with bound feet or even mentions it because the folk didn't do it. To the folk, binding women's feet was always the behavior of perverts."[35] Ben's defense of Pandora's work focuses on the appeal of Chinese culture to whites: "She creates a Chinese culture that is acceptable to whites by rewriting a little of this and a little of that, in order to show higher truths. . . . We are revealing the truth of the Chinese culture we reject and create a Chinese-American culture that is more humane, more considerate of women, more . . ."[36]

Taking exception to the feminist reconstructions of his work as well as Ben's assertion that Chinese culture oppresses women, Ulysses counters with a more heroic tradition: "The fact is that Chinese literature—the Three Brothers of the Oath of the Peach Garden, *Sam Gawk Yurn Yee*, The Romance of the Three Kingdoms, Fung Sun Bong and Kwan Kung—has nothing to do with your fiancée's strange tales. The stories she says are Chinese aren't and never were. She's not rewriting Chinese anything, man. She's just doing a rewrite of Pearl Buck and Charlie Chan and Fu Manchu."[37] Ulysses accuses Pandora of altering a heroic Chinese literary tradition filled with tales of male bonding and national loyalty. For example, he cites the brotherhood and loyalty central to the epic *Romance of the Three Kingdoms*, in which the Three Brothers, Liu Bei, Zhang Fei, and Guan Yu, take the Oath of the Peach Garden: "We three, though of separate ancestry, join in brotherhood here, combining strength and purpose, to relieve the present crisis. We will perform our duty to the Emperor and protect the common folk of the land."[38] By emphasizing the theme of brotherhood in Chinese literature, Ulysses places himself in opposition to an Asian American feminism represented by Pandora. King-kok Cheung echoes such a stance when she asserts that "the ability to perform violent acts implied in the concepts of warrior and epic hero is still all too often mistaken for manly courage; and men who have been historically subjugated are all the more tempted to adopt a militant stance to manifest their masculinity."[39]

More than just a philosophical disagreement, Ulysses links Pandora's reinterpretation to those of Pearl Buck and places her work on the level of racist literature that promotes reductive stereotypes. Buck's novel *The Good Earth* (1931) focuses on the life of a Chinese peasant farmer and his family. As an American writer, Buck allows common misperceptions of the Chinese to find their way into her novel, thus failing to challenge stereotypes of the Chinese in the United States. At best, she tries to tailor her representations to the expectations of white audiences; and Ulysses sees Pandora as doing the same thing with her work. Almost in retaliation, he resists Pandora's feminist reading in favor of a heroic interpretation that privileges the Asian man in the terms of racial pride. By looking at Chinese literature through a masculinist lens, Ulysses accuses Pandora of promoting a feminist agenda at the expense of Chinese culture and defines the Chinese literary tradition in predominantly masculine terms.

Ulysses's conflation of masculinity and ethnicity mirrors the gender dynamics of the Black Power movement. Some routinely criticized the Black Panther Party in its early days for its tendency to cast the revolution in masculine terms that marginalized black women. Charles E. Jones and Judson L. Jeffries recall, "Male Party members brought patriarchal norms with them to the organization," creating "macho cult behavior."[40] Tracye Matthews notes that the revolutionary message was initially targeted at reimagining black masculinity:

> Men were the primary recruitment targets of early Panther campaigns. The language in this statement clearly asserted the role of Black men as protectors of women and children—self-defense was a man's job. . . . Statements such as these, along with the Party's paramilitaristic style and male dominated formal (national) leadership structures, suggested a particular definition of Black masculinity that assumed men had the skill, inclination, and obligation to be warriors, while conversely, women (and children) did not.[41]

This use of black masculinity to shore up racial pride often resulted in the denigration of women to complement the shaping of the revolutionary message in male terms. Robin Kelley notes, "In an age when metaphors for black liberation were increasingly masculinized and black movement leaders not only ignored but perpetuated gender oppression, even the most Marxist of the black nationalist movements belittled the 'Woman Question.' The BPP [Black Panther Party] was no exception."[42]

While Ulysses's attitudes echo sentiments of the Black Power Movement, his playwriting reflects elements of the Black Aesthetic or the Black Arts Movement, which advocated racial consciousness, often through a distinctly male lens. Larry Neal, one of the architects of the Black Aesthetic, notes: "Black Art is the aesthetic and spiritual sister of the Black Power concept. . . . The Black Arts and the Black Power concept both relate broadly to the Afro-American's desire for self-determination and nationhood. Both concepts are nationalistic."[43] The Black Aesthetic shares a focus on racial consciousness, but also deploys it through a distinctly male idiom. Neal's overview of the Black Aesthetic routinely refers to how such works relate to black masculinity. Neal cites Amiri Baraka (formerly LeRoi Jones) as the best practitioner of the Black Aesthetic, and notes that in one of his most notable plays, *The Dutchman*, the protagonist faces historical obstacles to black men: "Symbolically, and in fact, the relationship between Clay (Black America) and Lula (white America) is rooted in the historical castration of black manhood. And in the twisted psyche of white America, the Black man is both an object of love and hate."[44] Neal interprets the protagonist as a masculinized characterization of the nation when he equates Clay, a black man, with America. While the work centers on the African American family, Neal centralizes male dynamics in Ron Milner's *Who's Got His Own*, citing the central conflict as "rooted in the historical search for black manhood": "Thus unable to direct his violence against the oppressor, the Black man becomes more frustrated and the sense of powerlessness deepens. Lacking the strength to be a man in the white world, he turns against his family."[45] Such an overview shows how prevalent masculinity featured into this mode of black theater of the 1960s.

Ulysses embodies the strategies of a male-inflected black activist theater to articulate grievances about Chinese American representations in American culture. He learns to turn stereotypes to serve his own critical project, using satire to correct the erroneous representations of Chinese Americans by white writers. During rehearsals for his play, Ulysses offends some actors by singing the racist song, "Ching Chong Chinaman." He explains the critical nature of his appropriation: "Have you ever heard of satire? . . . Satire is where you make fun of how *they* think and what *they* say in order to make *them* look *stupid*."[46] Ulysses uses satire to expose the very stereotypes perpetuated by the dominant society and turn them on their heads. Neal encouraged black writers to do the same. Once the black writer recognizes the problems of dominant society, he "will then be forced to question the validity of the forms that have been forced upon him by society and construct new ones."[47] Amiri Baraka reflects such sentiments in his play *The Slave*, where his protagonist "becomes a caricature of the singing, dancing darkey down on the plantation, or the corner hood, so happy with drink that he forgets who the oppressor is, and that the goal of the fight is liberation."[48] Baraka engages in the very kind of satire that Ulysses engages to critique representations of Chinese Americans.

In fact, this appropriation of black masculinity by Chinese American culture crops up in Chin's own early aesthetic. Employing a bombastic and aggressive writing style, his early essays use African American culture as a way to illustrate the ways that the dominant American society oppresses Asian Americans. He admires the aggressive behavior of African American men. "In a world where manliness counts for everything," Chin admires "bad blacks" who "had a walk, a way of wearing their pants on the brink of disaster, a tongue, a kingdom of manly style everyone respected."[49] In his 1972 essay "Confessions of a Chinatown Cowboy," Chin argues: "White America is as securely indifferent about us as men, as Plantation owners were about their loyal house niggers. House niggers is what America has made of us, admiring us for being patient, submissive, esthetic, passive, accommodating essentially feminine in character."[50] By using the highly charged word "niggers," the comparison denotes just how much Chin believes mainstream society denigrates Asian American men. Just as plantation owners cast black men in subservient roles that demand docility, he suggests that American society uses a similar stereotype for Asian American men to rob them of their masculinity. He describes the degree to which white mainstream America denigrates Asian American men by using a term closely associated with the African American experience.

Ulysses's irreverent performances also link him to black activist theater of the 1960s, which deployed aggressive rhetoric and over-the-top characterizations and drew from stereotypes to challenge white expectations and move the audience to action. Ulysses's performance tries to deconstruct stereotypes of Chinese American men: "In the play, Fu Manchu tells the white captive to give up the secret of Kool-Aid. . . . But the white man defends the secret to Kool-Aid, and Fu's luscious daughter wheels the captive off to her silk-sheeted torture chamber. . . .When the director sees Ulysses off-stage watching, still in character, he tries putting Fu Manchu back onstage, reciting classical Japanese haiku of Issa and Basho, breathlessly watching his daughter torture the white man by seduction."[51] Not only is this plot scenario revolving around the secret of a popular childhood drink ridiculous, it seeks to shock the audience in its use of stereotypical figures like Fu Manchu and his lewd daughter. Robert G. Lee characterizes Fu Manchu as "the archetype of the sado-masochistic Asian male character in American popular culture narratives of the twentieth century," a figure that is "the very definition of the alien, an agent of the distant threat who resides among us."[52]

Ulysses's use of such irreverent performances echo black activist theater. Playwrights like Baraka argue that a revolutionary theater "should stagger through our universe correcting, insulting, preaching, spitting craziness. . . . The Revolutionary Theater must Accuse and Attack anything that can be accused and attacked."[53] The Black Aestheticians use theater to reveal the ways in which the dominant culture perpetuates images that strip men of color of agency. The point of this is to instill a sense of agency in black men. Neal quotes Baraka as saying: "Our theatre will show victims so that their brothers in the audience will be better able to understand that they are brothers of victims, and that they themselves are blood brothers."[54] Such tactics create what playwrights view as an assimilationist backlash. Hoyt Fuller, another significant figure in Black Aesthetic movement, reflects on the kind of reception black writers received from white critics: "The movement will be reviled as 'racism-in-reverse,' and its writers labeled 'racists' . . . . In order to look at Negro life unflinchingly, the white viewer either must relegate it to the realm of the subhuman, thereby justifying an attitude of indifference, or else the white viewer must confront the imputation of guilt against him. And no man who considers himself humane wishes to admit complicity in crimes against the human spirit."[55]

Chin re-creates a similar critical response to Ulysses's work in the novel. Missing the critical commentary on Chinese American masculinity, reviews of Ulysses's play focus on the rhetoric that challenges notions of propriety. Washington Flores expresses disdain at the fact that "Playwright Mo and his actor Kwan seem to be serious about their Fu Manchu's fanatical adherence to Chinese tradition, and the humiliation and subjugation of women. Do they seriously believe portraying Fu Manchu's daughter as a foul-mouthed nymphomaniac, using sex to torture the American into giving up the secret formula for Bisquick, is funny?"[56] The stereotypical figure of Fu Manchu appalls Flores and he misses the critical function of the figure. For him, context plays no role in changing the meaning of the figure. In fact, other critics argue that "Ulysses is trying to create an unrealistic macho-butch image of the Chinese man . . . playing Fu Manchu as an angry black man."[57] The critique emanates from a person of color, who castigates another person of color, for embodying the critical style of another ethnic group.

While Ulysses initially casts his lot in with African American masculinity, his infatuation with interracial male camaraderie is short-lived. He eventually rejects interethnic friendship, thereby enforcing distance between African American and Chinese American cultures. Despite his earlier inspiration by activist theater, Ulysses comes to express a sense of detachment from African Americans and their culture. Chin's own work foreshadows this ambivalence regarding connections between African

American and Chinese American masculinity. His 1972 play *Chickencoop Chinaman* follows the quest for a father-son relationship by its two Asian American male protagonists, Tam and Kenji. Finding their own Asian American fathers inadequate, they seek a replacement in Charley Popcorn, the father of black boxer Jack Ovaltine Dancer. Scholars have interpreted this as a failed search. Elaine Kim asserts that the play rejects "the myth that Asians could be like Blacks."[58] Patricia Chu argues that the failure lies in the suspicion on the part of Popcorn, who not only proves not to be Jack's father but also distrusts "Tam, whose Asian face is at odds with the 'black' voice he heard on the phone."[59] Chin's early forays in literature suggest a sense of ambivalence regarding Afro-Chinese male dynamics. Such ambivalence increases as *Gunga Din Highway* wears on. Ulysses's ultimate rejection of African American culture represents a rejection of interracial male camaraderie and reinforces the distance between African American and Chinese American cultures.

Despite his early participation in interracial camaraderie, Ulysses develops an ambivalent attitude toward American black culture. Such an attitude may be fueled in part by negative characterizations of African Americans by Chinese Americans that surround him. When Ulysses introduces Jason Peach to his family, "Ma shakes her head when she meets him, and my aunts come sit around me and try to talk me into telling Jason Peach we can't be friends."[60] Ulysses's Chinese American friend Milton reveals, "I was brought up to see them as ugly and beneath me. . . . [My mom] didn't want us playing with Negroes. . . . Your mother didn't discourage you forming any friendships with Negros [sic]?"[61] At the very least, friends and family members discourage Ulysses from participating in Afro-Chinese friendships. As an adult, Ulysses articulates his own ambivalent attitudes toward African Americans during Ulysses's coverage of a demonstration. As a result of reading his incendiary writing, Herman Schwartz, his African American boss at a local television station, sends him to cover the demonstration organized by black radicals in a black neighborhood. Herman believes Ulysses shares his perspectives on power relations in society: "Badmouthing all those pig movies in the *Seattle City* magazine. The badmouth that Kwannie lays on John Wayne I was sure was gonna get the niggah lynched from one of them bullshit plastic lanterns in Chinatown."[62] Because Herman believes that Ulysses shares a sense of outrage towards the dominant culture, he thinks Ulysses is the perfect person to send to meet the black radicals, who demand that no white reporters be sent to cover the demonstration. Perhaps Herman operates under a sense of interracial male camaraderie, but Ulysses has profound reservations about going into the black neighborhood and being associated politically with blacks: "If we are such brothers, why is it I know nothing about Herman's wife and baby till the instant he leaves me? It's a strange Lone Ranger who goes home to the wife and kid and leaves the guns and silver bullets with Tonto. I feel pretentious, icky and had."[63] Instead of trust, Ulysses expresses suspicion and feels exploited by Herman.

This feeling of exploitation lays the groundwork for Ulysses's later sense of detachment from African Americans during the demonstration. He feels alienated by his contact with the black residents. He muses to himself that he is a stranger: "I don't know this ghetto. This ghetto doesn't know me. . . . I'm a Chinaman. Why am I trying to feel like I've been here before?"[64] His coverage of the demonstration reflects this estrangement, as he assumes the position of the ultimate objective, detached observer. He describes his role in mechanistic terms: "thinking like a soulless machine, a pretentious camera-eye seeking the perfect man-machine relationship" and "working so hard to be the legs and organs of the camera."[65] As the machine rather than the individual who operates it, Ulysses has no emotional connection to the blacks he films.

His alienation turns into outright hostility toward black radical and political action. His assessment of the Black Panthers and Black Immortals, the two black radical organizations in the demonstration, focuses on appearance rather than social critique: "The local Prime Minister of the Black Panthers, in black leather jacket, black gloves, black shades, and black beret, and a field marshal of the Black Immortals, in a leather overcoat, black wrap-around shades, carrying a swagger stick, jointly issue a statement from the black community to white Seattle."[66] His description of the speech of the spokesman carries a tone of condescension and disbelief. The black radical representatives assert that "The TV news is out of control" and declare that "the media is the pig." They warn that if "white pig reporters from the imperialist pig media" remain to cover the holiday festivities, their presence will ignite "one of the first great battlefields in the Third World" and they will "consider [reporters] as the forces of the enemy making a war of invasion!" They feel justified in making such a statement because they speak "in the name of the coalition of the liberation forces of the oppressed peoples of America."[67]

From Ulysses's point of view, these representatives of black radical politics enter the text as actors in a performance. His description draws attention to their apparel as if it is a costume. He focuses on the part of the

Immortals spokesman's statement filled with rhetoric that seeks to incite the crowd rather than educate it: calling the media names and advocating a race war. As fiery and righteous as the statement seems, Ulysses's description does not motivate the reader to identify with the cause. While the media is the target of the black radical rant, the primary source of harm toward the black community is the police. Although officers have shot three black kids during the demonstration, Ulysses's representation of the speech says little about the police brutality. By having the black radical statement focus on the ill-advised intervention by a reporter rather than the brutality of the police, the novel makes the black radicals look petty, itching to get into a racial confrontation at the drop of a hat rather than engaging in substantive issues. Just as Ulysses embraced a masculinized form of black theater as part of his interracial camaraderie, his rejection of black radical politics translates into a rejection of interracial camaraderie.

Ulysses also disavows less controversial forms of African American protest. Ben Han discovers letters between Ulysses and the Berkeley branch of the NAACP, where Ulysses supports his boss's racist actions: "If the Storefront Theater actually does depend on a clientele composed in large by racially biased elements of the community . . . for its support, I would deem Mr. Blanchard justified in not hiring those people who in any way might threaten this means of support."[68] Ulysses thus rationalizes that because the theater depends on racist people for profits, it is justified in enacting discriminatory practices. He also attacks other progressive efforts to recognize racism in language and culture: "I do not agree with the omission of the word 'Black' from 'Little Black Sambo' or the abolition of minstrel shows, or the suppression of D. W. Griffith's *Birth of a Nation*. Such action to protect the Negro against discrimination seems ludicrous, even patronizing to the Negro."[69] While there is a complex argument that may be made regarding such racial cultural production, including the fact that the use of such terms are reflective of their historical context, Ulysses seems to make a more superficial argument. He casts such actions as efforts against discrimination rather than distorting tactics. By bypassing more substantive issues, Ulysses's argument seems to suggest that any action that recognizes inequity is ineffectual.

By taking stances against a range of black political perspectives, Ulysses puts himself at odds with a tradition of solidarity politics that Vijay Prashad links to the anti-imperial stance of Bruce Lee: "With his bare fists and his *nanchakus*, Bruce provided young people with the sense that we . . . could be victorious against the virulence of international capitalism."[70] As part of a tradition of Afro-Chinese radical politics, the Black Panther Party incorporated substantive ideas from China into their political thought and programs. Robin Kelley recalls Chairman Mao's April 1968 statement "In Support of the Afro-American Struggle Against Violent Repression," which "endowed the urban riots with historic importance in the world of revolutionary upheaval. His statement, as well as the general logic of Lin Biao's 'theory of new democratic revolution' justified support for black nationalist movements and their right of self-determination."[71] Black radicals like Robert Williams, Eldridge Cleaver, and Huey Newton recognized that "China offered black radicals a 'colored' or Third World Marxist model that enabled them to challenge a white and Western vision of class struggle."[72]

In turn, the Black Panther Party influenced the formation of Chinese American radical organizations. Prashad notes that the Red Guard Party, composed of Chinese American youths, formed under the consultation of the Black Panthers and developed programs that mirrored the outreach of the Panthers, including community fairs, free breakfast programs, and resistance to police brutality. Such common goals "enabled [the Red Guard Party] to make connections with the other anti-poverty, anti-capitalist organizations that struggled among the working class and working poor in their communities."[73]

Ulysses's stance against such coalitions establishes cultural distance between African American and Chinese American cultures in the novel. For Ulysses, Afro-Chinese cultural interaction is not the answer. Instead, Ulysses endorses a form of individualism derived from Chinese myth. Ulysses's loner status may initially resemble a quintessentially American individualism. Ben associates Ulysses's crafty skills with American invention: "Ulysses built things in his room. . . . [He] spent most of his time home up there making model airplanes. He spoke English like an American. There was nothing Chinese in Ulysses' voice. . . . But Ulysses was American, all-American and unafraid. No one told him what to do. He did what he wanted."[74] Ben describes Ulysses as a kind of founding father with a measure of ingenuity. He builds things, like American inventors Benjamin Franklin and the Wright Brothers. His English language skills also mark him as an American, as does his independent, can-do, take-no-prisoners attitude.

However, the novel provides much more evidence for characterizing Ulysses's shift toward individualism as a life course advocated by the

Chinese creation myths. Articulated in the author's note that precedes the novel proper, the first myth involves the creation of the world by Poon Gu (also Pangu), a giant who gains consciousness and emerges from an egg and creates heaven and earth: "When the sky stays up and the earth stays down, he dies and his breath becomes the atmosphere, one eye becomes the sun, the other, the moon; his blood runs clear and becomes the waters. Other parts of his body become different minerals and geographical features covering the stuff of the egg with soil, mountains, rivers, forests, and plains." The giant is responsible for much of the physical world that surrounds us. The other creation myth involves Nur Waw (also Nuwa), the "Mother of Humanity" who populates the new world created by Poon Gu: "She creates animals for six days, and on the seventh day, she creates human beings. . . . She invents music and retires to the wilderness." Responsible for bringing living beings to this world, she is also linked to culture through her creation of music.

Together, these mythical figures produce a world where the individual is embattled: "The world, the giant, and the Mother of Humanity create a world where every hero is an orphan, a failed scholar, an outlaw, an outcast, an exile on the road of life through danger, ignorance, deception and enlightenment." These myths suggest that humans enter into a hostile world where each person must depend on him- or herself. This world was created long before them and will exist long after them. If individuals have little effect on this world around them, they have to adapt to it by detaching from it. The myth suggests that individuals should be alone, alienated, failing in knowing the world around them, separated from others.

The personality that Ulysses settles on for the latter part of the novel reflects his attempt to enact this Chinese mythical mandate within an American context. He has always felt like an orphan, a literal outcast from his Chinese American family as well as from American society: "I am strange to the Chinese of my family, and strange to Sylvia's family, and am the stranger in town, the stranger in the family."[75] His outcast status empowers him, giving him a sense of freedom to make his own destiny, much like the hero in the Chinese myth. He learns such empowerment from his Chinese schoolteacher:

> You are the stone monkey come to life. To learn the difference between
> stone idea and living flesh and blood, you must learn everything Chinese
> and American there is to know, you must master all the knowledge of
> heaven and earth, become The Sage Equal to The Emperor of Heaven so as

to see the difference between the real and the fake, the knowledge of what being neither Chinese nor *bokgwai* (white European Americans) means.[76]

Rather than consigning his young charges to limbo between cultures, the teacher reveals the power that such marginality affords them. Ben Han realizes that by occupying this liminal space, "All things were possible. No guilt. We were pure self-invention."[77] For the Chinese American students, part of attaining that power means learning all things Chinese. Ulysses and his friends have carte blanche to interact with their environment in any way they want, a lesson taught to them using Chinese myth.

Part of this Chinese-based individualism manifests in a defiant attitude toward the Chinese American status quo. Ulysses and his friends declare themselves Brothers of the Oath of the Peach Garden, alluding to the *Romance of the Three Kingdoms*, where Liu Bei, Guan Yu, and Zhang Fei "swear to serve China and save the people" (73). Chin elaborates in an essay that Guan Yu, the brother Ulysses emulates in the novel, "is the exemplar of the universal man, a physically and morally self-sufficient soldier who is a pure ethic of private revenge."[78] Ulysses asserts such resistance in his response to his Chinese after-school teacher, who tries to silence him. "None of us had ever heard Ulysses or anyone talk back to a teacher like this. The only way I could describe Ulysses at the time was to say he talked to the Horse [Mr. Mah] as if he were the boss. Every day they argued. . . . Ulysses never gave an inch, never stopped fighting once he started."[79] Ulysses consistently defies Mr. Mah as a figure of authority.

While his resistance to Mr. Mah represents a defiance of the Chinese American status quo, Ulysses's rejection of his father, Longman Kwan, represents another dimension of his rejection of American authority in a quest for independence. He has serious issues with his own father's quest for assimilation into American culture, for Longman Kwan gravitates toward roles that reflect the expectations American culture has for him. Robert Lee notes that rather than reflecting the ways Asian Americans see themselves, such roles represent "a historical discourse of race that is embedded in the history of American social crises."[80] Whether he is a war hero or the detective's flunky son, Longman Kwan's roles demonstrate his preference to take on images fashioned for him. On one hand, he gains notoriety by playing a passive Asian man. He is often cast as The Chinaman Who Dies, a stock Asian role in war movies who always ends up dead to elicit a sentimental response from the audience: "I am the symbol of helpless, struggling China in the arms of William Bendix. He says I'm a 'cute little fella.' He names me 'Donald Duck.'"[81] Longman routinely plays a character without power, an infantilized figure that functions only to elicit an emotional response from white co-stars. His character is so weak that he must depend on the much stronger American. Anlauf Lorraine echoes this sentiment when he advises Longman on securing the role: "How can I tell you how you helped the war and brought the future absorption and assimilation of your people closer and closer every time you lived and died. It's very important to the United States of America, Kwannie. The more fondly America cherishes the memory of you dying, the less visible the Chinese in America will be. And the more quickly you'll be assimilated."[82] These roles function as cultural instruction, providing models for other Chinese Americans to fit into American culture. Such characters are created by white Americans to encourage Chinese Americans to be as they believe them to be.

On the other hand, Longman's recurrent role as Charlie Chan's Fourth Son and his own veneration of the Charlie Chan role further reinforce an image constructed by American culture that denies Asian Americans agency. The forty-four films that feature the detective style Charlie Chan as a round detective who sports a white suit. He is often called in as a consultant when a crime baffles law enforcement. His character affects a Chinese accent, speaks in broken English and seems unaware of certain American colloquialisms and customs, reinforcing the perception that he is exotic and foreign. His problem-solving skills are excellent, but are attributed to the mystery of Chinese culture rather than the deductive reasoning attributed to other fictional detectives like Sherlock Holmes. Asian American scholars find this problematic. Notwithstanding that the detective has always been portrayed by a white man in yellowface, Charlie Chan represents an alternative portrayal of Asian Americans by Earl Derr Biggers, a white American writer who sought a more sympathetic representation than Asian American villains like Fu Manchu in 1923. What passes for "sympathetic" is "a non-threatening, non-competitive, asexual ally of the white man, usually contrasted with a parade of Asians in secondary roles as cowardly servants and vicious gangsters."[83] Longman longs to be the first Chinese American to portray Charlie Chan because it would signal to him his arrival as an acceptable American icon. Laura Uba states that individuals like Longman who adhere to such assimilationist tendencies "completely prefer . . . to adopt the cultural values and lifestyles of Euro-Americans and, at the same time, consciously and unconsciously denigrate the physical and cultural characteristics of their minority group

. . . to elevate their status by identifying with members of the dominant group."[84] The role of Charlie Chan would allow Longman to accede to societal expectations by representing an image that is acceptable to mainstream white America but problematic to Asian Americans.

When Ulysses rejects Longman as his father, it is largely in part due to his quest for assimilation through the portrayal of Asian stereotypes in order to gain American acceptance. He hates his father, his roles, and his notoriety as one of Charlie Chan's sons. His failure to bond with Longman results in an alienation from his family in general. The combination of abandonment by his Chinese family and removal from the white vaudeville couple sets the stage for Ulysses's inability to trust the bonds between family members: "I didn't know what parents meant. I had no idea of what a mother and father were supposed to be, the proprietary rights they had over their child. I didn't grow up with that. . . . I had never even heard of a mother and father. I was somebody, something, that had no explanation, and needed none from the first of my memory."[85] Ulysses claims not to recognize these bonds, and more importantly, believes he does not need them. His familial rejection extends to his brother as well, whom Longman adores because of his success in white America: "What is a brother? My brother, Longman Kwan Jr., The Hero, is home. I don't know anything about brothers. . . . How come I have one? Ma can't explain."[86] Ulysses feels alienated from his own family, the one relationship that should make him feel as part of the group. His rejection of them should be read as part of his overall rejection of the kind of assimilation they represent.

After exploring various ways of relating to others (Chinese Americans, Americans, African Americans), Ulysses appears to sell out toward the end of the novel to his own benefit. He trades in his activist theater for Hollywood screenwriting that appeals to a broader audience, but also is devoid of any cultural critique or political message from an ethnic point of view. His screenplay for *Night of the Living Third World Dead* is loosely based on the Orpheus myth. In the film, the hero seeks to reanimate Eurydice, but something goes wrong:

> His recently dead wife, along with the remains of presidents and war heroes, rise from Arlington National Cemetery. Malcolm X, Martin Luther King, freedom riders long forgotten in unmarked graves, the consciences, the folksingers, and memories of the '60s, and all my brothers and sisters of the Third World Revolution Power to the People politics from the barrel-of-a-gun days have been secretly buried in Arlington by the FBI for the usual FBI

reasons of patriotism and paranoid schizo banzai gung ho arrogance and loyalty to the Bureau.[87]

Ulysses's past activist days become material for a B-movie, and in the process, lose all their cultural significance. He is happy to embrace what the paying public wants: "No more doing it for the people. No more agonized poetry. . . . If it makes $35 million I won't even have to worry about catastrophic illness."[88] Such financial gain will allow him to experience the freedom from obligation to others he has felt his whole life. Yet, this move to a cultural practice informed by American capitalism is not a neutral proposition. Historically, race-inflected work prevented people of color from fully reaping the benefits of participating in American capitalism, while cultural production that underplayed or eliminated racial difference were received much better by audiences.

However, Ulysses has other motives for his Hollywood playwriting. He seeks a life of isolation and independence. The success of the films will allow Ulysses to "be rich enough to be forgotten, to wander Chinatown, anonymous even to the Chinese, for the rest of my life." Not only does he profit personally from this venture, he also wins isolation and independence from community ties as well. His artistic production reflects this: "I can go back to writing art that goes nowhere, without ever again worrying about eating out and paying the rent."[89] Ulysses's use of the language of art for art's sake divorces him from a communal literary tradition; he wants to go it alone. When he decides to write zombie movies for a profit, he believes this is a way to escape ethnic associations that marginalize him and coerce him to participate in an ethnic community.

This shift in Ulysses's personality echoes Chin's emphasis on a heavily inflected Chinese identity within the United States. In his later work, Chin moves away from a discourse of Afro-Asian solidarity to one that emphasizes Chinese culture. He critiques popular Chinese American writers such as Maxine Hong Kingston, Amy Tan, and David Hwang because their work "is not informed by any Chinese intelligence," but rather "Confucian culture as seen through the interchangeable Chinese/Japanese/Korean/Vietnamese mix . . . of Hollywood."[90] He argues that the Chinese in America never forgot their connection to Chinese culture: "The values of Chinese fairy tales, the form and ethics of the classics of the heroic tradition, the names of the heroes, and the works themselves are written into the bylaws of the tongs and associations that run Chinatowns to this day. The characters of the fairy tale and the heroic tradition are found in figurines, statues and calendar art. Their stories are told through toys, on flash cards, and in homes and in Chinatowns."[91] Chinese culture informs not only a Chinese American past but also a Chinese American consciousness. Chin currently advocates his own identity as that of a "Chinese in America": "I'll swallow down my own thin, not really liquidy bile, without making a face or changing the look in my eyes. I have gotten into the humiliating habit of calling myself a 'Chinese-American.' 'Chinese-American' is not a conversation starter. Call myself a 'Chinaman' and fights start."[92]

This move to embrace a Chinese mode of individualism replicates a shift in the perception of the relationship between Chinese and Chinese American identity. It depends on a view of Chinese diaspora that retains ties between Chinese culture in the United States and Chinese culture in China. It begins with the arrival of Chinese immigrants on American shores in the mid-1800s, when a discourse emerged that made Chinese and Chinese Americans interchangeable in an effort to negatively characterize them. Najia Aarim-Heriot notes that there was the idea that the Chinese immigrant would be a perpetual foreigner. Newspaper writer Henry George opined in 1869 that "America was doomed with a permanent little China in its midst, inhabited by an army of 'utter heathens, treacherous, sensual, cowardly and cruel.' The Chinese would not assimilate totally as European immigrants had, or partially, as had African Americans."[93]

Even with the development of a Chinese American community in the early twentieth century, the negative tendency to establish links with other Asians rather than Asian Americans persisted. William Wei points to stereotypes: "The majority of stereotypes apply to Asian nationals, rather than Asian Americans, but because most Americans are unable or unwilling to distinguish one from the other, they have been readily transferred to Asian Americans."[94] Such perceptions continue to make unfavorable connections between Chinese and Chinese Americans. During the late 1980s, incidents like the Wen Ho Lee case, where a naturalized Chinese American scientist was accused of spying for the Chinese government, raised negative specters about the relationship between China and the Chinese in America. Frank Wu states that the prosecution was, in part, motivated by the reasoning that "the Chinese government seek[s] out Chinese Americans for its ignoble purposes, playing on racial sympathies."[95]

However, the 1990s witnessed a reconceptualization that recognizes a positive relationship between Asians and Asian Americans in diasporic terms. Sau-ling Wong suggests that the recent trend of denationalization was the result of changing attitudes regarding Asians and Asian Americans.

While dominant America linked Asian Americans to Asians in stereotype, Wong notes that Asian Americans themselves made more positive links through global phenomena like the Vietnam War and international postcolonial movements. In more contemporary times, the blurring of boundaries between "what is Asian American and what is 'Asian' have material bases, chief among them the ascendancy of Asia as an economic power of global impact, the coalescence of the Pacific Rim as a geoeconomic entity, and the circulation of Asian transnational capital." Wong adds that such economic transformations increase "cultural dissemination, maintenance and transformation for Asian Americans" through "the advent of cheap jet travel, fax and e-mail, pocket translators, long-distance phone services competing for clients with multilingual support, satellite-typeset Asian-language newspapers, and video and laserdisc rental outlets featuring Asian films."[96] David Palumbo-Liu sees connections between such identity formations and transnational capitalism: "We should understand that the historical reality of Asian America has been produced by a number of factors, including but not limited to the ongoing influence of Asian national identity, America's continued identification of Asians as not Americans, and transnational capital's persistent merging and delinking of the interests of 'Asia' and 'America.'"[97]

Ultimately, Ulysses places a premium on the cultural discourses centered on the individual rather than the community. While such a discourse resembles the American myth of the self-made man, it is actually grounded in the world of Chinese myth. This kind of Chinese myth transforms the loner into an empowered outcast, free to determine his/her own destiny. This emphasis on Chinese individualism should not surprise readers, for it is prefaced by a rejection of the interracial male camaraderie narrative. Ulysses detaches from African American culture, and then expresses full-blown hostility toward black radical political positions. Such cultural distance represents a stark departure from the Afro-Chinese dynamics that inform the beginning of the novel, where African American and Chinese American men share a common marginalization by American society, as well as strategies to cope with such marginalization. The novel ends with Ulysses alone.

Gunga Din Highway's pessimistic view of interethnic cultural dynamics challenges the more optimistic scenario posited by Bruce Lee's *Enter the Dragon*. Part of that challenge comes from the limits the novel places on interethnic friendship. Ulysses's decision to embrace a Chinese individualism over Afro-Chinese interaction translates into a reliance on a monolithic perception of ethnic culture. He gives up circulating between two cultures, each with transnational ties, for just one that serves his individual needs. While one could argue that Ulysses confronts a transnational context, his failure to do so at the expense of cross-cultural dynamics results in his distance from multiple ethnic cultures. The novel invokes Chinese culture but within the context of American society, and emphasizes transnationality only in terms of a diasporic Chinese identity. African American and Chinese American characters interact within the bounds of the United States, and the novel never considers how that dynamic may be affected by interaction with a global culture like the kind considered by Vijay Prashad, who associates Lee with possibilities between ethnic cultures on a global scale: "Bruce did not claim his power from his inherited kung fu lineage . . . but he wanted others to bow to his street-fighting prowess. . . . In other words, anyone with dedicated tutelage can be a master, can be a *sifu*. Kung fu gives oppressed young people an immense sense of personal worth and the skills for collective struggle."[98] Prashad suggests that, by eliminating the power hierarchy, Lee's vision also eliminates other barriers, like national boundaries, to encourage camaraderie in the struggle. While Chin downplays the theme of interracial camaraderie, post-1990 contemporary films make the interethnic male friendships central in locations outside the United States.

"They Don't Like Tourists Here, So Try to Blend In": New Chinese Connections in *Rush Hour 2* and *Unleashed*

While *Gunga Din Highway* ultimately rejects the theme of interethnic male camaraderie established by *Enter the Dragon*, the novel does recognize the transnational to a certain extent. Contemporary Afro-Asian films build on Lee's legacy and Chin's intervention. Both *Rush Hour 2* and *Unleashed* feature full-fledged friendships between their African American and Chinese leads in locales outside the United States. The pairs of friends envision themselves in relationships described in familial terms, but with very different outcomes. *Rush Hour 2* embraces an interethnic male friendship based on a reductive notion of national identity that reinforces distance between the African American and Chinese leads. Even as they both suffer the shame of being kicked off the case by an FBI agent, Detective Carter, portrayed by African American comic actor Chris Tucker, and Detective Lee, portrayed by action star Jackie

Chan, see themselves sharing a bond as the sons of fallen police officers. The comedic value of the difference they both represent derives primarily from their respective national identities rather than ethnic identities. The setting of Hong Kong allows those national differences to be distinct, while racial differences fall to the background. Based on narrow characterizations of national identity, the friendship ensures distinctions remain between African American and Chinese characters. As a result, their dynamics embody cultural emulsion.

However, in *Unleashed*, the interethnic friendship emphasizes the similarities between Sam, portrayed by veteran African American actor Morgan Freeman, and Danny, portrayed by action star Jet Li. Their friendship, based on a shared legacy of subjugation, heals the psychic damage caused by Danny's enslavement to Bart, a British hood played by Bob Hoskins. Danny and Bart's relationship mirrors the dynamic between China and Britain. But Danny and Sam's friendship operates on a shared understanding and counteracts its negative effects, resulting in cultural exchange.

The Afro-Chinese male friendships that underscore *Rush Hour 2* and *Unleashed* represent an alternative to cinematic interracial male friendships. Melvin Donalson identifies an interracial buddy pattern exemplified by the relationships between black and white men in film. More than just fluff for the plot, he argues that the interracial dynamic is central, for the lives of the men of different races are intertwined and not limited to casual friendship: "The two males achieve a union that acknowledges personal sharing and sacrifice for one another—personal demands that go beyond the conveniences of a friendship. . . . This closeness can be expressed in action, verbal banter, physical touching, and shared space."[99]

While the buddy dynamic can be found in a wide array of films, Donalson argues that when it involves black and white men, it often conforms to the same pattern. Films ranging from *Lethal Weapon* (1987) to *48 Hours* (1982) demonstrate how black men historically act as foils to white male characters: "The characters of color have been rendered to make white males appear more courageous, tolerant, heroic, intelligent, etc., in the narrative. . . . This delineation often resulted in a racial hierarchy that assigned positive and laudable qualities to white characters by virtue of race."[100] Donalson maintains that this pattern that perennially places black men in the supporting role to the white partner derives from the historic way white men define their own masculinity using general black/white racial dynamics. Scholars such as Michael Kaplan establish that comparisons to black masculinity inform the way white men view themselves, dating back at least to the antebellum age: "Racism was central to white working-class identity in antebellum New York. Young workingmen gained a sense of power and democratic brotherhood among themselves by excluding and persecuting African Americans."[101] Eric Lott suggests similar dynamics inform blackface minstrelsy around the same period: "A certain dynamic of masculinity or, conversely, 'unmanning' seems to have been at work here" based on "codes of black and white manhood."[102] In both instances, white men assume a status of superiority, a status that gets adapted to interracial dynamics between black and white men.

However, Donalson only alludes to an alternative to this interracial male dynamic, one where both parties are members of ethnic minorities: "American cinema allows this special dispensation because both men belong to the racial 'other' and therefore are already on a equal footing from the dominant group's perspective. Likewise, in a form of vindication of the dominant group, if people of color espouse racial epithets about one another, the attitudes that frame those statements do not belong solely to the dominant group, thereby turning racial slurs into merely another form of entertainment."[103] However, Donalson sees this othering outside of any historical or cultural context and fails to realize how such othering can produce uneven dynamics between men of different ethnic cultures. Ethnic men represent a different kind of racial other, and while they may occupy equal footing in the dominant group's perspective, they may not do so in a perspective that takes into consideration past interaction.

For example, during Reconstruction, African Americans encountered attempts to curtail their rights, but at the same time were perceived as preferable to Chinese immigrants. Najia Aarim-Heriot cites the logic of Henry George in a letter to the editor of the *New York Tribune* in 1869: "With the exception of African Americans, he stated, Americans had successfully melded into a homogenous people. The Asian newcomer, George observed, differed from Americans "by as strongly marked characteristics as do the Negroes." He believed, however, that the Chinese had "a civilization and history of their own." . . . "The Chinese would not assimilate totally, as European immigrants had, or partially, as had African Americans."[104] Given past situations where hierarchies are established among ethnic groups, the question arises: Do interracial male friendships between men of color revert to traditional interracial male dynamics or establish new patterns of interaction?

Rush Hour 2 provides a partial answer to that question, while at the same time, extending the interracial camaraderie suggested by *Enter the*

Dragon. The film draws from the franchise formula that uses the hilarity that is supposed to ensue from frequent misconceptions between the two. In *Rush Hour,* Inspector Lee, a Chinese national, comes to the United States to find the kidnapped daughter of a consul representative in Los Angeles. During the course of the investigation, he encounters and befriends African American Los Angeles police officer James Carter. *Rush Hour 2* continues the comedic plot by making Carter the outsider who arrives in Hong Kong for a vacation, but finds Lee embroiled in a case. Sparked by an explosion at the American embassy that kills two Americans, the case revolves around Ricky Tan, Lee's father's traitorous expartner. Lee tries to show Carter the sights while covertly investigating Tan's involvement, but Carter's very public antics spoil Lee's attempts to conduct a quiet investigation. American FBI officials take over the investigation and warn Lee and Carter not to interfere, a warning they promptly ignore. Their covert investigation uncovers Tan's relationship with Steven Reign, a white, wealthy Los Angeles developer, whom they follow back to the United States. In Los Angeles, Carter uses his connections to discover that the case is really about undetectable counterfeit money. Reign works with Ricky Tan to distribute the fake bills via a casino in Los Angeles. During the climactic final scenes of the film at a Las Vegas casino, Lee discovers that Ricky Tan faked his own death and escaped to the United States, where he betrays and murders Reign. Lee and Carter recover the counterfeit plates and save the day.

In a way, Carter and Lee's relationship extend the interracial camaraderie from *Enter the Dragon,* but in a way that is built on comedy. The careers of both Jackie Chan and Chris Tucker underscore the comedic intent of *Rush Hour 2.* Initially an extra in kung fu films of the 1970s (including Lee's *Enter the Dragon*), Jackie Chan made a conscious decision to embark on a comedic style of kung fu film. In his breakout role as a young Wong Fei Hung, beloved Cantonese folk hero, in *Drunken Master* (1978), Chan opted to play up his youthful innocence rather than a sense of reverence for the figure. Stephen Teo notes that "Chan was encouraged to go overboard with his fool characterization" and, as a result of his comic take, "the persona of the mischievous kung fu kid was to stay with him for several years."[105]

Chan's choice to develop a predominantly comic career was related in part to his desire to step out of Bruce Lee's shadow. Chan sought to carve out a new niche for himself, one that Lisa Stokes and Michael Hoover describe as the "anti-Bruce Lee": "Whereas Bruce Lee kicked high, Jackie

Chan kicks low. Lee broke through walls with a single punch; Chan hurts his hand when he strikes a wall. The former was serious; the latter is a comic."[106] Comedic performance become central to Chan's later films aimed at Western audiences, especially those with interracial elements. In *Rumble in the Bronx* (1994), the precipitating event that brings Chan's character to the United States is his uncle's desire to help with his business. The uncle's marriage to an African American woman is an odd element upon which the film never elaborates. Yet, hijinks ensue when Chan takes over the business while his uncle is on his honeymoon. In *Who Am I?* (1998), Chan's character, a secret agent, loses his memory on a mission and winds up in an African tribe. While he becomes a member of the tribe, he soon after regains his memory and the episode seems to have little bearing on the rest of the film.

By pursuing the comic route, Chan diverged from the recurrent themes of cross-cultural engagement and power struggles found in Bruce Lee's films. As one of several Chinese actors used by Hong Kong film producers to fill the vacuum left by Lee's untimely death, Chan quickly came to the conclusion that carrying on Lee's legacy would not assure him the international stardom he sought. He aspired to fame in the Hollywood of his youthful imagination: "America—the home of Hollywood, where filmmaking began—awaited. I had long watched American films with envy, wishing I had the budgets and resources they boasted with every frame; I'd danced along with Fred Astaire, hummed to Frank Sinatra and Julie Andrews, laughed at Chaplin and Keaton and Lloyd, the great comics of the silent classics. 'Now, someday soon I'd join them in Hollywood's galaxy of stars.'"[107] Chan measured success by making it in Hollywood, as opposed to Hong Kong. He also identified with a comic tradition in American film, which tends to overlook more nuanced elements of the interracial backdrop of some of his films.

Similarly, Chris Tucker's career had been characterized by taking on comedic roles. He had portrayed a series of characters that function as comic relief. His early roles placed him squarely within African American culture, including his first role as Smokey in *Friday* (1995) opposite Ice Cube. A frequent partaker of illicit substances, Smokey implicates his friend Craig when he uses a shipment of drugs for his local dealer. Upon discovering this, the drug dealer gives Smokey until the end of the day to rectify the situation. Yet from the midst of this potentially serious subject matter of inner city experience emerges Tucker's constant wisecracking, which becomes his hallmark in later films. In *Money Talks* (1997), Tucker makes use of his wisecracking, fast-talking personality as a hustler who finds himself mixed up in a jailbreak with two diamond smugglers.

The Fifth Element (1997) showcases Tucker's comedic stylings most prominently. Tucker portrays Ruby Rhod, a larger-than-life intergalactic radio personality. Korben Dallas, portrayed by Bruce Willis, is the reluctant winner of a trip on a luxury space liner. Unaware of Dallas's role in preventing an intergalactic incident, Ruby constantly uses his fast-talking ways to make Dallas part of his radio show, attempts that are rebuffed by Dallas. Ruby is a showman, but also a coward. As the aliens attack the liner, he continues to broadcast not just the play-by-play, but also his own cowardice in the face of danger. Whining and a marked reluctance to enter the fray replace his bravado. All the while, Tucker demonstrates the comedic style for which he is known: he insults the aliens by calling them ugly, hides under tables to avoid danger, and demonstrates his utter inability to fire a weapon.

The combination of Tucker and Chan ensures that comedy will underscore the dynamics of their friendship in *Rush Hour 2*. The first scenes that Carter and Lee share establish them as friends who often engage in banter designed to elicit laughs. In the car on the way back from the airport, they demonstrate shared interests by enthusiastically singing "California Girls" by the Beach Boys. Carter notes that "the Beach Boys are dope," while Lee says he loves the group. This scene also establishes one of the most recurrent elements of their friendship, namely, the putdowns that constantly issue from Carter's nonstop mouth. However, these insults never bother Lee, who seems to take it as part of their friendship dynamic. When Carter threatens to "slap you so hard you will end up in the Ming dynasty," Lee merely smiles.[108] Audiences are meant to see such exchanges as comedic elements of their friendship, for J. H. Park et al. note that "racial jokes in the film cross color lines, creating an impression that all races are subject to stereotypes."[109]

Beneath the comedy lies the interethnic friendship. During the fighting scenes, the choreography often is devised to show Carter and Lee working together. In the fight in the massage parlor, several shots show Carter saving Lee from deadly punches, and Lee physically using Carter to attack the enemy. We also see Lee's reaction when he believes that Carter has died in an explosion. Stunned when he leaves the station, in his car he happens upon Puff Daddy's 1997 tribute to Notorious B.I.G., "I'll Be Missing You." The lyrics of the song reflect the loss of a friend but also the loss of a duo. Lyrics such as "Seems like yesterday we used to rock the show /

I laced the track, you locked the flow" suggest the kind of teamwork that Carter and Lee shared, each with their own talents that complemented the other.[110] Lee's subsequent snake-dancing in the car recalls happier times between himself and Carter. The song helps to underscore the connection between Carter and Lee.

While Lee and Carter actually collaborate, their dynamics continue to be governed primarily by differences that stem from national identity rather than ethnicity while the duo remain in Hong Kong. In Lee's film, Hong Kong acts as a transnational backdrop that sets the stage for an interrogation of national interests over ethnic concerns in a way that links *Rush Hour 2* to *Enter the Dragon*. In *Enter the Dragon*, Williams notes the enduring, debilitating effects of economic disparity in Hong Kong while taking a small boat to the martial arts tournament. Lee also highlights Hong Kong's role in competing national interests when he acts as a spy on behalf of the British government, who has a stake in the tournament but must act behind the scenes. The complicated legacy of British colonization also looms over Lee's mission. Han's island is located near Hong Kong, but not subject to any country's jurisdiction. Here, the islands of Hong Kong function, not on their own, but as part of international intrigue.

Similarly, *Rush Hour 2*'s Hong Kong operates as a site of contrasts, which underscores the outsider status of Carter. The film opens with establishing shots that characterize Hong Kong as a more exotic location than the United States, thereby emphasizing its national associations. Opening credits start with a series of overhead panning shots of a lush green forest, which morphs into the skyline of a city, which a caption later identifies as Hong Kong. Images of modernity, like the skyscraper-dotted skylines, exist alongside those that suggest antiquity, like Buddha statues and traditional Chinese sailing vessels in the harbor. These shots suggest that Hong Kong is a city of contradictions and establish it as a different national space into which Carter enters as an American. Kwai-Cheung Lo reminds us that it is in Hong Kong that Carter asserts "his superior American identity to the Asian girls" and "boasts about himself as a First World handsome," calling Chan "the Third World ugly."[111] Once in Hong Kong, Carter is defined more by his American identity than his ethnicity. Characters repeatedly respond to Carter as an American tourist. At the karaoke club Lee warns Carter, "They don't like tourists here, so try to blend in." At the Chinese massage parlor he introduces Carter as "his American friend" and remarks, "Americans are funny."[112] All of these instances emphasize Carter's national association. He is rarely referred to as Lee's black friend in Hong Kong. It is his identity as an American that makes him different.

The film uses Hong Kong to reinforce stereotypes regarding Carter's national identity, and in doing so, utilizes strategies similar to those of the first film in the franchise. American audiences instantly grasp the multiracial politics of the Los Angeles setting of the first film, which reinforce Lee's identity as a Chinese national. Kwai-Cheung Lo describes Lee as a "prodigal son" who "is immediately assigned the huge mission of saving China's future (Consul Chan's little daughter) and also of protecting China's past (the antiques that Chan fights to prevent from being smashed by gangsters in the final confrontation)."[113] The film emphasizes his difference using national terms, reflecting American anxiety about his foreignness. This anxiety undermines cultural exchange, for Frank Wu notes that a "perpetual foreigner syndrome . . . depicts Asian immigrants as inassimilable."[114] By defining Asians as different and unknowable, American discourse contains its fear around its own constructions of Asia as "a homogenous continent of cultural and economic marauders."[115] Lee's outsider status excludes him from an American identity and plays on his inability to participate fully in the American (and African American) culture that surrounds him, just as it does for Carter in Hong Kong.

Carter's own behavior also marks him as an American. His frequent miscommunication with the Chinese reinforces his role as bumbling American tourist. As they depart from the airport in Hong Kong, Carter and Lee drive up next to two Asian women who are blasting hip-hop music at a stoplight. Lee and Carter are bopping to "California Girls" by the Beach Boys. Carter tries to invite the ladies out for a drink in Chinese, but is puzzled when they rebuff his offer. In fact, they appear to be offended. Lee explains that Carter's inept use of Chinese actually invited them to get naked. Carter's fast-and-loose use suggests a disregard for the proper use of the Chinese language.

Later, Carter emulates a legacy of American objectification and commodification of Asian women. Asian women figure prominently into Carter's quest to have fun on his vacation. At the massage parlor, Carter literally gets his pick of women, as if they are only objects there for his consumption. Rather than choosing one companion, he chooses five. In response to Lee's attempts to rush him, Carter replies, "You don't jump in front of a black man in a buffet line."[116] This scene echoes the one in *Enter the Dragon* previously discussed, in which the black character Williams chooses four women. Carter's "acquisition" of the women underscores his

American identity because of the historic link between American men and financial exchange. This objectification of women through monetary exchange mirrors the way Western men, especially American men, historically viewed and interacted with Asian women. Legislation in the nineteenth century, such as the Page Law of 1875, equated all Chinese women with prostitutes as part of its exclusionary practices. This stereotype of the sexually available Chinese woman for purchase survives to the twentieth century, for Park et al. note that "the Chinese women at the massage parlor embody the stereotype of obedient Oriental dolls readily fulfilling Americans' sexual desire and fantasies."[117] While the scene alludes to ethnic male stereotypes, it also reinforces Carter's identity as an American male.

In addition to his objectification of Asian women, Carter also performs an American identity through his association with Los Angeles Police Department. Despite Lee's suggestion that they keep a low profile in the karaoke club, Carter uses his LAPD credentials to try to gain the information they need. After questioning Lee's more subtle tactics ("who taught you how to roust a bar?"), Carter flashes his badge. He declares, "I'm from Los Angeles, we invented gangs," a statement that represents an example of American bravado that suggests that Americans do everything bigger and better.[118] Given its involvement in high-profile cases, the LAPD functions as a well-known representation of American law enforcement. The United States already has a characterization of being a "cowboy" state, and the LAPD's image draws upon that. Carter's association reinforces an American identity, downplaying the problems that the LAPD has with ethnic groups in the United States, particularly with African Americans. An overwhelmingly white police force that has routinely been linked to racial profiling and police brutality, the LAPD has a reputation for targeting African American males as the primary participants in criminal activity. Park et al. observe that by associating himself with law enforcement, Carter acts "in service of White America by defeating those who challenge White patriarchal power."[119]

Because the film reinforces his national identity in a reductive way, it contributes to the distance between African American and Chinese cultures, despite the transnational location. Carter is unable to blend into Hong Kong society because of his American behavior. His repeated misuse of the language fails to endear him to any of the Chinese characters. He continues to swagger through his interactions with others and takes on some of the worst traits commonly ascribed to American tourists. The Afro-Chinese male friendship operates on the difference generated by

Carter's difference, which is based on national identity. The whole point of the relationship between Carter and Lee is that they are different. It drives the comedic value of the films. They have to be different so that they can come together and work together despite their differences. Carter's American identity undermines his friendship with Lee while in Hong Kong. They are hardly together in the scenes in Hong Kong. Much of the action follows Carter's antics on his own while Lee pursues his own personal investigation of Ricky Tan. Carter explores the Chinese market by himself. He buys a Chinese suit on his own. He remains uninterested in Lee's investigation for the bulk of his vacation.

When Carter's ethnicity comes into play in Hong Kong, it serves to qualify a particular brand of American identity. Ji Hoon Park et al. suggest that Carter does not pose a threat because of his bumbling antics and "minority status": "Because people of color are usually portrayed as victims rather than perpetrators of racism, they are not perceived as having power over the others (as opposed to a White character having power over a minority character)."[120] Carter's American identity contrasts with a more dominant form represented by Agent Sterling, the white FBI agent who arrives in Hong Kong to take over the investigation of the American embassy bombings. Rather than working as equals who respect each other, Sterling insists that the Hong Kong police force provide support, "whatever they need." The Hong Kong police commander is consistently overruled by Sterling. Sterling represents the type of American to whom the Chinese defer, culturally arrogant in their enactment of authority. Claire Conceison argues that this kind of American "is often a 'significant other,' a privileged marginalized Other rather than a dominated colonial subject. . . . When a white American or European is 'Othered' in China, it is as likely to be in the form of being pushed to the front of the line as to the back."[121] Whiteness plays a major role in this mode of American identity, for "although White characters only have small roles in Rush Hour 2, they still occupy key 'overseeing' positions in the storyline, regardless of whether they are good or evil."[122] Thus, Sterling is a different kind of American from Carter.

Just as Carter's identity is tied to his nationality, Lee's function as a Hong Kong inspector is tied primarily to national tensions. With the film set in Hong Kong, a nation where Lee is no longer the outsider, his differences with his environment are subdued. In the first film Lee functioned as a fish out of water because he was a Chinese national working a case in Los Angeles. His difference was shown in relief in his inability to grasp some of the nuances of language and cultural gestures. However, as a member of the majority national group in *Rush Hour 2*, Lee is not different at all. The film does not have a vocabulary for ethnic Chinese distinctions—everyone in Hong Kong is Chinese. Any attempt at ethnic identification is erased.

When it comes to being an outsider in *Rush Hour 2*, place matters. When the action shifts to the United States, ethnicity resurfaces as the more important marker of difference for Carter and Lee. In the Las Vegas casino, Carter attracts attention to himself by accusing the dealer of racial discrimination, and goes into a tirade that evokes the civil rights era:

> Dealer: Sir, are you aware that there is a $50,000 buy-in this evening?
> Carter: If that's the case, give me $100,000 in chips. Let me have a diet Pepsi and some hot wings.
> Dealer: Give him the chips.
> Carter: Whoo! Ima get me some of this money. Whoa! What's this?
> Dealer: $500 chips sir.
> Carter: You gave me $500 chips because I'm black?
> Dealer: Ah, no sir. I did not. I just assumed . . .
> Carter: You assume that a brother coming in here could only afford $500 a roll, is that it?
> Dealer: No, I didn't think that at all.
> Carter: You a racist?
> Dealer: No, I'm not.
> Carter: How come everybody else around the table got $1000 chips, and the black man got a nickel?
> Dealer: I don't know, I'm sorry.
> Carter: How did that happen? It just happened, didn't it? You think my people suffered 362 years of slavery so you could send us back to the cotton fields with $500 chips? Do I look like Chicken George to you? What the hell is that?

This tirade only escalates when Lee needs a further diversion:

> Carter: How come ain't no black people performing in this hotel? We ain't good enough for you people?
> Security Guard: We got Lionel Richie performing here tonight.
> Carter: Lionel Richie ain't been black since the Commodores, man. What about Peaches and Herb? Gladys Knight and the Pips? Ike and Tina? They can get back together. This is crazy.

Security Guard: Sir, why don't you calm down, win some money, and have some fun?

Carter: I ain't calming down no more. I'm sick of you trying to calm me down. . . . I have a dream that white people and black people and even Chinese people can gamble together without getting different chips![123]

This speech resonates in the United States because ethnic identity functions as a primary marker of difference. It has a legacy that includes Martin Luther King's words. Back in the United States, national association matters little for him as an American. Rather, he invokes an ethnic history that forms the basis for difference.

While *Rush Hour 2* embraces an Afro-Chinese male friendship to reinforce the distance between African American and Chinese cultures, *Unleashed* suggests an interethnic male camaraderie where African American and Chinese men share experiences based on both national association and ethnic identity, resulting in cultural exchange. The film uses elements of a discourse of slavery to underscore a modern-day Chinese coolie experience, which relies on both ethnic identity and national association and results in more cultural exchange. *Unleashed* tells the story of modern-day slavery with a Chinese character as the slave. Jet Li's character, Danny, is the enforcer for the illegal protection racket operated by British hood, Bart, portrayed by Bob Hoskins. Bart "obtains" Danny as a very young child after he murders his mother, a Chinese piano student who refuses to work for him as a prostitute. From that time, Bart uses deprivation to "train" Danny to do his bidding. When Danny grows up, Bart enters him into underground fighting competitions where people wager on the outcome. One day, Danny meets Sam, an African American blind piano tuner portrayed by Morgan Freeman and strikes up a friendship. After a car accident, an injured Danny finds his way back to the warehouse where he met Sam, who takes him home. While recuperating at Sam's home, Danny begins to shed his enslaved personality with the help of Sam's adopted daughter, Victoria. He learns to eat with proper table manners, appreciate music, and has new experiences such as eating ice cream, cooking, and grocery shopping. But Danny cannot leave his former life behind. He bumps into one of Bart's henchmen, who threatens to harm Sam and Victoria if he does not return to his former life. When Bart attempts to force Danny to return to the underground fights, he reluctantly complies, and then runs away. Bart sends several henchmen to retrieve him. The pursuit ends at the apartment of Sam and Victoria and, after a climatic fight, Danny resolutely leaves Bart, refusing to kill him even after Bart goads him. The film ends with Sam and Danny attending Victoria's piano performance as a family in New York.

The decidedly darker subject matter of *Unleashed* may reflect different career trajectories of Li and Freeman as compared to the comedy-infused work of Chan and Tucker. While Chan's films are often governed by comedy, Jet Li's career echoed earlier Bruce Lee films that engaged national identity. Jet Li portrayed a more serious Wong Fei Hung in *Once Upon a Time in China* (1996), which emphasizes the figure's resistance to British imperial forces and assimilation. Set in 1875, the film encompasses the tensions between the Chinese and Europeans, corruption in the Chinese government, general lawlessness in the form of local gangs, and American attempts to exploit Chinese labor. The opening scenes of the film begin with a misunderstanding between Chinese and French ships. While conducting a dragon ceremony, the nearby French ship mistakes firecrackers for gunfire and proceeds to fire on the Chinese ship. As the result of this multinational incident, the Chinese commander secures Wong Fei Hung's help in developing a militia to defend China against what he sees as an inevitable foreign attack. To solidify their agreement, he hands Fei Hung a fan with all of the Unequal Treaties on it. This set of treaties, including the Treaty of Nanking (1842) (with Britain) and Treaty of Tientsin (1858) (with France, Britain, Russia, and United States), primarily opened up parts of China for trade and missionary activity. China felt humiliated in the wake of these treaties because of their conditions; John S. Gregory admits that the "treaties became more oppressive than its original architects anticipated or intended."[124]

Recurring tensions between the Chinese and the various Western powers that encroach upon them carries the plot of the film. Fei Hung reflects this in his suspicions regarding Western philosophy, protecting the Chinese peasants who have been captured as coolie labor by the British and openly criticizing imperialism. Li's Fei Hung also protects Chinese culture. Corrupt Chinese officials, seeking to curry favor with the British and the Americans, encourage local groups to terrorize his Chinese martial arts school. They eventually force its closure. When Fei Hung battles the gang, he also fights to preserve his culture. In Tsui Hark's *Once Upon a Time in China* series, "Li's folk hero not only celebrates Chinese cultural identity and humanistic ideals (defending the weak, championing justice, and redressing the wrongs of the oppressed); he also denounces imperialism and considers loaded issues of modernization, progress and the future."[125]

While casting Li introduces national identity into *Unleashed*, the casting of Morgan Freeman injects ethnicity. A venerated actor who often appears in Oscar-worthy fare, Freeman has come to be known for the wise, supporting character that aids other characters in finding their moral center. Freeman portrays Hoke, a chauffeur for a wealthy Southern white woman portrayed by Jessica Tandy in *Driving Miss Daisy* (1989). When Miss Daisy can no longer drive her car, her son hires Hoke to perform this service. From the beginning, he is polite and obliging to Miss Daisy, even in uncomfortable situations where segregationist mores of the South enforce the racial separation between them. Because of Hoke's patient and long-suffering nature, Miss Daisy and Hoke form a special relationship. When Miss Daisy begins to show signs of senility, it is Hoke who comes to her rescue and visits her in the nursing home. Freeman has also become known for his roles that place him in a position of leadership. When the world is in eminent danger from a rogue comet in *Deep Impact* (1998), it is Freeman as president who assures the inhabitants of earth that "we will survive." In *Seven* (1995), Freeman portrays a cop on the verge of retirement, working his last case involving a serial killer who murders according to the seven deadly sins. His character is methodical and pays attention to detail, while his new partner, portrayed by Brad Pitt, is gung-ho to find the killer and make him pay. In *Glory* (1989), Freeman's character guides the younger characters onto the right path. He plays an older soldier in the all-black regiment under Robert Gould Shaw, who explains the motives behind the behavior of the black soldiers, including the apparent desertion of Private Trip, portrayed by Denzel Washington. Shaw brutally exacts military justice by having Washington's character whipped in front of the entire regiment, but later regrets it when informed by Freeman's character that he went looking for shoes which the soldiers were sorely lacking. Freeman's characters are often the repository of wisdom and knowledge for younger characters in films.

Unlike Chan and Tucker in *Rush Hour 2*, the combination of Li and Freeman in *Unleashed* sets a tone that depends on interpersonal development supplemented by action, rather than laughs. Director Louis Leterrier set out to make an atypical actioner, maintaining that he "was really intrigued of doing something strange, something we hadn't seen before." He may be referring to the sinister nature of the film: "I was really excited about the noir aspect of it—the film noir—the dark, underground, dirty, grimy aspect of it all. It was an action film with a twist."[126] That "twist" also depends on themes of subjugation and economic inequity. Against the backdrop of Glasgow, the interethnic friendship between Sam and Danny emerges from the confluence of ethnic culture and national association. Danny functions as a modern-day Chinese slave in the hands of the British mob boss Bart. His subjugation to Bart re-enacts China's subjugation to Britain and its subsequent damage to the national psyche of China. The film invites the audience to view the dynamic between Danny and Bart through the lens of national identity. Danny's subjugation by Bart reflects not just the damage of the Chinese national psyche, but also mirrors the psychological damage inflicted on enslaved Africans during the transatlantic slave trade of the eighteenth century. Danny's interethnic friendship with Sam resolves the psychic distress caused by his incarceration by Bart. A black man, Sam recognizes and addresses Danny's plight because they share a legacy of subjugation, an ethnic understanding that results in cultural exchange. Overall, Sam's friendship solves Danny's problem, one with national overtones, using sympathy based on a common ethnic experience.

Against the ethnic monolith that is Glasgow, Danny and his mother certainly stand out. Danny's mother was not a native to Glasgow; she was an exchange student studying at the conservatory music school. The viewer gets no information on her home country. Moreover, the film is also silent on specifics regarding Danny's own nationality. Both appear to be Asian and, although the film never specifies their nationality, the casting of Li leads audiences to surmise that both are Chinese nationals. Up to this point in his career, Li had never portrayed a non-Chinese character. Moreover, Danny and his mother appear to be Chinese nationals in economic distress. Danny's mother's financial issues bring her into contact with Bart and contribute to her exploitation by him. While a benign music exchange program places Danny and his mother in Glasgow, their brush with the criminal underworld severs Danny from his mother and introduces him to a life of subjugation defined by violence and economic inequity.

Danny functions as a modern-day Chinese slave. Separated from his mother, Danny is made the literal slave of Bart for the rest of his life. He receives no compensation for his work and lives in horrible conditions. Audiences would be able to gauge the brutality of Danny's experience by making such connections to the violence of human trafficking. *Unleashed* also characterizes Danny's incarceration as a violent economic exploitation of his labor. Although Danny is a member of a criminal organization, he resides at the bottom of the hierarchy. Often called upon to assault others, he functions as the muscle of the organization, working with his hands.

The opening sequence of the film sets this tone. Set into motion by Bart's command to "get them," the sequence shows Danny attacking several men at once. This is an important first sequence because it defines Danny's function to Bart: a worker. It is repeated several times throughout the film; this is all that Danny does. His trade is the violence and pain he inflicts on others. The fight sequences choreographed by Yuen Wo Ping are far more gritty and far less graceful than his martial arts work in films like *Hero* (2002). For example, a key sequence in this Chinese swordplay film between Li and martial arts star Donnie Yen occurs in the rain at a teahouse, where a blind musician accompanies the fight on his zither. For much of the encounter, there is very little movement, and when the fight commences, it is shot in slow motion to emphasize the grace of the movement. So subtle is the choreography, when Li delivers what appears to be the fatal blow to his opponent, the audience scarcely realizes it. There is no bloodshed.

In contrast, fight scenes in *Unleashed* are brutal. Danny's first appearance in an underground fighting match takes place in the submerged space of an empty swimming pool. The cheering, bloodthirsty crowd resembles observers at a Roman gladiator fight. Instead of elegant weapons, Danny has to face spiked bats, which clang noisily against the concrete of the swimming pool. Participants get slashed and visibly bleed during this fight to the death. The audience gets to see much of the contact made with hands against bodies. Li recognizes the brutality of the fight scenes: "You know, usually, you fight with five guys, you'll punch this one, you'll kick that one. But a dog is nuts. A dog just focuses on one. He knock you down first. Even if four guys behind him beating him up, he doesn't care. He just beat you up."[127] Such a brutal fight scene underscores the violence of Danny's "work." Not only is Danny's "work" violent, he is also economically exploited while he performs it. He receives no compensation for his dangerous labor. Bart uses it to outfit himself in fine, white suits while Danny is consigned to grungy, dirty garb. Danny is confined to a sparse, underground cage illuminated by a bare bulb while Bart lives lavishly. Danny functions as Bart's own source of profit in an unequal financial relationship enforced by violence and intimidation.

While Danny is not spirited away from his homeland by a ship to a foreign land, his modern-day experience with violence and economic exploitation also remarkably resembles that of a certain group of Chinese immigrants known as coolies in the nineteenth century. Robert Irick makes a distinction between "the coolie trade," which he equates to "a slave trade in Chinese labourers," and "the voluntary emigration of Chinese labor abroad under contracts."[128] Pressing labor needs in the Western hemisphere created an extreme demand for labor. While the participants in the coolie trade were Chinese, the trade itself was affected by two factors: the California gold rush that demanded large numbers of laborers to work the mines, and "the need for cheap unskilled labor in the Central and South American colonies following the general international renunciation of the African slave trade."[129] Countries like China with a large population were key targets for new labor and unscrupulous practices. Local agents resorted to kidnapping Chinese peasants. Once secured, Chinese laborers were herded into former warehouse space where "all egress was blocked and prohibited." Once aboard the ships, the Chinese "were herded below deck into quarters . . . [and placed in] dungeons [that] contained irons to keep the coolies in place."[130] Coolies were economically exploited for their labor under bad circumstances. Shipped to locations like Central and South America, they shared the fate of African slaves shipped before them. In the American West, in occupations like mining, Chinese workers experienced unequal pay as well as violence. Sucheng Chan recounts that violence, including "the maiming and wonton murder of individuals" and "spontaneous attacks against and the destruction (usually by fire) of Chinatowns."[131]

Danny's experience not only mirrored this combination of violence and economic exploitation, but also echoed the national relationship between Britain and China in the eighteenth and nineteenth century. As part of the "informal empire," China was coerced to hand over its resources, material and human, to the profit of Britain. Military force enforced this arrangement. Resat Kasaba notes that this arrangement was achieved as a result of military incursion: "Ultimately, the British, along with the French, fought two more wars, forced their way into Beijing and burned and looted the emperor's summer palace in order to gain the ratification of a series of free trade treaties."[132] In addition, diplomatic pressures represented by those treaties resulted in British economic exploitation of the Chinese. Referred to as the Unequal Treaties by the Chinese, they gave the Chinese the short end of the stick. The Treaty of Nanking (1842) forced China to cede Hong Kong to the British and open treaty ports; the Treaty of Tientsin (1858) forced open more ports to Western countries and allowed foreigners to travel into the interior regions of China. Such liberties disregarded China's sovereignty and bred inequities between the British and Chinese: "The relationship [between Europeans and Chinese] was permeated with suspicions that reflected its hierarchal nature, fed on cultural misunderstandings, and drew on the difficult relations between Europeans and Chinese at all levels under the old Canton system."[133]

More than just using a country for resources, there developed a discourse where Britain saw violence as crucial to maintaining its economic control over the course of the imperial relationship between Britain and China. Kasaba cites a British official who described: "Their minds are too shallow to receive an Impression that will last longer than some such period, and warning is of little use. They care little for words and they must not only see the Stick but actually feel it on their Shoulders."[134] The Chinese themselves began to see such impositions in terms of incarceration. Wang notes that in the 1920s, Chinese political agents adopted discourse using Chinese terms "which are easily intelligible to a broad audience and with a strong emotive charge. To the general public, words such as *daili* (agents), *zougou* (running dogs), *maishenqi* (self-selling indenture), *nuli shenfen* (slave status), *hushenfu* (amulet), *quaiwu* (monster) and *jiasuo* (shackles) were much easier to understand."[135] Sun Yat-sen linked the Unequal Treaties to nationalist discourse using more powerful rhetoric after 1923: "The phrase *bupingdeng tiaoyue* developed a series of confrontational and class-infected connotations such as 'threat,' 'slavery' and 'misery,' inflicted upon China by 'imperialism' and its 'agent' (*daili*) 'militarism.'"[136] The relationship between Bart and Danny parallels the violent economic exploitation figured in the dynamic between Britain and China.

Danny's subjugation to Bart also results in psychological damage through the use of physical restraint and mental control. Bart is able to secure Danny's labor through the use of a dog collar. The opening shots of the film feature close-ups of Danny that initially obscure details of his face and surroundings. The first clear shot focuses on Bart releasing the metal collar around Danny's neck. The collar is spring-loaded and rusty in some places and has left scars on his neck, indicating that Danny has been subdued with it for many years. It represents the physical manifestation of captivity and the power that Bart exerts over him. When Danny escapes Bart and wakes up in Sam's home, his inability to take the collar off demonstrates how he has internalized his incarceration. He has to learn to function without it, for while he wears it he is not truly free.

This physical restraint represents the primary metaphor for Danny's loss of humanity. As a result of being collared, Danny's eyes are lifeless when Bart takes him to collect protection money. His demeanor signals that he is unaware of what is going on around him. He only comes to life upon the removal of the collar, signaling him to attack others. Danny has no sense of self, no role independent of his function as enforcer, provided by Bart. After one fight, he does not even realize that he is bleeding from a cut on his head. He eats, and practices sparring with a weight bag, which develops a hole where sand starts to run out. Danny stands there, unsure of what to do with the gauze tape that one of Bart's henchmen gave him for his cut. He seems to understand that the hole in the bag is a wound, and that he also has a wound, but rather than bandage himself, he bandages the bag. He fails to take care of himself, demonstrating his lack of self-worth.

Not only does Danny have little regard for himself, he has difficulty developing bonds with others. Wary of those unfamiliar to him, Danny hides under the bed when Sam brings him a meal in his apartment. Leterrier wanted the film to support this kind of character development in Danny: "When you cast Jet Li, it becomes a martial arts film, and people are expecting something that I didn't wanna give them this time. And Jet didn't want to give them. He wanted to go further. He wanted to give some fights, but he wanted to make them more brutal, truer, harder, and then step away from this and become an actor afterwards."[137]

Such lack of self-worth results from Bart's attempt to give Danny a self-image of his own design. Bart constantly reminds Danny that he not only controls every aspect of his existence, but he also has created him. When a potential victim marvels at the way Bart "basically turned a man into a dog," Bart explains, "When you get them young enough, the possibilities are endless." He takes particular delight in shaping every aspect of Danny's development. Like slave masters, he provides the basic necessities in order "to make you the man that you are." When encountering Danny after his second escape, Bart seems enraged that Danny is going beyond the role and function Bart has fashioned for him. He taunts Danny by telling him, "You'll never escape what I made you."[138]

Bart not only robs Danny of an independent self, he also advocates a warped sense of family that establishes Danny as subhuman. Bart tells Danny that he is part of a family and even designates himself as Danny's uncle. But Bart promotes a dysfunctional notion of family based on hierarchy and dehumanization. Bart constantly reinforces himself as Danny's master rather than a family member. With Bart as master, Danny becomes the dehumanized dog, emphasized by one of the alternative titles of the film, *Danny the Dog*. Bart treats Danny as a pet. He keeps a collar on him (a point reinforced by a brief scene where Danny sees a dog with a collar while riding on a public transportation) and keeps him in a cage. Clearly, Bart has not taught Danny manners, because he eats his food without benefit of utensils. The one time that Danny fails to prevent an attack on Bart, he dehumanizes Danny even further by complaining, "even a dog has the brains to come to his master's defense."[139]

This kind of psychological damage echoes national metaphors that describe China as the "sick man of Asia" in a "century of humiliation." The phrase, "sick man of Asia," plays on the imagery of the phrase "sick man of Europe" in reference to the Ottoman Empire and its failure under pressure from other political powers. In the case of China, it points to a weakened China in the nineteenth and twentieth centuries as a result of internal schisms and pressures from Western powers (through the Unequal Treaties). Scholars such as Peter Gries examine the period using psychological terms to describe the impact on the Chinese psyche:

> Narratives about the "Century of Humiliation" frame the ways that Chinese understand themselves today. Most educated Chinese today are painfully aware of the "unequal treaties" signed with the British in 1842 and the Japanese in 1895. Unilateral concessions forced on the Chinese in treaties signed at those times such as indemnities, extra-territoriality, and foreign settlements in the treaty ports, are still perceived as humiliating losses of sovereignty. . . . The "Century," furthermore, is a traumatic and foundational moment because it fundamentally de-centered Chinese views of the world. In Chinese eyes, earlier invaders were Sinicized, and barbarians beyond the border paid humble tribute to "civilization" (*wenming*), reinforcing the Sino-centric view of Chinese civilization as universal and superior.[140]

This psychic harm echoes the low self-esteem Danny experiences at the hands of Bart.

Danny's psychological state not only reflects the damage to Chinese national pride, but also mirrors the psychological damage of enslaved Africans during the transatlantic slave trade in the eighteenth century. We can draw direct parallels between Danny's subjugation and that of Africans. While slavery existed in various forms around the world, the transatlantic slave trade became known for the lifelong status of the slave, and for the destruction of families, particularly in the United States. Once they were violently torn from their homes, African slaves were treated violently once they arrived in the Caribbean. One of the frequent modes of violence utilized was the whip: "In the hands of a stern overseer it could draw blood through the breeches of a slave. At times the floggings were so severe as to inflict wounds so large that a man's finger could be inserted in them."[141] Under threat of punishment, slaves worked sunup to sundown in backbreaking agricultural work with few breaks and inadequate food and clothing. It was this system that plantations in the United States sought preserve when states passed laws to institute lifelong servitude. Ronald Takaki argues that "where earlier it had been more expensive to invest in blacks as slaves than in whites as indentured servants, it became less of a risk as longevity increased for everyone. Lifetime servitude had become more profitable."[142]

As a result, slavery was all some could expect, a slavery experience with no economic compensation and punctuated with violence, just like the one Danny has. The use of physical objects like the metal dog collar that secures his subjugation hearkens back to the physical restraints of enslaved Africans. Such physical restraints were standard in the transatlantic slave trade of the eighteenth and nineteenth centuries. While middlemen secured Africans using many strategies, "slaves brought to the post for sale were always chained." Africans were also restrained in ships packed to capacity: "Chained together by twos, hands and feet, the slaves had no room in which to move about and no freedom to exercise their bodies even in the slightest."[143] Metal restraints became one of the most common used pieces of material culture used to denote the legacy of the transatlantic slave trade. Physical restraint defines the transatlantic slave trade, just as a metal collar controls Danny's movements.

Such physical bonds had the same psychological consequences we see in Danny. Like Bart, slavemasters used such devices to break the spirit of enslaved Africans and gain greater control over their charges. Takaki reminds us that "employing psychological reins, masters tried to brainwash their slaves into believing they were racially inferior and racially suited for bondage. Kept illiterate and ignorant, they were told they were incapable of caring for themselves."[144] Slavemasters took such measures to ensure the dividing line between slaves, whom they considered savage, and themselves, whom they considered civilized. Takaki uses Caliban from Shakespeare's *The Tempest* as a metaphor to explain the racialization of savagery: "To the theatergoers, Caliban represented what Europeans had been when they were lower on the scale of development. To be civilized, they believed, required denial of wholeness—the repression of the instinctual forces of human nature." Additionally, "Caliban appeared onstage at a time when the English were reading about associations between apes and Africans."[145] Given the perception on the part of slave-masters that slaves were inferior, their treatment represented attempts at dehumanization.

Danny's interethnic friendship with Sam resolves the psychic distress caused by his incarceration by Bart. A black man, Sam recognizes and addresses Danny's plight because they share a legacy of subjugation, an understanding that results in cultural exchange. The film parallels Danny and Sam early on to emphasize their similarities and set up their later relationship. In Glasgow, the largest city in Scotland, both Danny and Sam are outsiders. Sam is a black American who finds himself in Glasgow solely to secure a musical education for his stepdaughter. He is a temporary resident who intends to return to his permanent home in New York City. Given that Sam is one of only a handful of blacks shown in the film, the audience can infer that Glasgow is a predominantly white city. Director Louis Leterrier describes the setting of the film as postindustrial British working-class town: "To find a location—we went to London, which has a nice feel, but we've seen it before. I wanted something smaller. I wanted something more like—sort of like a small-time Gotham City. And then we found Glasgow, and that was it. Glasgow is such an amazing city for, like dark, grimy action."[146]

This location would deem Sam as an outsider because he is African American, but also because he makes his living not doing manual labor but performing a skill: tuning pianos. Danny also seems similarly out of place. Like Sam, Danny's Chinese identity makes him unusual within the context of the film. There are no other Chinese characters within his circle. Like Sam, Danny's "profession" further distances him from Glasgow's residents. In fact, Danny spends most of his time with Bart and his goons. Not only does he participate in the marginalized, underground world of criminal activity, he also occupies the lowest position in Bart's criminal organization. He is the muscle of the organization, and does not receive equitable compensation for his work.

More in keeping with the Afro-Chinese male friendship established by *Enter the Dragon*, Sam establishes a helpful position vis-à-vis Danny, ostensibly because he recognizes the ramifications of Danny's slave experience as an African American who bears a similar legacy. Whereas Danny does not acknowledge any of the victims of Bart's illegal enterprise, and barely acknowledges Bart's henchmen, the first time Danny speaks is to

Sam. This suggests that he feels that it is safe to do so. This scene suggests that Danny and Sam share something in common that Danny and Bart do not. From their initial meeting, it is clear that the dynamic between Danny and Sam is radically different from that between Sam and Bart. Sam immediately recognizes Danny's humanity. Inviting Danny over to help him, he explains, "Pianos are a lot like people. You pound on a person, they can get out of tune." Unlike Bart, Sam recognizes the destructive ramifications of violence. He recognizes Danny's reticence to initially get to know him: "It is as if something or someone has made him shut down his feelings so hard he can barely get in touch with them."[147] Sam observes that Danny's fear in his new environment in his apartment stems from his experience of being incarcerated. In response, Sam provides Danny with an environment where he is free. He gives Danny his own room with a bed. He provides pajamas as well as day clothes. Danny can come and go as he pleases; there are no locks on the door at Sam's apartment. Sam imposes few restrictions on Danny, a radical departure from the life of control exerted by Bart. Sam himself seems to know the value of a free life; a black man, his profession as a musician has allowed him to travel, and take employment that suits him. It would stand to reason that such a life was not easy to attain, thus making its value that much greater. As a result, Sam seeks to provide an environment where Danny too can experience such freedom.

Sam also provides a life filled with more upbuilding activities, in contrast to his violent life with Bart. Rather than dingy and blood-soaked underground fighting arenas and shady business deals that take place in darkly lit places, Danny's life with Sam is more domestic, at a distinctly less frenetic pace that takes place in brightly lit places and outdoor settings. Scenes with Bart are characterized by quick cuts from one violent encounter to another, with loud music to punctuate the brutality, whereas scenes with Sam are slower with more soothing music in the background. Danny is enticed out of his room by music. It is his fascination with music in the form of the piano that leads him to Sam in the first place. Victoria gets him to open up by sharing the piano with him, and he later declares that his life was literally saved by music. Such a domestic setting also leads to economic enfranchisement for Danny. While Bart forces Danny to act as muscle to attack delinquent clients, Sam invites Danny to help him tuning pianos. He teaches Danny a marketable skill. When Danny starts going out on calls with Sam and they tune pianos together, Sam makes a point to count out Danny's share, assuring him that they are "fifty-fifty, partners, you and me."[148] This is an economic relationship based on equity rather than exploitation.

Most importantly, Sam helps restore Danny's humanity. When Danny first shows up, he is very afraid, and cannot even bear to be touched. To coax out his personality, Sam speaks to Danny in soothing, inviting tones, a distinct difference from Bart, who only yells at him. He involves Danny in several nurturing activities, such as cooking, and invites him to eat dinner at the table. In addition, Sam uses the rhetoric of family, signaling that he acknowledges Danny's humanity as he would he own. Unlike Bart, who treats Danny as a pet, Sam sees Danny as family: "We've come to think of you as family." "That's what families do, they stick together."[149] If the discourse of slavery provides a link between Sam and Danny, then family is central. Sam and Victoria, his stepdaughter, already embody a nontraditional family brought together by circumstance. Sam marries Victoria's mother after her father dies, and soon after, Victoria's mother is also off the scene. Not blood related yet still family, this notion of extended family is prevalent in the transatlantic slave trade, where the separation of individuals from the same tribe prior to the Middle Passage and subsequent separation of families on American plantations fostered a more expansive way of thinking about family. It is through this lens that Sam views Danny.

Danny also has been separated from his family and placed in a life of servitude. The centrality of music to Sam and Victoria's lives allow Danny to remember his own mother's playing and love for him. Key to Danny's rehumanization is connecting to his past, a past obscured and distorted by Bart. Bart lies to Danny, telling him that he found him on the street and stresses that "no one cared whether he lived or died." When Danny asks about his background, Bart tells him: "Don't dwell on the past, look to the future; the past is behind you."[150] Conversely, Sam encourages Danny to discover his past. He takes Danny to the conservatory where his mother studied. While Bart tries to control the way Danny processes this information by telling him that his mother was a prostitute, Victoria instead directs his attention to the musical talent that she possessed. It is within Sam's family that Danny reconnects with his own family and regains a large measure of his humanity.

It is clear that Sam's efforts heal Danny's physical and psychic wounds inflicted by Bart. Danny slowly comes out of his shell, slowly develops likes and dislikes. More importantly, he decides that he no longer wants to participate in the violent world of his past. When Bart tries to force him to fight, he says he "doesn't want to hurt people anymore."[151] He further exercises his own newly developed agency by purposely wrecking the car to escape from Bart a second time and taking off his own collar, never to wear it again. Danny also exhibits the kind of compassion he learns from Sam by not killing Bart, despite his goading to do so. Significantly, this interaction between Sam and Danny creates a new trajectory in the Afro-Chinese buddy relationship. While Sam acts as a mentor to Danny, he really teaches him to be human. More importantly, Sam's ability to reach Danny is related to how Sam understands Danny's plight, as a person descended from enslaved Africans.

Just as in *Enter the Dragon*, a transnational location has huge impact on the types of interethnic dynamics that occur between African American and Chinese men. In Glasgow, Sam and Danny are outsiders but share a legacy of subjugation. If Danny's relationship with Bart is in part understood as a national dynamic, then it is an ethnic dynamic, the relationship between Danny and Sam, that counteracts its negative effects. Conversely, Carter and Lee in *Rush Hour 2* fall back on clichéd dynamics because their relationship relies on comedy based on differences grounded largely in national identity. Their relationship remains one clouded in distance, never allowing the characters to have true cultural exchange.

One may argue that the Afro-Chinese manifestation of the buddy arrangement is so pervasive because it is a dynamic that American audiences understand, in no small part, due to the success of *Enter the Dragon*. However, it is not the only form of Afro-Asian cultural dynamics to occur within a global context. Because Asian and Asian American cultures are different, it stands to reason that different combinations of Afro-Asian cultural production produce different results. As part of the appeal of his work, Lee's other films consider how the Chinese culture relates to another ethnic culture within an imperial context.

"Scheming, Treacherous, and Out for Revenge"

Ethnic Imperialism

While Bruce Lee's *Enter the Dragon* prefigures a theme of Afro-Chinese male friendship, *The Chinese Connection* (1972) (also known as *Fist of Fury*) interrogates a theme of ethnic imperialism. Set against the backdrop of Shanghai in 1908, tensions between Japan and China drive the action. While the previous chapter examined the impact of the "century of humiliation," largely attributed to the influence of Western powers, one cannot forget the impact Japanese incursions had on the Chinese psyche. While the Japanese and Chinese experienced cultural exchanges, tensions flared in the late 1800s over Korea, resulting in the First Sino-Japanese War (1894–95). China's loss in this conflict demonstrated the weakness of the Qing dynasty and foreshadowed its impending fall as well as the perpetuation of the notion of China as the "sick man of Asia."

The Chinese Connection takes advantage of these historical tensions, and weaves a story (loosely based on real events) of national pride and personal revenge. The film opens with Lee's character, Chen Zhen, who arrives by rickshaw in the rain to attend the funeral of his kung fu teacher, Huo Yuanjia. At the sight of the coffin, he is so overcome with emotion that he prostrates himself and must be knocked unconscious and carried away. When he comes to, he persists in his belief that someone murdered his teacher. While the Chinese martial arts school mourns the loss of their leader, representatives from the rival Japanese judo school arrive and disrupt their somber proceedings. Their interpreter, Mr. Hu, presents a sign that reads "Sick Man of Asia" and questions the masculinity of the mostly male student population. Many of the students are eager to fight, but the elders urge nonviolence. Unable to let the incident go, Chen Zhen visits the dojo and destroys the sign in a violent encounter with the leader of the judo school and their students. After leaving the school, he has an encounter with Japanese tourists at a park. Upon being refused entry by the Sikh guarding the gate and insulted by the Japanese patrons who are allowed to enter, he assaults the Japanese and destroys the "No Chinese or Dogs Allowed" sign.

Meanwhile, the judo school retaliates for Chen Zhen's earlier assault by attacking the Chinese martial arts school, injuring many of the students. The students are then faced with the decision to turn Chen Zhen over to the authorities for punishment. In the meantime, Chen Zhen overhears a conversation between two spies sent by the judo school to pose as students. They admit to poisoning his teacher at the behest of Suzuki, the leader of the judo school. In a rage, he kills them both and hangs their bodies from a lamppost in town. Despite the additional pressure from law enforcement this act brings, he continues his campaign of vengeance. He kills Hu, the Chinese translator, as well as Suzuki. Afterwards, he returns to the Chinese school to discover the deadly attack by the judo school. Realizing that he can end the violence against his brothers if he sacrifices himself, he surrenders himself to the police. The film ends with a still of Chen Zhen in a midair kick with the sound of a barrage of bullets in the background.

The Chinese Connection revolves around an attempt at ethnic imperialism by the Japanese, where the Chinese viewed the Japanese as foreigners encroaching on their sovereignty and resources. While the film focuses on the tensions between the Japanese and the Chinese, it also invokes the shadowy influence of the West, making the plot a nexus of relationships involving three cultures and nations. These international tensions are reflected in the historical significance of Huo Yuanjia, the subject of the funeral that opens the film. The real-life Huo was co-founder of the Jingwu Athletic Association and became known as a historic figure who used martial arts to defend China's reputation in a series of international competitions. Reportedly, after Huo defeated several representatives from Western countries, he was poisoned before his match with a Japanese master, and died during the tournament. The allusion to his suspicious death opens *The Chinese Connection* and introduces ethnic imperialism as a running undercurrent in the film. The film highlights tensions between the Chinese and Japanese martial arts schools. When Hu brings the Chinese school a sign that reads "Sick Man of Asia," he disrespects Huo's memory and antagonizes his students by challenging their masculinity, implying that the school and its students are weak. Hu also implies that Chinese culture is weak and that Japanese culture is superior.

The judo school seeks to eradicate the Chinese school in an effort to erase Chinese culture.

The Chinese Connection crafts the theme of ethnic imperialism by providing a sense of agency to the Chinese. Chen Zhen's course of revenge represents retaliation for the murder of his teacher as well as a defense of Chinese national character. The elders admonish him to refrain from retaliation, but this is not an option when he discovers that infiltrators from the judo school intentionally poisoned Huo. He embarks on a massive quest for revenge, targeting everyone from the Japanese assassins to Hu the interpreter and Suzuki himself. Everyone involved with the Japanese are implicated and must be punished. Just as the initial insults to Chinese culture can be read in nationalist terms, so too can Chen's retaliation.

Japanese cultural imperialism depicted in the film also symbolizes global forces. After fighting at the Japanese martial arts school and returning the sign, Chen Zhen visits a park. The Sikh gatekeeper denies him entry, pointing to the iconic sign of the film that reads: "No Dogs or Chinese Allowed." However, he allows a woman in Western garb to enter with her dog. When Chen Zhen questions his decision, the guard replies, "You're the wrong color, so beat it."[1] Soon after, a group of Japanese offers to take him in if he pretends to be a dog. Unable to contain his outrage any longer, he assaults the Japanese. With a spectacular kick, he breaks the "No Dogs or Chinese Allowed" sign into many pieces.

This act challenges the cultural erasure represented by Japanese imperialism, but in order to understand the full transnational ramifications of this act we need to understand the real-life significance of the park itself. Huangpu Park limited Chinese entry to servants of Westerners and Chinese law enforcement. As a result of complaints from Europeans, the policy changed until it settled on the famous articulation found in 1894 signage, namely, that most Chinese were to be barred and, later, that "These Gardens are reserved exclusively for the foreign community."[2] While Robert Bickers and Jeffrey Wasserstrom demonstrate that the sign never read "No Dogs and Chinese Allowed," they also reveal that the segregation of the park emanated from Western imperialism. The parks were "administered by the foreign-controlled Shanghai Municipal Council of the International Settlement in Shanghai" and that "the kind of prejudice that descriptions of the notice are typically used to conjure up certainly did exist, and that niceties of wording aside, native residents of old Shanghai unquestionably had good reason for finding the rules offensive, and for feeling that they were being treated as second-class citizens, even though the city they lived in was on Chinese soil."³ As a result, the ethnic imperialism has a third component involving Western powers.

The film transfers the characterization of imperialism from Western powers to the Japanese to underscore Chinese resistance to it. In the film, other Asians function as obstacles of entry in service to the Japanese, including the Sikh policeman who points out the sign and insults Chen Zhen and the Japanese officers who want him to act like a dog. The Western element is nearly invisible in the film, while the tensions between the Chinese and Japanese remain in the foreground. Chen Zhen's victory with the destruction of the sign signals an empowerment of the Chinese in the face of Japanese oppression. Stephen Teo notes that Lee's characters in films like *The Chinese Connection* fight for a cause "based on racial awareness, on the quest to make the Chinese character a dignified, respected and honoured figure."⁴

The characterization of the Japanese as imperial enemy resonated with African American culture in the 1970s. Like the Chinese, African American culture was subject to efforts at containment. The government infiltrated African American organizations, like the Black Panthers, and conspiracies abounded in the assassinations of major African American leaders like Malcolm X and Martin Luther King Jr. Chen Zhen's revenge against the Japanese, particularly the public hanging of their dead bodies from lampposts, represents a transnational echo of racial violence experienced by African Americans in the South in the United States. So while the audience surmises that he dies in a hail of bullets heard in the final frame of the film, the overall impression is one of victory over imperial forces.

From *The Chinese Connection* emerges a theme of ethnic imperialism, where the Japanese are characterized as an overriding and controlling force. The characterization of the Japanese as enemy reemerged in the late 1990s, where economic successes underscored images of the Japanese as conquering hordes. In the 1980s media and film had described the Japanese as faceless figures who sought to take over the United States through businesses and corporations. Post-1990 Afro-Asian cultural production reproduces and challenges this manifestation of ethnic imperialism. In his novel *Japanese by Spring* (1992), Ishmael Reed uses Japanese economic imperialism that ultimately relies on national association and maintains distance between African American and Japanese cultures. Conversely, *Samurai Champloo* (2004), the Japanese anime series, uses African American hip-hop to articulate youth-driven Japanese individualism. Because the series addresses both ethnic and national dynamics, it reinforces the synergy between the two cultures. *The Chinese Connection* establishes a model of Afro-Japanese dynamics that characterizes the Japanese as an imperial enemy. Using the Chinese as the object of Japanese cultural imperialism, the film employs a transnational dynamic. It brings together ethnic identity and national association in a way that prompts a variety of responses in Afro-Asian cultural production.

Black Dragon Society: Japanese Allies and Enemies in Ishmael Reed's *Japanese by Spring*

The Chinese Connection prefigures the theme of ethnic imperialism, with the Japanese as the antagonists who represent a colonizing power bent on erasing Chinese culture and imposing Japanese culture upon the citizens. Hu, the Japanese translator, taunts the Chinese martial arts students by calling China "the sick man of Asia." Reed's *Japanese by Spring* revisits this mode of ethnic imperialism involving the Japanese. By citing the largely unfamiliar history of Afro-Japanese solidarity from the early twentieth century, the novel highlights parallels in American perceptions of African Americans and Japanese as threats to the social fabric. Ultimately, the novel uses post-1990 Japanese "imperialism" to enforce distance between African American and Japanese cultures, deemphasizing Afro-Japanese solidarity even after recovering its history. Cultural distance results from this reliance on national association rather than ethnic culture.

Whether or not you agree with Ishmael Reed that he is the only true practicing multiculturalist, it is hard to deny that he has been a consistent voice calling attention to the interplay among multiple ethnic groups throughout his career. As someone "who for years has aired the dirty laundry of the black, white, yellow and the brown community," Reed feels free to critique ethnic American culture with impunity.[5] In addition to being a unique voice of African American culture, Reed is one of the only major African American writers who emerged during the 1960s to place his own literary vision vis-à-vis an Asian American one. Early in his career, Reed utilizes a "writing is fighting" style that directly addresses power inequities in ways that reclaim masculinity for black men. Such aggressive language provides a model for ethnic masculinity taken up by Asian American writers like Frank Chin. "In a world where manliness counts for everything," Chin admires "bad blacks" who "had a walk, a way of wearing their pants on the brink of disaster, a tongue, a kingdom of manly style everyone respected."[6] At the same time, Reed finds in Asian myth complements to his own work, sharing common ground with writers like Chin who used Chinese heroism: "I got a clue from Frank Chin about the parallels between ancient tales from China and African American folktales. That life is war, survival, and how one uses tactics and strategies."[7] These cultural exchanges demonstrate that Reed is interested, not only in including other ethnic cultures in his work, but in the ways that the ethnic cultures interact.

Reed's specific interest in the dynamics between blacks and Asian Americans is reflected in his own publication projects as well. He seems particularly drawn to Asian American writers like Chin and Shawn Wong, two outspoken and prolific Asian American writers. Two of the writers dubbed the "Four Horsemen of Asian American Literature," they "combine their experience with that of other ethnic groups" and "[are] influenced by black and white culture" while maintaining their own ethnic identity.[8] In 1974 Reed worked on *Yardbird Reader III* with Chin and Wong. In 1979 he edited and contributed to *Calafia: The California Poetry*, a multicultural anthology that featured Wong as an advisor on Asian American literature and Al Young as an advisor on African American literature. Reed also cofounded the Before Columbus Foundation, which has produced multicultural anthologies in poetry and fiction. With these publications, Amritjit Singh and Bruce Dick assert that Reed anticipates an art that "would reflect the new demographic realities which are sure to emerge with new immigration from Asia, Africa and the Americas."[9] Sharon Jessee lauds the fact that he "envisions the multiculture as sort of collective consciousness to be created through cultural exchanges between individuals and groups which will revitalize not only their individual experiences but their culture as well."[10]

The dynamics between African American and Asian and Asian American cultures form a consistent trend in Reed's fiction. The Chinese bookend Reed's first novel, *The Free-Lance Pallbearers* (1967). The early pages of the novel portrayed Chinese men as a dangerous contingent in the fictional land of HARRY SAM: "DEM CHINAMEN DONE GALLOPED INTO THE SUBURBS ON WERWOLF SANDALS/KIDNAPPING HEEL-KICK-ING HOUSEWIVES HANGING OUT DA WASH."[11] The novel ends with a flashing sign of the "new" regime "WRITTEN IN CHINESE NO LESS."[12] HARRY SAM, the name of both the city and the dictator who runs it, represents a dominant culture that manipulates various elements in its efforts to control the public. The Chinese function as one means of manipulation by the powers-that-be. The dominant powers use the image of the yellow peril, reflective of the rise of Communism in China in the late 1960s, to scare the public at the beginning of the novel. Rather than suggesting that the Chinese are a menace, Reed uses them to illustrate the ways that the dominant culture manipulates the masses. In doing so, he shows how one culture uses another culture for a particular effect.

Reed's 1982 novel *The Terrible Twos* prefigures his interest in Japanese forays into American culture. In one scene, two businessmen give their opinion about the impact of the Japanese on the American economy during a parade: "That's why the Japs are ahead of us. Did you see that little Jap sucker on TV the other night? He said that America can't be good at everything all the time and that we must allow some nations to be at least pretty good at some things. I felt like pushing my fist right through the TV and mashing in that little Jap's face."[13] The businessmen's use of the derogatory term "Jap" reflects an anti-Japanese sentiment that ran rampant in the United States in the 1980s. Often, the critiques revolved around Japanese business practices during a time that witnessed Japanese economic ascendancy and American economic stagnation. Kan Ito asserts, "Many Americans would like to believe these days that they are innocent victims of Japan's trade and investment activities, which are variously described as unbalanced, unfair, aggressive, one-sided and predatory."[14] Reed does not include the Japanese in his fiction merely for multicultural flair. He contextualizes them to make a point about the larger American perspective. He will take this one step further by figuring such sentiments in relation to African Americans in *Japanese by Spring*.

Reed further distinguishes himself by focusing on the interplay among ethnic groups, which has often been overlooked by scholars. Many scholars recognize his multicultural impulse. Robert Eliot Fox asserts that Reed's "recognition of the fact that the American pie has been baked from a variety of recipes and ingredients led [him] into a perspective that could aptly be termed multicultural with a 'minority' emphasis."[15] Fox's focus on Reed's use of multiple ethnic cultures fails to articulate the ethnic cultures he uses. He ascribes to Reed a generalized multicultural impulse that functions on mere inclusion. Other critics insist on characterizing his multicultural move as essentially Afrocentric. Chester J. Fontenot acknowledges that Reed uses Asian myth, but insists that "his importance to us as we consider the way in which Reed constructs a new system of thought lies in his synthesis of various aspects of African diasporic culture."[16] While an African diasporic orientation can be complex in itself,

Fontenot alludes to it in a unified way and privileges it over Reed's clear use of Asian myth. While Fontenot and Fox both note that he engages multiple ethnic cultures, they fail to acknowledge the interplay among different cultures in Reed's work.

While the Chinese and Japanese only make small appearances in his previous novels, Reed turns his full attention to the dynamic between the Japanese and American blacks in *Japanese by Spring*. The novel follows the exploits of a conservative black professor, Benjamin "Chappie" Puttbutt, as he attempts to secure tenure at predominantly white Jack London College in California. To better position himself, Puttbutt consciously subscribes to positions he thinks will improve his worth. He takes Japanese lessons from Dr. Yamato, a private teacher, in order to prepare himself for what he views as the coming ascendancy of the Japanese on the world stage. He espouses feminist theories to curry favor with the faculty in Women's Studies. He hides his contempt for the fighting factions within the African American Studies department. Most importantly, he carefully grooms himself to be the definitive conservative voice on black America by focusing on the "dysfunction" within black communities, to the delight of many traditionalists within and outside the Department of Humanity.

Puttbutt's world is turned upside down when the college denies his bid for tenure. Ironically, financial woes make the college ripe for a takeover by Japanese businessmen and the college inaugurates a Japanese administration led by Dr. Yamato. Chappie finds himself in a position to retaliate against all who thwarted his academic aspirations. He delights in calling out the intolerance of the feminists and the shoddy scholarship of the traditionalists. However, when Chappie sees Dr. Yamato enacting repressive measures against both students and faculty, he switches sides again in a last-ditch effort to oust Dr. Yamato. That revolution is short-lived, for Major Puttbutt, Chappie's high-ranking military father, arrests Dr. Yamato for conspiracy to kill the Japanese prime minister. Chappie exits the text after receiving a plum assignment acting as a translator for his parents, who have been assigned to Japan by the United States government.

Reed's novel recovers an unfamiliar legacy of Afro-Japanese cooperation and creates a character capable of navigating that complex landscape, who can operate in several ethnic spheres. Not only is Chappie well versed in the various factions on the Jack London campus, he also embodies the complexity of a black man in academia. Despite his quest to be the "true" voice of the African American experience, willing to expose its flaws, Chappie reflects the tensions of double consciousness and the anxiety that comes from having to bend to the low expectations of others. It is this complex personality that makes Chappie amenable to navigating the Afro-Japanese landscape created by Reed.

In order to navigate a landscape populated by African American, American, and Japanese cultures, Reed creates a protagonist with a degree of moral flexibility, which makes him the ideal vehicle to expose the ways that African American and Japanese cultures come together. Reed's persona in the novel refers to Chappie as "The Schmoo of American Culture": "Al Capp's creature, who was an all-purpose thing. . . . Chappie wasn't for any group. He was for Chappie, which is what he meant when he was always referring to himself as an existentialist, the hip philosophy for the individualist."[17] Lacking a fixed sense of self, Chappie's allegiances seem to change with the circumstances. Motivated by self-interest, he possesses an ability to ascertain expectations of others and manipulate those expectations: "When the Black Power thing was in, Puttbutt was into that. When the backlash on Black Power settled in, with its code words like reverse discrimination, he joined that. He'd been a feminist when they were in power."[18] Chappie's ability to perform such ideological shifts makes him the ideal vehicle to navigate a terrain where African American and Japanese cultures interact with one another.

Chappie justifies his role as an aficionado of African American culture by claiming expertise in the knowledge of American blacks. His critique of African Americans reflects his knowledge of their experiences as well as his knowledge of critics of a progressive African American political agenda. The contortion of his personality to fit the expectations of his more traditional colleagues shows that he knows what certain sectors of higher education value. He plays to his colleagues' expectations about race: "It was the biggest literary hustle going and Puttbutt decided that he was going to get his. He had written a dozen or so articles about affirmative action. About how your white colleagues don't respect you. About how you feel stigmatized. About how you feel inferior. You know, the usual. All of these speeches, op-eds and lectures, he felt, would get him where he wanted to be. Would get him tenure."[19] In fact, Chappie seeks to build a career in being the African American "go-to guy on racial matters, a person that doesn't ruffle the sensibilities of whites in power":

Puttbutt was a member of the growing anti-affirmative action industry. A black pathology merchant. Throw together a three-hundred-page book with graphs and articles about illegitimacy, welfare dependency, single-family households, drugs and violence; paint the inner cities as the circles of hell in the American paradise—the suburban and rural Americas which were, in the media's imagination, wonderlands with sets by Disney—and you could write your way to the top of the best-sellers list. Get on C-SPAN.[20]

Chappie understands that issues such as welfare dependency play into mainstream American fears about inequity. By reinforcing images of the inner city as dangerous and mostly populated by blacks, Chappie shows his knowledge about anxieties surrounding violence in America. His actions demonstrate his knowledge of how to play the academic game.

Such schemes not only demonstrate Chappie's intimate knowledge of mainstream American culture, but also his ability to use that knowledge to manipulate those around him. His actions are calculated to get him ahead in academic circles, knowing that his opposition to programs that seek to address inequities puts him in allegiance with more powerfully situated academics. When he criticizes a program for blacks or justifies some political issue that continues inequity, he notes that "his colleagues would often congratulate him on his position that blacks were their own worst enemies" and give him props "for saying the truth" the way they see it.[21] But Chappie consciously spews such opinions to gain their favor: "It was almost a formula. He knew the formula well. Say that the blacks were lowering the standards of American education. Jimmy some facts about test scores. Argue that the blacks desired multicultural education because they couldn't cut it with the tough Eurocentric curriculum. Justify the Eurocore curriculum by arguing that American liberal values arise from the West."[22] Chappie consciously distorts these issues facing African Americans. He knows that blacks face inequities in education, but he blames their lack of motivation. He understands the movement to include more African American perspectives in subject matter in academia, but characterizes the motives as insincere. Not only does Chappie know the contours of dominant cultural discourses poised against diversity, he also knows how to deploy their arguments for maximum effect.

However, Chappie pays a price for his knowledge and manipulation. His efforts to advance his position within the American mainstream create internal tension between Chappie's public conservative persona and his black radical background. It shows another element of the double consciousness that W. E. B. Du Bois eloquently describes. The "twoness" that Du Bois describes is the effect of a "warring body"; the perceptions from without and from within, when not aligned, produce a sense of instability.

In Chappie's case, this tension makes it difficult for him to shed his more ethnically informed past. Prior to arriving at Jack London College, Chappie challenged the status quo and advanced militant black causes. When a white female student asks about his credentials, Chappie thinks: "In the 1960s, when he was a TA with a huge Afro and addicted to blackness, . . . when he was a black militant firebrand and chairperson of the black caucus at the Air Force Academy, he would have told her to kiss his deguchi."[23]

In his younger days, Chappie embraced a confrontational brand of blackness. Branded as a troublemaker by the administration, the ideals of black nationalism are symbolized by his Afro, which "was so big that once some blackbirds tried to make a nest in it," much like the Afro Jim Kelly sports as Williams in *Enter the Dragon*.[24] Chappie never fully suppresses his radical personality and sometimes loses his composure as a result of the inner struggle to maintain the conservative mask. A number of what appears to be stress-related ailments clearly stem from his repression of this more radical black self: "Puttbutt's gum problems intensified during the semester when he taught. He experienced heart palpitations and insomnia. He got indigestion a lot and had to keep a box of baking soda on hand."[25] These physical problems are exacerbated when he has to encounter white students who undermine his authority in class, challenge his credentials, and generally disrespect him as a professor. Following the conclusion of a meeting with a student responsible for a racist cartoon involving Chappie, where the student calls black academics Chappie's "jungle bunny friends," he can hardly stand: "He felt as though he were suffocating. His chest felt stuffed. He felt lightheaded. He had to hold on to a desk to avoid passing out."[26] The pressure of maintaining the mask is too much for him because he is not entirely comfortable with his deracinated public persona. As Kenneth Womack observes, the reaction represents "Puttbutt's secret accord with the multicultural project, despite his monocultural public persona."[27]

This struggle matters, for not only does it inform Chappie as a character, it underscores his function as a liaison between African American and Japanese cultures. His black radical origins coincide with his first interactions with Japanese culture, which provide the foundation for the later discovery of a historical Afro-Japanese legacy. He begins his study of the Japanese language as an Air Force Academy cadet. As an academic, Chappie continues to place value on his study of the Japanese language: "Puttbutt figured that with Japanese under his belt he would adjust to the new realities of the coming postsettler era, a time when the domination of the United

States by people of the same background would come to an end. . . . If the Asian thing was going to fly he wanted to at least be in coach. . . . Studying Japanese would put him where the yen was."[28]

Chappie's forays into African American, American, and Japanese cultures are intertwined and transnational in nature. Rather than merely pitting these cultures against one another, *Japanese by Spring* notes their parallels and reveals a hidden history in the process. Chappie is pivotal to the way the novel reveals the ways that American culture similarly constructs African Americans and the Japanese as threats against the social fabric of the United States that must be contained. Both American blacks and the Japanese are constructed as military threats. Using figurative military language derived from the World War II era to describe the two groups in contemporary times, the novel constructs both as threats because they represent ethnic differences that have the potential to disrupt the notion of a monocultural America. Such anxieties are transnational in nature, focused on the parallels in construction of African Americans and the Japanese (rather than Japanese Americans) and a largely unfamiliar history of Afro-Japanese cooperation.

American characterizations of the Japanese as military threats based on foreign status can be traced to the 1930s and 1940s. Prior to that time, the Japanese had a careful relationship with the United States, as demonstrated through such diplomatic relationships as the Gentlemen's Agreement of 1907. While the United States enacted specific immigration laws to severely limit the influx of Chinese immigrants, the Gentlemen's Agreement permitted certain forms of Japanese immigration. However, by the interwar period, the United States began to construct a more sinister image of the Japanese, one contextualized by a military discourse based on the Japanese as enemy combatants. The 1905 Japanese victory over Russia and subsequent military attacks on Pearl Harbor caused dominant American culture to characterize the Japanese as a military threat based on their status as a foreign power.

By the 1940s the Japanese were consistently conferred an enemy status attributed to their nationality, and nowhere was this more apparent than during Japanese internment during World War II. In justifying Executive Order 9066, which created the interment, General John L. De Witt, head of the Western Defense Command, reflected a characterization of the Japanese as enemy based on their foreign status: "[There are] approximately 288,000 enemy aliens . . . which we have to watch. . . . I have little confidence that the enemy aliens are law abiding or loyal in any sense of the word. Some of them yes; many, no. Particularly the Japanese. I have no confidence in their loyalty whatsoever. I am speaking now of the native born Japanese—117,000—and 42,000 in California alone."[29] DeWitt's use of the phrase "enemy aliens" placed stress on national origin as the cause for military concern. He even goes further to single out "native born Japanese" as the group he sees as the most dangerous. Moreover, nationalist societies such as The Black Dragon Society (Kokuryukai) and Dark Ocean Society (Genyosha) caused a great deal of anxiety for the American military. Herbert Norman describes such organizations as Japanese "patriotic societies" concerned with "declaiming against the government, foreigners, Korea, pension commutation and other targets of reactionary abuse."[30] In essence, they wanted to build up Japan, seeking support within both Japan and the United States. As we will discover later in the chapter, the United States documented multiple instances of recruitment efforts among African Americans within the United States.

The construction of the Japanese as nonwhite also contributed to the concept of the military threat they posed. According to Marc Gallicchio, the military was highly suspicious of the Pacific Movement of the Eastern World, a pro-Japanese organization within the United States, and he characterized its activities this way: "The idea . . . is that Japan is the international leader of the colored races—yellow, black and brown in the forthcoming challenge of the colored races to white supremacy and the duty of the colored population in white territory is to strike in the rear the white overlords when Japan is assailed by any white power."[31] The military saw such organizations as promoting the nationalistic cause of Japan, a quest that also promoted the racial superiority of Japan. Such discourse became more prevalent during the early twentieth century within the context of World War II. Theodor Geisel, best known as Dr. Seuss, created scores of editorial cartoons deriding the totalitarian regimes of Russia, Italy, and Japan. The ones that featured figures from Japan play on racial stereotypes. They are consistently depicted as cats, to emphasize their untrustworthy nature, and in large numbers, which pointed to the "yellow peril" fear. So, the 1940s contextualized the characterization of the Japanese as military threats based on race and national association.

Reed's novel uses this characterization from the early twentieth century to describe post-1990 U.S.–Japanese dynamics, in which the Japanese again come off as military threats long after the world wars are over. Major Puttbutt uses a military context when trying to convince Chappie about his suspicions about the Japanese presence in the United States.

He couches his allusions to the rise of Japan's influence in the 1980s in militaristic terms from the 1940s: "Whether you know it or not, there's real trouble ahead for this Japanese-American alliance that's been going on since the end of the war. We may have to fight them again. There might be another Pearl Harbor."[32] Major Puttbutt envisions a continuous, unchanging postwar era stretching from the end of World War II to the present. His statement does not acknowledge any shifts in the dynamics between the United States and Japan, nor any change in the internal cultural dynamics of Japan. Major Puttbutt also reveals how he personally feels about the Japanese. A high ranking member of the U.S. military, he demonstrates condescension towards the Japanese as a people by referring to them as "Nips"—a derogatory slang term derived from Nipponese, a Japanese name for the Japanese people that gained widespread usage by the military during the 1940s—in front of his own Japanese American assistant. He does not even realize his degradation of the Japanese when he refers to them in this manner.

Major Puttbutt is not the only one. Others who are suspicious about the Japanese in the novel also resort to using military language from the 1940s that characterize the Japanese as military threat in the present. President Stool of Jack London College reflects the same sentiments in his racist comments: "Seems that some of the money that UC Berkeley received recently was traced to that Jap mob. The Yakuza. God, isn't it awful. I'm dreaming about Japs a lot since they bought Rockefeller Center and Radio City Music Hall. . . . To think that my dad did the Long March at Bataan, and now the yellow monkeys are taking over the place. They came swarming on us in Korea, too. Human waves."[33] Stool begins by characterizing Japanese businessmen as members of the criminal underworld and seamlessly transitions to using "Japs," another derogatory term from the 1940s to describe Japanese businessmen. He is even more straightforward, using images that directly play on the fear of the yellow peril.

The Japanese and African Americans in the novel share the characterization as threats to the American social fabric. The novel echoes how contemporary American society characterizes African Americans as combatants in a military engagement that promotes a sense of fear similar to that caused by the Japanese. Urban American blacks are characterized as a threat to domestic interests: "Relying on the enemy class to save one's ass wasn't new in history. There was an element of truth in what the grandfather said. Both politicians and scholars on the right were equating the multiculturalists, the 'rebels' and 'rioters' who took to the streets after the Simi Valley jurors acquitted the four policemen who brutalized Rodney King, with barbarians."[34] The narrator links the characterization of the Japanese during WWII to commentary about blacks in Los Angeles in the 1990s. Against the backdrop of the riots, blacks are the enemy. By calling them barbarians, these commentators suggest that blacks represent outsiders who pose a threat. Some accounts of the 1992 Los Angeles uprising characterized African Americans as a destructive force disrupting the calm of American society, much like a ravaging horde. Darnell Hunt quotes a white respondent who explains: "If I was that young and I saw it, you know, a bunch of African Americans just beating up on white people and just like running, you know, just like starting fires and everything . . . I'd just be so scared of black people after that."[35] Such characteristics depict blacks as dangerous elements in the United States.

It is perhaps these similarities that make Chappie's grandfather's loyalty to Japan relevant in the contemporary day. He recalls the "trickeration" of his day, where African Americans recognized efforts by mainstream America to obstruct an ethnic alliance: "Back there in Detroit. Me and my friends didn't think like the rest of the blacks in those days. Bowing and scraping to the white man and worshiping Jesus. We were ahead of our time. Proud. All the rest of these niggers were spellbound by the trickeration of these white people."[36] Chappie's grandfather refers to the lesser-known narrative of sympathy between African Americans and the Japanese during the 1940s. He sees a promising alternative in an alliance with the Japanese: "Son, you can't trust these devils. They got you thinking the way they think. They tried to take over Asia, but the Japanese people stopped them. Japan was the only country that wasn't colonized by them. That's what World War II was all about. Pearl Harbor. Hell, ain't nobody told the white man to come to Hawaii. Had no business having his ships there. All these other niggers was sorry when the Japanese hit those ships, those fools. Me and my friends was glad and we said so. Look, Grandson. The Japanese were standing up for the concept of Pan-Asia, just as the blacks were fighting for Pan-Africa. There ain't no difference."[37]

Chappie's grandfather's contemporary loyalties to the Japanese echo the ways that African Americans came to see the Japanese not as an enemy, but as a symbol of the need for racial equality in the world during the early twentieth century. African Americans perceived the Japanese as the "champions of the colored people" of the world following the defeat of Russia in the Russo-Japanese War of 1905. In a survey of African

American newspapers, Reginald Kearney found that the favorable perception of the Japanese by African Americans reached their height as a result of such factors as "Japan's role in China, reports of Japan's efforts to aid Ethiopia in its war with Italy, certain goodwill gestures of the Japanese, the despair felt by southern agricultural workers, and a visit to Japan by W. E. B. Du Bois."[38] In addition to newspaper coverage, African Americans formed Afro-Japanese organizations to support a perceived solidarity.

Interest in Japan on the part of African Americans also brought them into contact with Japanese nationalist societies. The participation of student members of Kokuryukai, the Black Dragon Society, a patriotic Japanese group, in efforts to convince Tokyo to enter the war on Ethiopia's behalf impressed African American readers of the *Pittsburgh Courier* in 1935. The Ethiopian Pacific Movement was initially launched "to foster an alliance between the darker races, starting with the superpatriots of the Black Dragon Society."[39]

Such sympathies also took on a military cast during the 1930s. While American military leaders viewed the Japanese invasion of Manchuria as evidence of imperial ambitions that could eventually reach the United States, African Americans believed that "aggression of the Japanese in China was mean to bring together the colored peoples of the world in some kind of anti-imperialist coalition."[40] Rather than casting the Japanese as enemies, some African Americans viewed them as allies in a common struggle against racism and colonization. This was evident in groups that brought together African Americans and Japanese of like mind. Kearney notes links between the Kokuryukai and African Americans concerned with the fate of Ethiopia. While Italy threatened Ethiopia, African Americans perceived that Japan, and groups like the Kokuryukai, protected it from such Western incursions: "The ordinary people of Japan clamored to support the regime of Haile Selassie. Americans who regarded it as a sinister organization 'conjectured that the Black Dragon Society [was] attempting to influence the Japanese government to intercede on behalf on Ethiopia.'"[41] The rhetoric used to describe such affinities challenged the American military rhetoric that cast the Japanese as enemy: "The very name of the Black Dragon Society disturbed, perhaps even shocked white American psyches. . . . African Americans, however, liked the image of strength connoted in the symbol of a black dragon. [They] . . . liked the symbolic imagery of a Japanese black dragon doing battle with the American eagle or British lion."[42] Seeing the Japanese as an ally rather than an enemy countered the prevailing notion of mainstream America. African Americans viewed the Japanese as fellow workers against white power structures.

African American newspapers echoed this same sentiment in the 1940s, challenging mainstream American characterizations of the Japanese. Kearney notes that African Americans identified as segregationist legislation directed toward the Japanese in the early twentieth century: "These actions of the San Francisco school board and the California legislature made blacks and Japanese fellow victims of racism. Clearly this was an opportunity for African Americans to identify with the Japanese in a fashion less remote than the precarious associations made during the war between Japan and Russia."[43] Kearney explains that African Americans were drawn to the Japanese because such an identification placed them "in a context in which people of color determined their own destinies, built their own institutions, and drew upon their own heritage."[44] In this way, Chappie's grandfather interprets the attack on Pearl Harbor as an attack on a racist country by a force sympathetic to his own sensibilities. This link between Pan-African and Pan-Asian ideas gestures toward the emerging global sensibilities among American blacks regarding nationalism, whose "cries would echo across the vast continent of mother Africa."[45]

Chappie's grandfather also brings such sentiments into the contemporary day, altering the characterization of African Americans and Japanese as enemies to the United States by focusing on a kind of Afro-Japanese alliance where the United States engages in bad behavior. He casts contemporary financial actions by the Japanese as reminiscent of their actions during the 1930s and 1940s: "The Japanese are buying Amerika. Hell, they just bought the Sheraton Place across the bridge in San Francisco. They're not acting like somebody who lost the war." The grandfather continues to cast Japanese actions in a militaristic, yet positive, light, using a rhetoric of Afro-Japanese alliance:

> It just ain't going to work. Even if all of the black people became prosperous tomorrow, there's no reason why they won't take it away from them. . . .
> They took it away from the Cherokee, our ancestors, when they became middle class, they even took it away from the Nikkei-jin who were trying to be so goody-goody. Kissing up to the white man. Even fought in the war on the American side against their own people. Assisted in the American Occupation of Japan. Now what makes you think that they won't take it way from us?[46]

The grandfather cites a recognizable pattern of economic inequity shared by blacks and the Japanese. He rationalizes that in America's contemporary economic shift, the same economic disfranchisement could befall blacks. All the while, he references the same militaristic rhetoric that characterizes both the Japanese and African Americans as threats.

It is important to note that *Japanese by Spring* consistently characterizes the Japanese as Japanese, rather than Japanese Americans, to reinforce the transnational anxiety. Clearly identified Asian American characters make relatively few appearances in the novel, and when they do, it spares little space to concretely deal with their complex impact on race relations in general and African Americans in particular. For example, Reed depicts Muzukashii, a second-generation Japanese American student, as an individual defined by his attempts to ingratiate himself with whites. Declaring that "the distance between him and his Japanese heritage was about the distance between the tortoise and the moon," Muzukashii seeks every opportunity to insult Puttbutt in class in order to impress the white kids and become accepted by them.[47] The novel fails to elaborate on the antagonism between Muzukashii and Puttbutt that clearly alludes to instances in which various Asian American groups are used as a leverage ethnic group against blacks. Muzukashii evokes the "model minority" myth often applied to Asian Americans. According to Frank Wu, the myth depends in part on other racial minorities: "[Asian Americans] are placed in the awkward position of buffer or intermediary, elevated as the preferred racial minority at the expense of denigrating African Americans."[48] The novel passes up the opportunity to delve into the notion that Asian Americans use their status as model minorities to ingratiate themselves with whites at the expense of Blacks. Vijay Prashad says rather bluntly that Asian Americans "are not simply a solution for black America, but, most pointedly, a *weapon* deployed against it."[49] The novel sets up a situation where a Japanese American denigrates a black American in order to curry favor with whites, yet neglects to explore the impact of those dynamics on more general African American/Asian American relations.

Chappie's grandfather's observations reveal the similar construction of both the Japanese and African Americans as military and economic threats and uncover the history of sympathy between the two. However, recognizing such parallels does not necessarily translate into cultural exchange. In fact, the novel fails to capitalize on its unveiling of the obscure history of Afro-Japanese solidarity. Initially, Chappie is part of the Japanese takeover of Jack London College and supports policies designed to dismantle oppressive white power at the school. However, the novel divides Chappie and Yamato, making it impossible for Chappie to follow his agenda. While the novel uses rhetoric that envisions them as active agents of cultural exchange, and sees them as common victims of national identity emanating from the United States, it keeps alive the specter of distrust between the two. This ultimately results in cultural distance between African American and Japanese cultures.

At first, the novel points to a contemporary Afro-Japanese alliance when Dr. Yamato appoints Chappie to a high-level post in his administration. It seems they are on the same page. When Chappie asks, "Why would you need my help?" Yamato replies, "I need somebody with whom I can communicate. Somebody that I can trust."[50] He tries to instill a curriculum that is not Eurocentric: "Changes are in order. We will help them. Try to civilize them. Show them that there are some things that all educated people must know in order to be culturally literate."[51] He plans to move the Department of Humanity into Ethnic Studies, despite his belief that "all [the courses] accomplish for these people is to glory some mythic past and to promote such dubious claims that Europe is the birthplace of science, religion, technology and philosophy."[52] He also intends to beef up the teaching of Japanese culture. He will quantify the IQ level of faculty and students using a measure that caters to Japanese-centered cultural values, such as the former names of Japanese cities and the plots of Kabuki plays. He explains his rationale this way: "The whites are complaining because, let's face it, they want easy questions so as to mask their inferiority. They want questions that will allow them to continue to mythologize about the greatness of Europe. They like the SAT tests because they can afford to provide their idiot children with coaches. They're even claiming that the ancient Egyptians were white when everybody knows that they were members of an Asiatic race."[53] Yamato's plans address the kinds of problems Chappie has had with his own department's intellectual exclusion.

In fact, Chappie relishes his role carrying out Yamato's wishes, settling old scores along the way. He uses the new administration as a catalyst for critiques he felt he could not previously make. For example, Dr. Crabtree, a Shakespearean in the English department, had unearthed information that tanked Chappie's bid for tenure: "Your article on *Othello* I felt, wasn't first-rate. Your thesis that race relations in this country haven't changed since Shakespeare's time. The play was written in sixteen-three. That's preposterous. And to call Shakespeare a racist is really overdoing it, don't you think? What claptrap!"[54] In pointing out the relevance of Shakespeare to black perspectives, Chappie identifies the kind of Western cultural chauvinism pointed out by Yamato and represented by Crabtree's notions: "Like many Eurocentric professors, as they were being called in the newspapers, he regarded Shakespeare as little more than a cultural hammer to be used to intimidate the infidels."[55] In his administrative position, Chappie smugly offers Crabtree a course in freshman composition rather than his usual course on Middle English: "Dr. Yamato believes that such courses constitute Anglo-Saxon ethnic cheerleading and feelgoodism."[56]

Chappie does the same thing to Marsha Marx, chairwoman of Women's Studies. She had opposed Chappie's tenure because he rented porn as part of a research project: "The private is the political. You men do all of your oppression in the dark. It is our right to shine a light upon your black deeds."[57] Using Marx's suggestion that sexism and racism should unite them in a fight against patriarchy after the change in administration, Chappie now challenges her feminism: "Explain to me why black and brown women are worse off than white women. Why there are few women of color in the main feminist organizations and why the black and brown women are always accusing you of racism."[58] He further castigates the women's studies field by contrasting its monolithic nature with the diversity he finds in Japanese culture:

> You white people make me sick with your homogeneity. You're the ones who are into some kind of narrow-assed homogeneity. . . . they have Korean components in their culture. They absorbed English during the occupation. They have a special Katakana set aside for English. They read books by Western writers. They trade with the world. And you call them homogeneous. You're the ones who are homogeneous. No matter how high a white may rise in this society's intellectual circles, with few exceptions they're still monolingual and culturally restricted crackers.[59]

Chappie's alliance with Yamato signals a potential contemporary Afro-Japanese solidarity in the rhetoric of *Japanese by Spring*. The Reed persona links contemporary blacks and Japanese. Chappie still had a healthy "respect for the Japanese, regardless of the silly and primitive racist attitudes of some of its leaders towards black Americans. As Quincy Troupe said, 'As a black man he could identity with Japan. The destiny of the Japanese and his African ancestors had been affected by the arrival of ships manned by the Portuguese during the fifteenth century.'"[60]

However, Chappie's severing of alliances does not lead to greater cultural exchange between African American and Japanese cultures. Being placed well within the new administration does not mean that he is in a position to accomplish his grandfather's dream of Afro-Asian solidarity. In fact, Yamato's later policies create a wedge between himself and Yamato, undermining any contemporary solidarity. For example, Yamato takes a page from the Japanese nationalist playbook of oppression. Major Puttbutt explains that he was born in Fukuoka, "a hotbed of extreme nationalistic activity" and "the birthplace of Genyosha" who "were fanatically opposed to Western influences in Asia."[61] E. Herbert Norman characterizes Fukuoka as "the spiritual home of the most rabid brand of Japanese nationalism and imperialism."[62] Believing that Western cultural values were antithetical to the Japanese way of life, Genyosha strove to stem their influence by reducing those who spoke in favor of them and against their nationalist ideas. Members of Genyosha resorted to "the stifling of free expression, the smashing of all organizations potentially dangerous to a militaristic government" as a way to stop the spread of foreign influences.[63] Yamato uses similar tactics to eliminate growing dissent at Jack London College with a harsh crackdown. When students present him with their list of demands, "Dr. Yamato had smiled contemptuously, balled the paper on which the list was written in his fist, and flung it into the wastepaper basket."[64] He does not care about their reaction to his new policies and does not seek their input or feedback. After expelling students who protest, Yamato makes his administration's discourse the only discourse. "Where once the students would mill about a noisy courtyard, there was silence and decorum. Sororities and fraternities were closed. In their place were friendship clubs where students would meet under the supervision of chaperones and discuss Nihon-no [sic] art and culture."[65] With those who promote a different point of view eliminated, he ensures acquiescence by having cultural overseers reinforce the culture he wants.

Yamato uses violence and aggressive tactics to mold public opinion, further quelling dissent. His early association with Genyosha also provides an education in using violence. Hilary Conroy describes Korean annexation supporters in Genyosha who engaged in "ronin tactics," which "meant not only strong stands, impatience with diplomacy and politics, and 'direct action' plots and coups, but also an active and restless searching out of the 'problem' areas of Asia." Such individuals practiced an imperialism that "begins in 'defense of the frontier'" where "they identify trends they dislike in their own society with the 'alien' advances."[66] Genyosha also had a reputation for supporting military engagement with others, whether it be the war with China in 1894 or acts of terrorism in Korea.[67] Yamato uses similar violent tactics during his presidency to control unruly students: "Suddenly there were some swift movements. Legs flying. Hands clapping. A knife flashed. After a fierce and murderous melee that lasted less than sixty seconds, Bass's former allies were lying on the ground moaning. Wounded. . . . Were these the extra measures that Yamato had in mind when he said that he would bring order and stability to the campus?"[68]

Chappie does not approve of Yamato's tactics, and his critiques land him on the side of Yamato's opposers, effectively undermining any contemporary Afro-Japanese solidarity. When he renames the university after Japanese war criminals, Chappie questions his logic. Even after he reminds Chappie that "they were lynching black people America in those days," Chappie suspects his motives in ways he had not previously: "But Puttbutt didn't feel right. Yamato had revealed a side that he'd never seen. Yamato was tough. Something that he wasn't. And to think that he had humiliated Crabtree and Obi. Had sent Matata packing, while doing the bidding of a man who was far more chauvinistic in his values than they."[69] Chappie now regrets settling his old scores with those who denied him tenure, and begins to see Yamato as the adversary. In changing his attitude, Chappie forgets any ethnic solidarity, and falls back on national association. After Yamato expels Muzukashii for being an American-born Japanese, Chappie draws the line: "It was time to join ranks. To restore Jack London to the American people. To rename the college after the author who admired Frederick Nietzsche. Jack London."[70]

In part, this failure of Afro-Japanese solidarity is fueled by suspicion based on a privileging of national association over ethnic culture. Chappie asserts his solidarity with other Americans: "Before he left for his showdown with Dr. Yamato, he fastened an American flag tie clip to his neckwear and tied a yellow ribbon around the tree in his front yard."[71] Such actions parallel early African American suspicions of the Japanese in the black press. Reginald Kearney notes that African Americans shared some views with mainstream white American media: "[Editorials about immigration] were at times hostile. . . . African Americans sometimes shared the general anti-Asian prejudice common to Americans. . . . The fear of job competition from Asians, at times, generated in the black press as well as the white media fantastic statistics about supposedly 'swarming millions of Asiatic coolies.'"[72] For some African Americans, the Japanese represented a threat to their livelihoods as import labor because of their numbers. Especially in the wake of the attack on Pearl Harbor, sentiment from African Americans coalesced around the notion of the Japanese as enemy: "Engulfed in the surge of national unity, some African Americans quickly pledged solidarity with the rest of the nation and condemned the Japanese for launching one of the most 'dastardly, cunning and deceptive attacks ever recorded on the infamous pages of human crime.'"[73] Other black newspapers described blacks as supporting this national sentiment: "The *California Eagle* vowed that African Americans stood 'solidly phalanxed,' prepared to join in the 'titanic struggle to defeat a common enemy.'" The *Amsterdam Star-News* promoted this opinion on its editorial page: "The diabolical treachery of the Japanese attack will find but one clear answer from all Americans. We will show those Japs and Nazis that as one nation indivisible, we fight the battle for democracy. We fight to win!'"[74]

Even direct interactions with individuals articulating support for African Americans could be read with suspicion. In addition to helping form the Ethiopia Pacific League, Hikida Yasuichi translated Walter White's *Fire in the Flint* into Japanese; regularly attended meetings of the Urban League, the NAACP, and the Association for the Study of Negro Life and History; and helped make arrangements for Du Bois's 1936 trip to Asia.[75] Gallicchio acknowledges the ambivalence that surrounded the motives of Japanese operatives like Hikida, for "it is difficult to determine if Hikida acted as a paid propagandist for the Japanese government for most of his stay in the United States or if he decided to employ his knowledge of African American life and personal contacts with black leaders in the service of his country only after political relations between Japan and the United States began to deteriorate."[76] Suspicions emerged within African American circles, for "most black Americans were quite willing to criticize what they saw as American hypocrisy in Asia, but that did not mean they were ready to join the Black Internationale," which also supported Japan's primacy in a co-prosperity sphere in Asia.[77]

While *Japanese By Spring* initially challenges the notion of Japanese ethnic imperialism by recovering the history of Afro-Japanese solidarity, it ultimately paints contemporary Japanese as modern-day cultural chauvinists, just as *The Chinese Connection*. In Lee's film, the Japanese function as imperialists, seeking to destroy cultures different from their own. Reed taps into American cultural sentiment that fueled Japan-bashing in the early 1990s as a result of their economic gains and involvement in a global economy. The result is cultural estrangement between African American and Japanese cultures. However, *Samurai Champloo* offers an alternative to the ethnic imperialism prefigured by *The Chinese Connection* and promulgated by Reed's novel.

Representin' in Feudal Times in *Samurai Champloo*

While Reed's novel echoes *The Chinese Connection*, the Japanese anime series *Samurai Champloo* presents a more cosmopolitan and globally engaged Japan, positioning it as an imagined site where multiple cultures meet and participate in exchange rather than ethnic imperialism. According to *Samurai Champloo: Roman Album*, "Champloo is a word from the Ryukyu dialect that means 'to mix.'"[78] The series does exactly that by using African American hip-hop to re-envision eighteenth-century Japan as an imagined site where youth have more opportunities for individual expression. The anime series shows how African American hip-hop aesthetics complement Japanese cultural expression. It also uses hip-hop to privilege a contemporary Japanese individualism that counters a more traditional contemporary discourse of conformity. By engaging both African American and Japanese cultures, *Samurai Champloo* sheds light on contemporary Japanese youth who use African American culture to challenge notions of Japanese conformity.

Samurai Champloo is a 26-episode series, part of the anime genre that represents one of the most prolific and popular forms of global culture. The term "anime" originally referred to Japanese animation, which initially took its cues in the 1960s from American animation pioneers like Walt Disney. In 1962 Osamu Tezuka founded Mushi Productions in Japan, and in 1963 released *Astro Boy* (*Tetsuwan Atomu*). However, anime diverged from the American animation model by focusing on subject matter aimed at both children and adults. Susan Napier explains that it "works to include everything that Western audiences are accustomed to seeing in live-action films—romance, comedy, tragedy, adventure, even psychological probing of a kind seldom attempted in recent mass-culture Western film or television."[79] Since the 1960s, anime has come to the forefront as a mode of global culture with stories that function as sites of cross-cultural exchange.

Anime not only represents an industry where cultural production itself flows through transnational capital, its content also caters to wide global appeal. Napier notes that anime faces competition from American films, and its dependence on Japanese manga, or graphic novels, is key to its cultural resonance. In addition to storylines, ideas, and audience, anime and manga share a visual style: "Their culture's tradition of picto-centrism is definitely an influence behind the ubiquitousness of anime and manga."[80] The focus on the visual in anime, I would argue, makes it even more amenable to cultural translation. Anime "is explicitly nonreferential. Other cinema and photography are both based on an outside reality—even if they use special effects to change that reality; animation stresses to the viewer that it is separate from reality, or perhaps even an alternative real-ity."[81] Because the visual is central, language becomes secondary to what the eyes see, and overcomes linguistic barriers. This is even more so the case with anime of the late twentieth century, which has developed into a form of cultural production most conducive to cross-cultural dynamics:

> By the late 1990s, it was clear that anime both influenced and was influenced by a plethora of Western cultural products. . . . [Japanese consumers of anime] are as equally interested in and influenced by Western cultural influ-ences as they are by specifically Japanese ones. . . . Despite its indisputably Japanese origins, anime increasingly exists at a nexus point in global culture; this position allows it to inhabit an amorphous new media territory that crosses and even intermingles national boundaries.[82]

Napier notes that anime functions as a cultural experimentation lab that brings all kinds of disparate things together: "The anime medium . . . offers a space for identity exploration in which the audience can revel in a safe form of Otherness unmatched by any other contemporary medium."[83] Interestingly, anime has also developed into a site for Afro-Asian cultural interaction. While most Japanese anime series do not feature storylines that bring together blacks and Japanese, they do feature African American cultural expression.

Such experimentation can be seen in the classic anime series, *Cow-boy Bebop* (1998), which follows several characters on a spaceship fol-lowing the breakdown of galactic travel technology in 2071. One of the protagonists, Spike Spiegel, is a classic pessimist with no future goals or ambition. The jazz style used in the title influences not just the name of the spaceship, but also the use of music in the series. Napier notes that Spike "is literally and symbolically adrift in a universe that sustains him physically but offers him no emotional or spiritual nourishment. . . . This drifting state is reflected in the music *Cowboy Bebop* uses to underline its themes. . . . it most frequently turns to wistful jazz or blues themes whose plaintive, fleeting quality is a subtle echo of the ephemeral drifting space that *Bebop* embodies."[84]

The same kind of mixing of Japanese and African American culture can be seen in *Afro Samurai*, a Japanese manga created by Takashi Okazaki and later developed into an American anime series. The manga's central character is Afro, a black man with a blocking-out-the-sun Afro who seeks to find the man who killed his father, and in the process claim the Number One headband to signal his fighting prowess. The American anime mini-series features the voices of Samuel L. Jackson, Ron Perlman, and Kelly Hu. The series combines the visual style and bleak tone of the manga with the swagger of black masculinity, thereby infusing it with a sense of African American culture. Moreover, Rza, of the African American hip-hop group Wu-Tang Clan, created the music for the anime series.

Samurai Champloo uses even more African American culture to re-envision eighteenth-century Japan as a site where youth have more opportunities for individual expression. *Samurai Champloo* revolves around the adventures of three primary characters: Fuu, a young girl; Mugen, a young man who has taken to wandering; and Jin, a highly trained swordsman. Their adventures begin in a restaurant where Fuu, an overworked waitress, falls into the clutches of the local governor's son, who threatens to take one of her fingers for accidentally spilling an order on him. Mugen offers to "take care of the trouble" for fifty dumplings.[85] Fuu offers him 100 dumplings to save her from the local governor's son, and Mugen proceeds to make good on his word by attacking the governor's son. At the same time in another part of town, Jin enters into an altercation of his own, attempting to save a worker from financial extortion by a construction foreman, who also works for the governor. Jin's interference sparks a fight with the governor's henchmen. The two events collide when Jin chases one of the governor's henchmen into Fuu's restaurant. Jin and Mugen mistake each other for the enemy, and proceed to battle, even as the restaurant burns down. They vow to have a battle to the death, but are captured instead. While awaiting execution, Fuu visits them and offers them a deal: agree to do a favor for her and she will free them. Fuu creates a distraction that allows Jin and Mugen to fight their way out of the governor's clutches. Per their arrangement, Jin and Mugen are duty bound to help Fuu find "the samurai who smells of sunflowers."[86]

As they embark on this search, they have various adventures that provide insight into the trio. Fuu actually searches for her father, who (for unexplained reasons) left when she was young. She finds a sense of safety traveling with Mugen and Jin. Mugen, an escapee from the Ryukyu islands, refuses to trust anyone, but comes to form bonds with Jin and Fuu. Jin's quest to perfect his swordsmanship also reveals his need to have friends as well. Their travels include intriguing encounters in eighteenth-century Japan. They have run-ins with the yakuza, Japanese organized crime, and Japanese law enforcement. They encounter a variety of individuals whom they help on the way, often saving the weak from those who dominate them. They bicker among themselves, all the while coming closer to finding Fuu's father.

In the final episodes of the series, Fuu discovers that her father is Seizo Kasumi, who helped the hidden Christians escape government eradication. Jin faces the man who forced his master to end his own life in order to protect his students from having their skills exploited as hired assassins. Mugen confronts the individuals who betrayed him on the Ryukyu Islands and again in an attempted heist on a sugar ship that almost ended his life. Each of the trio confronts and triumphs over their past, and when their quest is done, they go their separate ways.

We should not be surprised that *Samurai Champloo* makes liberal use of African American aesthetics. Shinichiro Watanabe produced the *Cowboy Bebop* series and subsequent movie. He was adamant about the use of African American hip-hop as the musical background for *Samurai Champloo*, recalling that "when we made a demo CD for *Champloo*, I wrote *Beats for SAMURAI CHAMPLOO* on it. That's how important beat was."[87] *Samurai Champloo* takes aesthetic elements from African American hip-hop and blends it with eighteenth-century Japanese culture in a complementary way. Such cultural translation can be seen in the appropriation of icons, music, and style from African American hip-hop.

Samurai Champloo is set during the Tokugawa era—a historical period characterized by increasing efforts at seclusion—but transforms this period into one more amenable to the inclusion of African American culture. During the Tokugawa era, national seclusion, or *sakoku*, was in effect. This policy was supposed to severely reduce the access of foreign powers to Japan. Foreigners were not allowed in and Japanese residents could not leave. It provided limits to contact through trade and other foreign relations. Trade with the Netherlands, China, and Korea were limited to certain port cities. L. M. Cullen notes that, while "Westerners had long seen a policy of exclusion as either irrational or unnatural," there were clear benefits of the policy at the time: "Sakoku gave Japan two and a half centuries of peace and a remarkable freedom from external complications.

Japan's economic vitality was powerful; intellectually, thought had been free to the point of anarchy . . . expansive internal trade meant that its tea and silk, inadequate in the seventeenth century, were able to command new markets when unexpectedly such markets appeared after 1860."[88]

However, the series depicts the Japan of the Tokugawa era as downright cosmopolitan, making it amenable to the incorporation of elements from African American hip-hop. *Samurai Champloo* captures a cosmopolitan Japan in the "Stranger Searching" episode, which revolves around the presence of the Dutch in Japan. The trio meets an errant Dutch governor who ditches his responsibilities in an attempt to blend in with the Japanese people in Edo, which has been transformed from a small town to a major metropolis and commerce center. Katsuhisa Moriya notes that "goods were shipped in an unending stream to the great consumption center."[89] Although Edo is a city of trade, it also maintains strict control on Europeans. Jouji, who is also known as Governor-General Izaac Titsingh, the chief merchant of the Dutch East India Company's Japan Branch, initially hides his identity, as do other Dutch officials who search for him. Despite this ruse, the episode uses other visual cues to distinguish them as non-Japanese. The episode opens with a scene where a phalanx of Dutch officials walk down street wearing basket-like hats that completely cover their faces and clunky clogs, as opposed to more traditional geta, or Japanese sandals. Jouji's claim to Japanese ancestry is also suspect. Not only does he wear the same clunky clogs as the Dutch search party, his appearance is completely out of place. Kazuto Nazakawa, one of the art directors for the series, explains that "he's Dutch, so he's huge."[90] He is referred to as a "mysterious giant" by the color announcer for the eating contest he enters, noting that his size is unusual for even the largest Japanese citizen. Once his own hat is removed, Mugen and Fu notice that Jouji has red hair, blue eyes, and "talks kinda funny." The subterfuge is necessary, for local law enforcement arrive on the scene because of "received reports that a European is wandering around here in disguise."[91] None of the citizens they question admit to having seen Jouji, who is difficult to miss, because they know that foreigners are not supposed to be there. However, the trio involve themselves in his activities, accepting his deal to give him the full tourist treatment of Edo in exchange for Jin and Mugen's swords, which they put up as their entry fee for the eating contest and forfeit to him as the winner.

In the "Unholy Union" episode, the trio's run-in with Jouji also sends them to Nagasaki, where they encounter Japanese Christians proselytized by the alleged grandson of Francis Xavier, a Spanish priest, who is credited with introducing Christianity into Japan. Christianity is identified as a non-indigenous religion, and its association with the Spanish priest represents another instance of cosmopolitanism in the series. Like Jouji, Xavier the Third's appearance distinguishes him from other Japanese characters. Even though he turns out to be Japanese, his disguise gives him a prominent nose and a Western-style beard designed to underscore his claims of being Xavier's descendant. Christianity initially spread quickly in Japan, for, according to Shinzaburo Oishi, "it was accompanied by muskets and other new items" which the daimyo in western Japan saw as "an instrument to help him suppress deeply entrenched Buddhist forces."[92] However, that attitude soon changed when the daimyo realized the Japanese converts were not loyal to him: "Understanding that converts believed Christ to be superior to all things, higher even than the national conqueror Hideyoshi himself, he concluded that Christianity was incompatible with his plan to establish his own political hegemony."[93] This is why the trio encounters secret pockets of Japanese Christians as they search for Fuu's father in the episode.

The protagonists encounter imperialistic white Americans in the "Baseball Blues" episode. While on their journey, the trio eats a meal at a restaurant. Mugen takes it upon himself to order a bevy of expensive dishes. When Fuu asks how they are going to pay for it, Mugen suggests that he has a plan, which involves skipping out on the meal. He runs out of the restaurant at top speed, leaving Jin and Fuu to face the consequences. He coincidentally runs past Kagemaru, a baseball enthusiast, who offers to pay their bill in exchange for their participation in a baseball game. Baseball functions as a metaphor for American imperial impulses towards Japan, representing another dimension to the cosmopolitan flair of the series. Kagemaru knows about baseball as a result of his time spent as a ninja in Kyushu, which "has always had a lot of dealings with foreign countries." He identifies the game as "a sport from across the sea."[94] In this sense, baseball represents a cultural exchange as a result of the cosmopolitanism the series enjoys. At the same time, baseball reveals tensions between the countries. The Americans show condescending attitudes toward the Japanese. When their ship runs aground, they show disdain for Japan, calling it a "country of savages." During the game, the American players refer to the Japanese by the derogatory term "Japs," and play more aggressively, which results in injuring Japanese players. The stakes are even higher, for they involve national pride. Kagemaru describes the contest as "a battle that our country's future is riding on." The Japanese announcer declares, "In this battle, the national prestige of America and Japan is on the line."[95]

The episode indeed has international resonances, as it also represents a reimagining of Commodore Perry's visit to Japan in 1853. The appearance of American sailors, led by Commodore Joey Cartwright, commander of the United States Far East Indies Fleet, and his interpreter Doubleday put Japan's policy regarding foreigners in full view in the episode. Nazakawa based his illustration of Cartwright on a picture of Perry. Cullen notes that Perry's initial trip "was intended to overawe the Japanese" and on his subsequent trip a year later, he "returned in the spring with nine vessels, a quarter of the entire American navy, in what was intended to impress the Japanese even more than had the guns of his first squadron."[96] The showy display of advanced weaponry signaled a threat to the Japanese that was managed by treaties allowing limited trade. Japanese art depicts Perry's ships as demonic, black, and menacing. An anonymous woodblock print entitled "A Foreign Ship" suggests that the Japanese saw Perry's ship as a terrifying black demon churning in the ocean with deadly black smoke from the steam engine. Such imagery in the series underscores the notion that all encounters with foreign cultures are not benign.

As a result of normalizing the presence of the Dutch, Christians, and Americans, the appearance of identifiably black people in Edo Japan fails to raise eyebrows for viewers. Anime already manipulates visual conventions to denote difference. Large eyes, the most often remarked feature of this visual style, represent a holdover from the early days of anime, itself influenced by early American animation. In terms of Japanese anime, "large eyes more easily express sadness, anger, happiness. . . . Large eyes are often used to express innocence, and younger characters will often have eyes larger than those of the adults."[97] This is true in *Samurai Champloo*, for Fuu is the only one of the trio with large eyes, and this reflects her age (early teens) as well as her general disposition (naive). Eyes, hair, and other general physical attributes usually work to differentiate characteristics because, as Gilles Poitras notes, "in a space story taking place in the future, not everyone can be Japanese."[98]

Just as large eyes denote difference within the visual language of anime, other physical changes identify African American characters. Character design and chief animator Kazuto Nakazawa states that "Ishimatsu and Rikiei are drawn as black men" in the episodes "Hellhounds for Hire" Parts 1 and 2, the only episodes that include characters that look like black people.[99] The two black characters have features that identify them as such: darker skin, facial features (including a broad nose), and textured hair. Both characters are also part of criminal organizations, which is true of many characters in the series, and possess a strong sense of self that can be linked to masculinity and black urban culture. The image of the gangster derived from urban black culture also represents one of several in a repertoire of identities that Imani Perry argues "stand in for the experiences of black men" and "constitute gestures of black masculinity under construction and definition in US society."[100]

Such characterizations do not just apply to black men, but are consciously constructed by them as well. Rikiei comes off as a cold-hearted gangster, interested only in power and money. Eric K. Watts notes that the gangster's identity "is constituted through a near-seamless rapport with a street code composed of a consumer-dominated rationality. . . . a commodified street code encourages the kind of behavior that translates into ghettoized profit and power."[101] Rikiei is only interested in using Mugen to increase his influence in the town's underworld. He tells Mugen: "There are only two kinds of people in this world. The rulers and the ruled."[102] This disregard for "the ruled" also suggests his easy use of violence, an "ends-means rationale" that not only "binds him to the street orientation" but also "demonstrates an utter lack of consideration for the welfare of anyone."[103] He pushes aside his longtime righthand man, Ishimatsu, in favor of Mugen, and when Mugen fails to be useful as a henchman, casually orders his elimination.

The other black character, Ishimastu, fights with Mugen, but later discovers they share the same philosophy of life, a sense of self. Perhaps it is this unspoken shared sense of self to which the title of the episode refers. The Japanese title, "Ishin Denshin," refers to "a phrase from Buddhism that denotes the passing of meaning and truth that cannot be expressed in words, from heart to heart. It thus also means to understand without having to be told."[104] Mugen says, "I don't believe in anything but my own skills." Ishimastu says he does not believe in anything but his own skills either, but when he tries to qualify the statement, Mugen retorts, "YOU'RE the one who decides how to live your life."[105] This emphasized form of reliance on oneself is one that permeates African American hip-hop, which will be discussed later in the chapter in connection with Japanese samurai culture.

The inclusion of black characters acts as a reimagining of the narrative that brings representations of people of African descent to Japan. While individuals from the eastern coast of Africa engaged brisk trade with China and Japan, Commodore Perry brought a negative image of African

Americans to Japan in 1853. Andrea D. Barnwell recalls the entertainment Perry used to commemorate the occasion: "For the finale, white sailors, after blackening their faces, performed to the delight of the Japanese Commissioners who 'enjoyed the imitations of the Negro and laughed very heartily.'"[106] This performance solidifies a certain negative image of Africans as foreign to Japanese culture. *Samurai Champloo* revises that image by placing it in its re-imaged Edo with echoes of contemporary black urban masculine culture created in part by black men.

In addition to black characters, *Samurai Champloo* relies on African American hip-hop aesthetics. The creators envision musical elements such as the break beat as key to the series. Writers like Dick Hebdige credit DJ Kool Herc with the invention of the "beats" or "break beats" that characterize hip-hop: "Gradually he developed a style that was so popular that he began buying records for the instrumental breaks rather than for the whole track. The lead guitar or bass riff or sequence of drumming that he wanted might only last fifteen seconds. Rather than play the whole record straight through he would play this same part several times over, cutting from one record deck to the other as he talked through the microphone."[107] Robert Farris Thompson quotes Afrika Bambaataa on the significance of the break beat for African American hip-hop: "Break music is that certain part of the record that you just be waiting for to come up and when that certain part comes, that percussion part with all those drums, congas, it makes you dance real wild."[108] To focus on the break beat is to focus on the most important part and mix it to form something new.

The centrality of the beat informs Watanabe's conception of *Samurai Champloo*: "Hip-hop has borrowed from older styles such as jazz and soul and folded them into a contemporary beat using sampling. In the same way, we've sampled from historical samurai dramas to make something new. That type of music fit the type of anime we were creating."[109] The beats in hip-hop also speak to the kind of tone Watanabe sets for the series in an attempt to capture danger and unexpectedness. The beat acts as a soundtrack for anticipation. Watanabe "wanted something more fragmented, something simple and wild with a strong beat. That is how I decided on hip-hop. Back in those days, everyone carried a sword—a deadly weapon—on their person. Innocently tapping the scabbards while passing could lead to a fight with those swords. I wanted a strong, edgy beat to help express the mood of the times."[110]

This guiding vision infuses hip-hop aesthetics throughout the collection. The menu of the DVD uses a scratching record as a transition between features. Transitions between parts of each episode feature visual variations on the title inspired by graffiti. "War of the Words (Master of Pen and Sword)" devotes an entire episode to graffiti and tagging. Hebdige reminds us:

> The wild style graffiti had grown out of the fad among street gangs for 'scribbling' their gang names on walls. In the hip-hop era this became an art form in its own right. Individual artists used magic markers and spray paint to scribble their "tags" (nicknames) on every surface they could find. Subway trains were a favorite target. Soon the grey carriages of the New York underground system were lost beneath a wild riot of dayglo colors and ornate script.[111]

The episode "War of the Words" makes use of this legacy in two parallel storylines. In the first, Mugen's illiteracy comes to light. Unfortunately for him, it happens in the presence of Bundai, a teacher who believes that words have the same power as a sword, and he literally kidnaps Mugen to teach him how to read. Despite Mugen's reluctance, Bundai overcomes his sense of pride by daring him to learn to read. After making him literate, Bundai tells him: "And now, use the letters you've learned to write your own story! Write it bigger than anyone else."[112]

In the second storyline, Jin discovers that the twin sons of a master he respects are members of a gang. He wants to teach them the honorable art of swordplay. Jin describes the dojo as "a place where those who strive to master the martial arts gather together."[113] However, the sons only care about their skills as graffiti artists. When a dispute emerges between the sons, Jin tries to mediate by suggesting they settle the dispute with a duel. One twin insists that graffiti is their preferred medium for reconciling their differences: "It might look like ordinary graffiti to you, but it's something that we've devoted our lives to. So in that sense, it's no different from the way Pop devoted himself to the sword. It's called 'tagging,' and it's like it proves that we're alive." The other twin adds: "We try to tag the most dangerous places, places that nobody else has ever tagged before. It's like the only time we're really alive is when we're experiencing that thrill."[114] These two storylines converge when, in the midst of the twins' tagging competition, Mugen surpasses them both by tagging the most dangerous place in town, Hiroshima Castle, which contains the powerful lord who humiliated the twins' father and drove him to suicide. Graffiti, an African American mode of expression, acts as a generationally coded mode of expression. While the old caretaker thinks that the twins disrespect their father's legacy and Bundai objects because "they are writing it wrong," the twins use graffiti to attain a measure of revenge on the lord who humiliated their father.[115] Mugen uses it as a mode of expression that previously eluded him. The classic Japanese themes of filial obligation and revenge are accomplished through the use of graffiti, a hip-hop visual style.

However, aesthetics represent just one mode by which the series uses elements of African American hip-hop. *Samurai Champloo* also uses hip-hop's emphasis on the individual to complement an emergent Japanese individualism. This hybrid mode of individualism counters the expectations of a conformist mode of Japanese culture. The series mixes a strong sense of individualism derived from samurai culture with the fierce sense of individualism derived from African American hip-hop. Both represent an individual spirit. The opening credits of each episode features a visual montage that features the three protagonists accompanied by the theme song, "Battlecry," by Japanese MC and music producer Shing02. Shing02 raps in English against a hip-hop beat, and his lyrics bring together Japanese samurai culture and African American hip-hop. The song emphasizes individual skill, central to both hip-hop and the samurai, as well as a samurai's quest for prestige: "Chip on my armor a sign of all-pro / The ultimate reward is honor not awards." Such prestige falls to the individual: "Wonder why a lone wolf can't run with a klan / Only trust your instincts and be one with the Plan."[116]

In hip-hop MCs gain a reputation for their ability to rap well; DJs gain a reputation for their abilities to put together beats in unusual ways. This focus on the skills of the individual parallels that found in the persona of the samurai that develops from 1960s and 1970s Japanese films and television series. Of particular note is the work of Shintaro Katsu, who gained international fame as the star of the long-running television series *Zatoichi*. In an interview, Watanabe, director of *Samurai Champloo*, states his desire to infuse the series with "Katsushin spirit": "He's the perfect example of someone who did not fit the mold. He was the nail that stuck out. . . . That type of life, one where you don't fear risk, is good. You stay off the safe path on purpose and bet everything on the moment. That was the type of characters I wanted to create."[117] The individualism that pervades the series is a hybrid of the individualism of hip-hop and the samurai. The *Samurai Champloo Roman* states: "The theme of this work is that we are all unique, different from any other. Each episode will feature characters with this type of fierce individuality. This feeling is very similar to what they call 'representing' in hip-hop."[118]

This individual spirit, informed by both Japanese and African American cultures, permeates the three main characters. The initial episode, "Tempestuous Temperaments," demonstrates that Fuu, Mugen, and Jin are strong individuals struggling against the strictures of Edo society. Their similarities are visually underscored by careful editing of a key sequence that places them in parallel situations. The switching between Fuu and Mugen in the restaurant and Jin in the nearby street show their similar orientation in challenging authority. They also demonstrate this individual spirit by transgressing the hierarchy of Edo Japan.

Sandy Kita describes *shinokosho*, derived from the Chinese characters for the four categories: warriors, farmers, artisans, and merchants. This classification categorized ranks in society: "The Tokugawa placed warriors such as themselves on top of their social order, farmers second, artisans third and merchants last."[119] Alain Silver notes, "An injunction against 'perambulation' prevented the *heimin* or commoner (that is, a non-samurai) from legally traveling more than a few miles from the place of his birth."[120] Given the social hierarchy of the Edo period, Fuu, Mugen, and Jin reject their class standing by traveling together. In the "Beatbox Bandits" episode, all three get arrested for not having the proper papers to cross a checkpoint and are subject to execution because of this lack of documentation. The journey also binds these characters together, further underscoring their common independent spirit. Every time they try to leave one another behind, they wind up back together. In "Hellhounds for Hire," Jin and Mugen abandon Fuu, but meet her again at a brothel, where Mugen notes: "This just means that no matter how hard we try to split up . . . it was always meant to turn out like this." Fuu not only searches for the samurai who smells of sunflowers, but her journey increasingly gets caught up in her fellow companions. In "Lullabies of the Lost," the trio goes their separate ways, during which a stranger tells Fuu: "Once you have traveled with someone, they become like family. Like brothers. You are not all alone in the world."

Such association further marginalizes them from the mainstream society of Edo and challenges authority. Their tendency to travel represents direct challenges to the government. Kita notes that "the merchant and artisan classes of Edo in the Tokugawa Period, collectively known as 'townsmen' or *chonin*, are considered oppressed because of the many sumptuary and other laws directed against them. These limited their dress, housing, and innumerable other aspects of their life."[121] While it initially appears to be a harmless journey, Fuu's search for her father and Jin and Mugen's accompaniment includes many instances where they challenge not only the social order of the Tokugawa era, but the government structure behind it. In the first episode, both Jin and Mugen, independent of one another, embarrass government officials. Fuu's quest for "the samurai who smells of sunflowers" puts her in the crosshairs of a government looking to crack down on Christian missionary work in Japanese history: "To prevent any influx of ideas which might threaten the status quo, the Tokugawa gradually closed the door of the island state to all outsiders, inaugurating in the 16th century, culminating with the suppression of an armed Christian force and the Shimabara uprising in 1637–38."[122]

While collectively they go against the strictures of Japanese society, Fuu, Mugen, and Jin each embody a personality that establishes them as individuals in different ways. Mugen is the character that most obviously exhibits a problem with authority. In the opening credits to the series, Mugen literally appears cocky against a background of roosters. He sits with his head cocked back and a frown on his face. Such visuals prefigure his behavior in the series. He is unpredictable, right down to his fighting style: "He has instincts like a wild animal, and superhuman reflexes. . . . He chooses a different line of attack in each situation using his intuition and instinct. He wasn't trained this way; it's his own personal style. . . . Put simply, his fighting style is a reflection of his personality."[123] His origins on the islands in the Ryukyus underscore his uncontainable nature. A small group of islands to the south of the mainland of Japan, the Ryukyus' history constructs it as outside of the mainstream:

> In 1429, Ryukyu emerged as a commercial crossroads, where merchants, pirates, and slave traders from China, Japan, Korea and Southeast Asia came together. . . . Throughout the Tokugawa period, Ryukyu remained in an ambivalent diplomatic position, a tributary of both China and Satsuma (and hence indirectly of the Tokugawa shogunate), while at the same time it retained a measure of autonomy over its internal affairs and a distinct cultural identity.[124]

The Ryukyu Islands' position and history mark them as outside the mainstream. Watanabe notes the relationship between marginal peoples such as those in the Ryukyus and the Edo mainstream: "From the start of the imperial system, and especially in the Edo Period, those who did not fit into the view of society held by the ruling classes were gradually made to disappear. They were pushed out to islands and deep into the mountains."[125] The cultural significance of these islands informs Mugen's personality in "Misguided Miscreants," an episode where the trio encounters Kozo and Mukuro, individuals from Mugen's past. They reveal that they all grew up on an island of exiled criminals, which makes Mugen doubly marginalized: a resident of outlying islands and the progeny of criminals. It is here that Mugen reveals a strong sense of self. He trusts Mukoro to get him off the island by robbing a sugar ship, but Mukoro betrays Mugen, leaving him to take the rap for the robbery, and escapes with Kozo. When facing his executioners, Mugen tells them: "I've lived my life without any help from anybody."[126] As a result of this betrayal, he learns to trust no one but himself. This can also account for his desire to fight everyone who crosses his path, for he construes everyone as a potential enemy.

Mugen is the one of the trio who is the most outspoken in challenging authority. In the first episode, "Tempestuous Temperaments," Mugen's first words involve talking smack to the official who is about the execute him. When asked about his last words, he insults his would-be executioners. It is this disrespect that has landed him in this predicament in the first place. He is sentenced to execution for insulting the governor's son and injuring his henchmen. In order to earn his compensation from Fuu, Mugen cuts off the arm of a guy who was going to cut off Fuu's fingers, and dares the henchmen to attack him, demonstrating his desire to fight against great odds. He confronts the governor's son, and before he can finish his sarcastic statement regarding how "folks who swing swords around in this day and age are nothing but anachronistic," Mugen cuts off his topknot, indicating that he does not care about his opinion, even if he is an official's son.[127] He then proceeds to break the governor's son's fingers. When Mugen tells him he's from the Ryukyu Islands, the governor's son is speechless, for he realizes that Mugen represents a force that can counter authority. He has nothing to lose, such as station in life or reputation among the elite. He is a rogue and that gives him power. All Mugen wants to do is fight. Nearly every episode has Mugen failing to show proper respect to authority figures, picking fights with other swordsmen, or simply doing the opposite of what others want him to do.

Others sense this strong sense of individualism from Mugen, but interestingly, it does not translate into a desire to attain power and use it against others. In "Beatbox Bandits," Mugen finds similarities between himself and the Tengu, warrior priests waiting for a chance to overthrow the government. Their leader makes a speech that may apply to Mugen, their captive, as well:

> There are only two kinds of dogs in this world, do you hear me? And those are strong dogs and pet dogs. Strong dogs, which in exchange for freedom wander in the rain and eat the food of uncertainty. Or pet dogs, which wear a collar and do nothing but eat the food of subjugation. . . . The ones who run the country now are stupid samurai who indulge in indolence . . . and are interested in nothing but maintaining their power! Them and their pet dogs who never question those samurai and simply do as they're told!

He then turns to Mugen and, noting his attitude, characterizes Mugen as a stray dog. So does the official who tells the story in retrospect. Mugen's rejection of power is echoed in "Hellhounds for Hire," when Mugen rejects his yakuza boss's assessment of the world: "So, this 'power' you keep talking about is the power to control other people? . . . I ain't the least bit interested in that crap. I don't wanna rule or BE ruled, either one."

While Mugen clearly functions as an individual, Fuu and Jin also challenge authority in their own ways, making them representative of the individuality underscored by samurai and hip-hop culture. At first sight, Fuu appears to be the run-of-the-mill teenaged anime girl. She has large eyes and seems to be in a perennially happy mood. With a high-pitched voice and very exaggerated expressions, she pays attention to her hair and overall appearance. Dependent on Jin and Mugen for protection, she possesses few fighting skills of her own. She constantly finds herself in potentially dangerous situations that require her rescue. In "Hellhounds for Hire," she is captured and sold to a brothel. In "Artistic Anarchy," she is the victim of a plot where ukiyo-e artist Moronobu lures her to be a model for him and helps traffickers put her in a barrel to be sold to Europeans. In "Unholy Union," Fuu is captured and incarcerated as labor for an illegal gun manufacturing scheme.

However, the series also reveals Fuu as a character that defies gender expectations. She demonstrates a lot of unladylike behavior, like her obsessive love of eating. In "Stranger Searching," Fuu enters an all-you-can-eat contest, besting both Jin and Mugen. When Jin and Mugen read her diary in "The Disorder Diaries," they find most of it devoted to her appreciation of food. In "Bogus Booty," Fuu eats so much that her appearance transforms from the svelte young girl to a rather zaftig young lady. Unlike many young women in anime, Fuu is not depicted as a sexualized object. Quite the opposite. The creators insist that Fuu is not a potential love interest for Jin or Mugen. Mugen cracks jokes about Fuu's lack of beauty. Both Jin and Mugen are always romantically linked with adult women through fleeting relationships and visits to brothels. Such behavior de-emphasizes Fuu as a sexualized object.

In fact, the series defines Fuu as a girl with initiative. Rather than being the meek waitress at the restaurant, she cops an attitude with the customers in the first episode. She does not think it is her duty to be nice to unruly customers. She thinks it is her duty to intervene on behalf of their victims. When the son of a local official disrespects an older patron by spilling tea on him, Fuu intends to rebuke him, but is quickly hustled out of the room by the older couple who owns the restaurant. She demonstrates her proactivity in other ways. She takes it upon herself to attempt to free Mugen and Jin from jail, and prompts their escape from the execution by setting off a huge fireworks display. While she comes off as the helpless young woman, she is clever, and manages to convince these two swordmasters to accompany her on her quest.

Fuu's character represents an anomaly in the Edo Japan portrayed in the series. In "Hellhounds for Hire," she gets captured and sent to a local brothel, where she meets Suzu, a woman who has also been sold to the brothel to cover her father's debts. Suzu is quiet and more demure than Fuu. While Suzu accepts her fate, preferring to stay due to her filial responsibility to her father, Fuu busily searches for a means of escape. She challenges Suzu's reasoning for staying: "Anyway, how come a daughter has to shoulder her father's debts?" Fuu escapes, only to become a dice roller in a gambling game, traditionally a male role. She literally rolls up her sleeves and rolls the dice. Her demeanor and personality is in sharp contrast with other women the trio encounters on their journey. In "Gamblers and Gallantry," Jin encounters Shino, a woman who experiences her last day of freedom before she reports to a local brothel to cover the debts of her husband, who is still gambling, putting them even further into debt. Her relationship with her husband is very different from Fuu's relationship with Jin and Mugen. While her husband consciously uses her so that he can continue to gamble, there is no exploitation of Fuu by Jin and Mugen. While Fuu leaves Jin and Mugen on several occasions, Shino cannot divorce her husband. Similarly, in "Misguided Miscreants," the trio encounters Kozo, a young woman who knew Mugen on the Ryukyu islands. Initially, she seems enamored of Mugen in a rather pathetic way. She is even more diminutive than Fuu, and she travels with cruel men because she believes she cannot survive on her own. However, the episode reveals how Kozo actually uses the men around her, pitting one against the other. She uses Jin to kill Mukoro to eliminate him as a partner so that she does not have to share the spoils of the heist of a sugar boat. Fuu may be dependent on Jin and Mugen for protection, but she never manipulates them in a exploitative way.

Like Fuu, Jin does not appear to challenge the status quo with an independent spirit. He seems to be the exact opposite of Mugen. Rarely causing disruption, Jin comes off as the picture of samurai restraint, with nice manners and low-key ways. Unlike Mugen's unruly appearance, Jin dresses in a reserved manner and wears glasses. He has very fine features: delicate hands, slim nose, and a thin frame. However, he is just as independent. Jin transgresses his social class. In the initial episode, Jin allies himself with Mugen. In "Tempestuous Tempers," the governor calls them both "vagrants," placing them in the same society-defying category. While Mugen is the most vocal in talking smack, Jin, in his quiet way, agrees with him. When Jin does so, he defies his identification with a higher class in Japanese society. Two swords mark Jin as a samurai, for Alain Silver notes that the shogunate "ordained that only a samurai could literally be a 'two-sword' man by forbidding members of the lower classes to carry more than one weapon, and that only of a limited blade length."[128]

The samurai were also closely identified with the ruling class through their service to a lord. The relationship between samurai and lord was defined by an intense loyalty: "Those trained to defend it were conditioned to place the welfare of the household over any personal ambitions, even gladly to forfeit their lives for it."[129] Such loyalty translated into a very limited existence for samurai, for "the first samurai was gradually constrained in his beliefs and actions by a ruling class seeking to preserve their control over the small amount of arable land available to a growing population in the mountainous island nation."[130] As a result of their service, they enjoyed the benefits of status. David L. Howell observes that the divisions between samurai and peasants "remained meaningful thanks to the powerful symbolic value of the use of surnames, the right to carry two swords, and other markers of warrior status."[131] In addition to status and privileges, physical barriers insured the separation of the samurai from the commoners. Chie Nakane notes there was a persistent "thorough-going segregation of samurai and peasants": "Samurai were forced to settle in castle towns. Peasants, denied weapons and required to till the land, lived in villages. The samurai, who were compelled to depend on stipends and gradually turned into administrators, were effectively prevented from establishing ties to the land."[132]

However, by the time Jin travels with Mugen and Fuu he becomes a ronin, a masterless samurai with no ties to any particular lord, a status that represents a display of his independent spirit. Ronin were "a group of wandering 'two-sword' men who sustained themselves by mercenary work for wealthy merchants or sometimes by criminality, and who personified for all a strong disaffection for the shogunate."[133] Jin is also an actual fugitive, having killed his own master. He becomes the target of other samurai who wish to see him dead. In "The Art of Altercation," Jin happens upon Ogura, a student at his former dojo who is bent on revenge. Jin defeats but does not kill him; however in "Lullabies of the Lost," Jin cannot shake the disgruntled student who insists on killing him in revenge, and must kill him to save his own life. Instead of being defined by their loyalty to their lord, ronin samurai existed outside of the royal order. This fall in status translated into a change in perception as well:

> The change in status of the *ronin* was a highly melodramatic one, a fall
> from the top rank of the four high castes to that of *chori* (outcast) or *hinin*
> (non-man), the substrata of untouchables in Japan's system. . . . the samurai
> who was reduced to one of their number but continued to act as if he were
> still a man of privilege found himself the object of enmity and persecu-
> tion by all the *shi-no-ko-sho*. An outlaw as well as an outcast, he was often
> equally scorned by the classless men who could not accept him as one of
> their own.[134]

As a ronin, Jin's personality is one of the loner. Reserved, he says little but does much. He has had to develop this personality, as he is a perennial outcast. Silver describes such ronin status as a kind of liberation: "Divested of social responsibility, unburdened of the heavy weight of *giri*—the absolute fealty owed to a lord—the former samurai carved out whatever place he could. As a man of rank, he had been inhibited by innumerable invisible ties. As a *ronin* who might become a *yakuza* (an '8-9-3' gambler) or *sanzuku* ('bandit'), he was as free as he dared to be."[135] However, Jin finds such freedom to be a burden. With the death of his master, he is forced to meet the world alone, until he finds Mugen and Fuu. Even though he is ostensibly the freest of the trio, he does not think so. In "The Disorder Diaries," a monk tells Jin: "Freedom is neither won through painful struggle nor can it be forced into existence. What's more, freedom has absolutely nothing to do with one's social status or profession. To simply accept yourself as you are, and as you live, to let it be. In this is freedom."[136]

Despite the internal struggles this causes, it also allows Jin to step out of the expectations of a samurai and help others. Samurai are bound to a lord and most ronin look out for themselves. As a result, such individuals develop a kind of arrogance. Silver notes: "The samurai was empowered to kill any of those lower castes, whose very function was to support the military hierarchy."[137] Moreover, samurai were seen as extensions of the government: "The clan retainer, no matter what his political inclination or his posture in previous eras, could only be identified as an accomplice of the oppressive minority of landed gentry."[138] When Jin embarks on the journey to protect Fuu on her quest, he defies societal expectations, often intervening when the weak are dominated by the strong. In the first episode, it is a worker whose tribute to the governor is deemed insufficient. In addition, the governor embarrasses the worker, who is pleading on his knees in the street. Jin insults the governor and makes quick work of his minions. After Jin wins, the governor remains speechlessness in encountering a force outside the influence of the society.

The hip-hop-infused Japanese individualism of Fuu, Mugen, and Jin speak to contemporary Japanese youth and a struggle against Japanese conformity. "Tempestuous Temperaments" uses script that resembles graffiti to introduce the series this way: "This work of fiction is not an accurate historical portrayal." A caption then adds: "Like we care. Now shut up and enjoy the show."[139] Immediately the series dismisses any claim to historical accuracy, which suggests that its themes are more relevant for a contemporary audience. A flashback takes the audience, not to eighteenth-century Edo Japan, but to a scene from contemporary urban Japan. It features modern-day automobiles in the foreground and an elevated train in the background. A figure in modern clothes, listening to headphones, crosses in the foreground, then the visual rewinds to reflect a rural scene more in keeping with Edo Japan. However, the juxtaposition of the two scenes indicates that the two settings are related, that Edo represents a cultural mirror for contemporary Japan.

The creators consistently use African American culture to underscore the significance of the series for contemporary Japan. The 2003 Project Roadmap for *Samurai Champloo* links urban African American culture that produces hip-hop, eighteenth-century Edo, and contemporary Japan: "[The series] will not portray the past, but a way of life that is suited for these times as seen through the samurai. . . . And, in order to depict a world where the taking of life is an everyday occurrence, the strong, edgy beat of hip-hop will be necessary."[140] It is important to note that the creators do not seek a mimetic representation of eighteenth- century Japan, but use in it in a contemporary enterprise: "This anime will also seek to create something new while sampling from 'samurai culture' and historical dramas."[141]

"These times" that require a hybrid hip-hop/samurai response include the societal conformity confronting Japanese youth in the 1990s. Sharon Kinsella notes:

> Individualism (kojinshugi) has, as we know now, been rejected as a formal political ideal in Japan. . . . Individualism has continued to be widely perceived as a kind of a social problem or modern disease throughout the postwar period. . . . Youth culture, symbolizing the threat of individualism, has provoked approximately the same degree of condescension and loathing among sections of the Japanese intelligentsia as far-left political parties and factions, symbolizing the threat of communism, have provoked in the United States and the United Kingdom.[142]

While youth cultures were often poised against society, in Japan, the term shinjinrui was used more and more to describe youth as "the irresponsible, passive consumers of leisure and cultural goods."[143] The creators of Samurai Champloo deploy hip-hop to counter such conformity. The roman declares, "The Japanese people . . . place importance on harmony above all else, fear offending others, pound the nail that sticks out, avoid overly stressing the self."[144] The creators consciously blend hip-hop and samurai culture as an alternative to the conformity of Japanese culture.

Rather than one ethnic culture eradicating another, as in The Chinese Connection or Japanese by Spring, Samurai Champloo features a blending of ethnic cultures. Watanabe specifically seeks to avoid the lapse into a dependence on national association, insisting on making Mugen "someone from the Ryukyus" and putting in "the bit about a person training in China," along with the presence of non-Japanese characters.[145] The reliance on both African American and Japanese cultures results in cultural exchange, rather than having the cultures remain apart. The hip-hop aesthetics complement the Japanese samurai culture. The Chinese Connection, Japanese by Spring, and Samurai Champloo all use Japanese culture to meditate, and in some instances, reject ethnic imperialism.

"Some Things Never Change, and Some Things Do"

Interethnic Conflict and Solidarity

While Bruce Lee's *The Chinese Connection* deals with ethnic imperialism by centralizing the antagonisms between the Japanese and Chinese in early-twentieth-century Shanghai, *The Big Boss* (1971), his first film, examines intra- and interethnic conflict as well as solidarity. In doing so, it prefigures cultural translations in Afro-Asian novels and films. *The Big Boss* follows the exploits of Lee's character Cheng Chao An, a Chinese immigrant who goes to Thailand to join others from his village who have gone abroad in search of work. Prior to his departure, Cheng promises his mother to refrain from fighting, a vow that his uncle urges him to honor as soon as he arrives. After meeting his fellow villagers, a group of young men led by Hsu Chien take him to the local ice factory where they all work. The "big boss" and his factory manager are both Chinese immigrants, but the henchmen are predominately local Thai muscle. On the way, Hsu Chien eagerly engages in a fight to help Uncle and Auntie Ma who are being bullied by a gang of thugs. When Uncle Ma goes broke gambling at the local establishment, Hsu Chien shows him how the dice are loaded, and loans them money to get by. This does not win him any friends among the local Thai underworld figures.

Soon after Hsu Chien gets Cheng a job at the ice factory, two of their fellow Chinese villagers go missing. When Hsu Chien inquires about their whereabouts, the factory manager puts him off. Since these are not the first workers to disappear, he takes his concerns to the "big boss," Hsiao Mi. When he threatens to report Hsiao Mi to the police and have him charged with murder as a result of his inaction, Hsiao Mi orders his henchmen to fight. They ultimately kill Hsu Chien. When he fails to return home, the workers go to the factory and threaten to strike unless true efforts are made to find their missing friends. In order to assuage them, the factory manager makes Cheng the new foreman. He takes him out to dinner, gets him drunk, and sets him up with a local prostitute in an effort to divert his attention from the missing workers. After he sobers up, Cheng goes back to the brothel, where the prostitute tells him, "There's something in the ice."[1] When Cheng goes to the factory to investigate, he not only discovers that the factory is a front for distributing drugs, but also a means of disposing of workers who find out the truth. He finds their remains in the ice. Hsiao Mi's Thai thugs show up, and they fight.

Meanwhile, Hsiao Chiun, the big boss's son, kidnaps Chiao Mei, Hsu's sister, and kills all the other ice factory workers that live in the house. By deciding to avenge their deaths, Cheng casts his lot in with his fellow villagers, thereby breaking the vow made to his mother. He shows up at the big boss's compound where the thrilling final fight takes place. Once freed, Chiao Mei leads the police to the compound. They arrest Cheng after he exacts his deadly revenge on Hsiao Mi.

The Big Boss constructs an immigrant experience that brings the Chinese into contact with another ethnic group, the Thai. Subtly, the film distinguishes between the Chinese workers who come to work in the ice factory and the Thai foremen who oversee their work. While it is never made explicit that the country is Thailand, the signage of the country identifies it as a location outside of China. The film also makes a point of distinguishing between the Chinese workers, the factory manager, and big boss on one hand, and the Thai foremen, one of whom is described as "the dark one," and the Thai maids and prostitutes who work at the brothel on the other.[2]

This is not merely a situation where Chinese immigrants struggle to assimilate into a new environment. These workers maintain links to their home country, form their own immigrant community, and view themselves as distinct. When Cheng and his uncle arrive, the workers have a small gathering to welcome them. They all live in one house, which cuts down on expenses. Each worker has a mat and a net. Uncle explains that their situation is common, for more people are leaving the country for the cities. While this Thai town is not a bustling metropolis like Hong Kong, relatively speaking, it functions as an urban site for immigrants. Later, Hsu Chien tells Cheng that if he works hard, he can make enough money to start a business back home. While they do not view their situation as permanent, they do view their time in Thailand as an economic endeavor, as immigrant groups often do.

The Big Boss demonstrates a variety of factors in interethnic conflict between groups, especially when one group is an immigrant group with less power than the dominant group. There are clashes between the Chinese immigrant workers and the Thai henchmen, who are in positions of authority. The Chinese immigrants work at the lowest level at the factory: cutting the ice and moving it onto trucks. The Thai foremen merely look on, boss the Chinese workers around, and generally treat them badly. When the workers accidentally break the ice and reveal a packet of drugs and Cheng tries to intervene, they hit him without provocation. Stephen Teo notes that Cheng responds out of ethnic loyalty: "Cheng is a character compelled to action for a reason. He fights for a cause. For better or worse, that cause is based on racial awareness, on the quest to make the Chinese character a dignified, respected and honored figure."[3] This ethnic conflict is further underscored by exploitation. The Thai exploit the Chinese by involving them in the drug trade, a criminal enterprise. The Chinese do not receive a cut of the profits, and when unsuspecting workers find out, they die. The Thai function as foremen at the factory and local muscle in social venues like the gambling house. Inequitable labor functions as the site where conflict emerges.

However, Hsiao Mi, his factory manager, and his son exploit the Chinese immigrant workers, resulting in intra-ethnic tension. Hsiao Mi uses Thai henchmen to oppress his fellow countrymen. He orders the Thai to oversee the gambling house that cheats the Chinese customers, act as muscle to intimidate the locals, and conduct the majority of the violence and murder. By using the Chinese workers in the drug trafficking business, Hsiao Mi rises socioeconomically. Hsu Chien's visit to his compound reveals the luxurious life that he accrues on the backs of his Chinese workers. Statuary tipped in gold pepper the grounds, along with a large wading pool and palm trees. The compound consists of several buildings, including a central building that serves as the big boss's home. It has a large indoor porch with hardwood floors. Inside, rooms are regaled with potted trees and animal heads from safari hunts. Maids, who are kept in line by the threat of harsh discipline, constantly attend Hsiao Mi. When one accidentally spills tea, he shoots a small dart into her chest to remind her to be more careful. Thus, when the workers feel resentment, they blame not only the Thai henchmen, but also the Chinese overbosses. This suggests ethnic conflict both between and within ethnic groups.

However, *The Big Boss* also features intra-ethnic solidarity. Despite his vow to his mother, Cheng decides to cast his lot in with the Chinese immigrant workers and fight on their behalf. After the death of Hsu Chien and the other workers, he feels deep remorse. He sees his fate as tied to theirs, and seeks to give them the justice the local police refuse to provide. Cheng's determination to bring Hsiao Mi to justice demonstrates solidarity within the ethnic group.

This theme of ethnic conflict re-emerges in post-1990 cultural production that responds to the 1992 Los Angeles riots. Many contextualized the riots with several prior high-profile clashes between African American patrons and Korean merchants, including the shooting of Latasha Harlins, an African American teenager, by Soon Ja Du, a Korean shopkeeper in Los Angeles, and boycotts by African American patrons of Korean stores in New York and Los Angeles. However, most pointed to the acquittal of four white Los Angeles policemen, accused in the beating of Rodney King on March 3, 1991, as the spark for the riots. During a traffic stop, the policemen pulled King over. Instead of arresting him without incident, they proceeded to assault him, an assault captured on video by George Holliday, and disseminated to the press. Many viewed the tape as incontrovertible evidence of excessive force on the part of the police officers. However, a predominantly white jury returned a "not guilty" verdict. Los Angeles erupted in riots, with over 700 million dollars in damages and almost sixty people killed.

While there are various explanations of the riots and their meaning, a recurrent interpretation emerges from the mainstream media that views the riots as the climax of long-simmering tensions between American blacks and Korean merchants. Such tensions allegedly represent larger fault lines between the groups. Nancy Abelmann and John Lie identify such a binary as "the ideological currents that bolster the 'black-Korean conflict' as a depiction of the two groups as antipodal minorities: the Asian American model minority epitomized by Korean entrepreneurial success and the urban underclass represented by the impoverished African American community."[4] Misrepresentative images range "from the striking image of gun-toting vigilantes to the pathetic figure of non-fluent Korean American merchants on talk shows."[5] Seeing the conflict in such bifurcated terms also results in comparisons to another significant urban uprising, the 1965 Watts riots: "While these riots revealed rising expectations of urban African Americans and their frustration with the Johnson administration and the 'nonviolent' civil rights movement, they also prompted Republicans to unleash a 'full-scale assault on liberal social policies.' . . . The 'race riots' thus set the stage for burning political debates over race, city, poverty and welfare."[6] Just as the urban unrest of Watts was described as a clash between blacks and whites in 1965, so too the 1992 riots generated a discourse of conflict between blacks and Koreans.

Basing the riots solely on ethnic conflict necessitates reductive characterizations of both ethnic groups. It assumes that all American blacks share the same antagonisms toward the Korean shopkeepers. Indeed, the coverage tends to paint all blacks with the same brush: rabid, violent participants in a riot beyond control. It also assumes that all Koreans share the same antagonism towards blacks, failing to take into consideration differences that generation or gender plays:

> Undoubtedly, a minority of African Americans, motivated by the Black Power ideology of community control, seeks to drive out Korean American merchants. Yet many others have made variable degrees of accommodation with Korean American merchants' presence in South Central Los Angeles. Just as some Korean American merchants contribute to community betterment, some African American customers welcome their presence. Otherwise, we cannot make sense of numerous instances of friendship and goodwill.[7]

The ethnic conflict metaphor in the wake of the riots fails to consider the role of immigration in ethnic interactions. Abelmann and Lie rightly point to how Korean immigrants learn perspectives about American blacks even before they arrive: "The pervasive American cultural presence in South Korea has contributed to Korean immigrants' racial attitudes. South Koreans note the (informally) segregated restaurants, bars, and brothels, and the black-white geography of the U.S. military in South Korea: the heavy concentration of African American troops at the demilitarized zone, and the 'whiter,' easier assignments in Seoul."[8]

The Big Boss prefigures an engagement with the ethnic conflict metaphor that emerges from the riots in the post-1990 era. Some contemporary Afro-Asian cultural production challenge the way the metaphor pits ethnicities and nationalities against each other by envisioning more cultural exchange. Paul Beatty's The White Boy Shuffle (1996) uses Asian and Asian American cultures to explain discourses in African American culture that challenge the ethnic conflict metaphor and expand the intra- and interethnic dynamics established in The Big Boss. The Matrix trilogy, composed of The Matrix (1999), The Matrix Reloaded (2003), and The Matrix Revolutions (2003), revolves around a revolution that pits blacks and Asians against forces characterized as white, a revolution that resembles the power dynamics of the Los Angeles riots. It employs an ethnic discourse, womanism, to enact Afro-Asian cooperation that crosses gender lines against forces represented as white, male, and in control. These films resolve ethnic conflict by positing the solidarity between Asian men and African American women, again expanding the parameters of *The Big Boss*.

"From Shanghai to Compton": Challenging the Ethnic Conflict Metaphor in Beatty's *The White Boy Shuffle*

Just as *The Big Boss* explores interethnic conflict, Paul Beatty's novel, *The White Boy Shuffle*, interrogates both ethnicity and national identity within the shadow of the 1992 Los Angeles riots. Beatty's novel uses Japanese puppet plays and postwar nihilism to explain contemporary African American despair brought on by the riots. It also employs the Japanese American internment experience to provide unexpected role models for young black men, models that act as bulwarks against the turmoil represented by the riots. Not to be confined by a unilateral consideration of cross-cultural dynamics, the novel also uses African American culture to provide alternative modes of acculturation for Korean and Japanese immigrants, modes that diverge from those implied by the Los Angeles riots. By interrogating both ethnicity and national identity, Beatty's novel engages in cultural translation that results in cultural exchange and rejects the reductive notions represented by the ethnic conflict metaphor.

Beatty's narrative sensibilities tap into poetic ones that reflect a multiculturality focused on the lateral relationships between ethnic groups as well as vertical relationships with a context that includes a dominant ethnic group. Coming to national attention as a result of his poetry, Beatty's brand of satire routinely targets all aspects of multiple ethnic cultures. Critics like Eric Murphy Selinger cite his dismissal of "any racial pledge of allegiance or intellectual move that would tell him what to say or fence him in or shut him down."[9] Beatty sets his sights on the most sacred cows of both American and African American culture. This is clear in a poem like "At Ease," in which he decries the deployment of uncritical modes of multiculturalism:

    y know
    its like multiculturalisms

the lefts right guard
of truth justice and the American way
       a spray-on deodorant
       against the stench of *isms*
           Contents under pressure
           extreme pressure.
       May explode
i understand the effort to prevent skin cancer
by removing epithets and fluorocarbons from the history texts
but multiculturalisms
sunblock jargon
       doesn't protect
       against big brother sun rays
       on days when niggas went to the beach and wore socks[10]

Often champions of the values of multiculturalism, the liberal left comes off as insincere and an obstacle to understanding the root causes of issues that affect people of color. The poem points out that the left focuses on superficial fluff like "removing epithets and fluorocarbons from the history texts" instead of "big brother sun rays," issues that really impact people of color. While certain modes of multiculturalism would try to co-opt Beatty, his caustic stance prevents it.

Beatty's poetry also features distinct Afro-Asian elements. After several positive references to icons of African American culture such as the Nicholas brothers, Michael Jordan, and Sarah Vaughn, Beatty turns his attention to other influential icons in "name of poem." The poem describes "lady kung fu / flyin roof to roof."[11] Beatty taps into the appeal of Asian martial arts films for African American urban youth, and goes one step further by highlighting not the swordsmen, but the swordswomen. "Lady kung-fu" alludes to martial arts films that feature women as martial arts masters. "Flyin roof to roof" suggests the fantastic movements of actors as they demonstrate their skill in the martial arts world in *wuxia*, or sword fantasy films, a genre whose most internationally recognized example is *Crouching Tiger, Hidden Dragon* (2000).

The martial arts film genre has a long history of female kung fu fighters. The first martial arts films of the 1920s featured women. Although men dominated Peking opera, on which the early films were based, women populated films because men considered the roles to be beneath them. The first successful martial arts film, *Burning of the Red Lotus Temple*

(1928–31), featured women in the title roles. Later martial arts films placed women front and center. King Hu's *Come Drink with Me* (1966) launched the career of Cheng Pei Pei (who would reappear in the wuxia genre in *Crouching Tiger, Hidden Dragon*), and tells the story of Golden Swallow's quest to find her brother. *Touch of Zen* (1969) centralizes a male protagonist, but also includes a more practical and proficient female martial artist who helps him. More modern manifestations of swordswomen include the revenge-seeking Wolf Girl in Ronny Yu's *The Bride with White Hair* (1993). By citing freedom-fighter swordswomen, Beatty underscores how the figure and the genre appeal to African Americans, as swordswomen function doubly as the underdog. In previous chapters, this book discussed the prominence of resistance to "imperialist aggressors" (the Japanese, Manchus) who force assimilation on the Chinese by outlawing Chinese martial arts in films popular among African Americans.

By the time Beatty pens his first novel, *The White Boy Shuffle*, he focuses his interrogation on the dynamics between African American and multiple Asian and Asian American cultures. The novel recounts the adventures of Gunnar Kaufman, Beatty's black male protagonist, who relates his tale in retrospect, from his current vantage point as a successful poet and reluctant leader of a mass suicide movement. The bulk of the novel relates his meteoric rise to fame and his increasing misgivings about the journey. As a teenager, Gunnar enjoys growing up in predominantly white suburban Santa Monica as "the cool black guy."[12] Relating to his friends on the basis of popular culture, only occasionally does his race raise an issue. Gunnar's perception of blackness echoes those around him. For him, "black was being a nigger who didn't know any other niggers."[13]

However, when Gunnar and his sister refuse to go to YMCA day camp because of the presence of other blacks, Gunnar's mother uproots them from their suburban bliss. Feeling that her family has lost touch with what it means to be black, she moves them to an inner-city neighborhood. In the new neighborhood, Gunnar finds himself in a place wholly alien to him: the 'hood. Hillside, a black community in West Los Angeles, forces him to adapt and carve out a place for himself. After several assaults, he uses his emerging poetic talents to secure a place as a bard for the local gang, the Gun Totin' Hooligans, led by the violent yet vocally talented Psycho Loco. At the same time, his friendship with Nicholas Scoby, jazz enthusiast and phenomenal basketball player, reveals Gunnar's own talents at the game. Several episodes ensue that form the backdrop for Gunnar's ever-changing consciousness, such as the 1992 Los Angeles uprising, the trials of teenage life, and his marriage to Yoshiko, a Japanese mail-order bride arranged by Psycho Loco. Both his poetic and athletic skills pique the interest of a university recruiter. Gunnar, Scoby, Psycho Loco, and Yoshiko travel to Boston University for more hijinks. It is here that Gunnar's challenge to blacks results in a mass suicide movement that earns him the title of the "Ebon Pied Piper." While Scoby takes him up on his offer, Gunnar, Psycho Loco, and Yoshiko return to Hillside for the birth of Yoshiko's child, Naomi. The novel ends with Gunnar alive and still pondering the vagaries of life.

The complexity of Gunnar's psyche makes it possible for the novel to use him as the vehicle for engaging multiple cultural realities. Rather than collapsing Asian and Asian American groups together in broad generalizations, the novel recognizes individual cultures and historical contexts. In order to do so, it imbues Gunnar with a complex personality that sheds light on multiple factors on intra- and interethnic dynamics. Gunnar sees himself as comprised of various elements: "I realized I was a cultural alloy, tin-hearted whiteness wrapped in blackened copper plating."[14] The language of metallurgy alludes to a personality made up of disparate elements. Gunnar sees himself not wholly black or white, but a melding of the two. Being such a "cultural alloy" makes him difficult to categorize. While Reed's protagonist Chappie attempts to repress the black elements of his persona even as he exploits those elements associated with the white dominant culture, Gunnar's psychology seems poised to accept and critique a variety of the assumptions we make about culture.

Gunnar's unique personality permits him to possess a complex response to the multicultural world that confronts him. On one hand, he challenges certain traditional norms, like the self-aggrandizing pedigree sometimes offered by African Americans to challenge the notion that they belong to a culture bereft of greatness. During the antebellum era, enslaved African women had children with white plantation owners. Paternal lineage was often obscured even though some children could trace relations to important families in the South. However, such relations were often denied, or at the very least not recognized, a situation that further underscored the low opinion the majority held of African Americans. By breaking up black families and failing to acknowledge relations between black and white families, proponents of the subjugation of African Americans advanced the notion that they held no legitimate place in American society. Under these circumstances, some African Americans sought to reclaim lost birthrights by situating themselves in a long line of distinguished ancestors in order to justify their own prominence.

Gunnar distances himself from this tendency by declaring, "I am not the seventh son of a seventh son of a seventh son," which cheats him of "my mythological inheritance, my aboriginal superpowers."[15] The designation of "seventh son" connotes specialness, given its relationship to extraordinary powers in folklore, and can be invoked to provide legitimacy and a connection to a community. Not only does Gunnar dismiss this strategy, the novel satirizes African Americans who go to absurd lengths to establish such legitimacy through genealogy. Gunnar's mother praises members of the Kaufman family, whose notoriety is based on questionable deeds: Euripides Kaufman, who sells out Crispus Attucks and contributes to his martyrdom; Swen Kaufman, the only black person to willingly run into slavery; Franz Von Kaufman, who is subservient from birth. Her use of such questionable history highlights Gunnar's ambivalence regarding this practice.

On the other hand, Gunnar also finds a sense of familiarity with black culture appealing. Although the African American community has its challenges, he finds it to be a refuge from the disparaging onslaught of the dominant culture. When his family moves to Hillside, Gunnar is desperate to assume his place among this black community: "I walked the dark streets of Hillside with my head down, looking for loose change and signs that would place me on the path to right-on soul brother righteousness."[16] His plea is answered when he meets Nicholas Scoby: "He called me 'nigger.' My euphoria was as palpable as the loud clap of our hands colliding in my first soul shake."[17] His relationship with Scoby introduces him to streetball and jazz. This friendship provides Gunnar "with alternative concepts of black cultural expression" that results in his "slow but conscious embrace of alternative or even highbrow forms of black cultural expression."[18]

However, Gunnar's powers of perception reach beyond dynamics among African Americans. He realizes that the larger context of white American dominant culture affects these dynamics. As an adolescent in Santa Monica, his perceptions of blackness are shaped by white culture: "Black was an unwanted dog abandoned in the forest who finds its way home . . . only to be taken for a car ride to the desert. Black was hating fried chicken even before I knew I was supposed to like it. . . . Black was a suffocating bully that tied my mind behind my back and shoved me into a walk-in closet."[19] Gunnar views blackness as the dominant culture does: something in need of repression, a nuisance and a hindrance that holds him back. This internalization has its greatest manifestation when Gunnar tells his mother that he does not want to go to an all-black summer camp "because they're different from us."[20] His failure to see himself as part of the "us" derives from internalizing how the dominant culture views blacks. The impact of dominant culture is complex in *The White Boy Shuffle*, for it also integral to Gunnar's later perceptions of race and interactions between races. After the Los Angeles riots, his mom forces him to attend a predominantly white school after his participation in a theft during the melee: "It was hoped that the reinfusion of white upper-class values would decrease the likelihood of my committing another felony, but the two miserable years I spent at El Campesino had the opposite effect. If you want to raise the consciousness of an inner-city colored child, send him to an all-white school."[21] Exposure to dominant society causes Gunnar to embrace a black perspective, produces skepticism about the authority of white society, and ironically serves to boost his ethnic confidence and self-esteem. He soon loses any sense of blind adoration: "I wasn't in arrears to the white race. No matter how much I felt indebted to white folks, I owed them nothing."[22] In both cases, white American culture impacts Gunnar's worldview regarding black culture.

In addition to engaging the traditional black-white racial dyad in complex ways, Gunnar also recognizes various Asian and Asian American cultures as part of his imaginary. On one hand, Gunnar uses Chinese culture to lift his own self-esteem. While he and his mom watch the production of a rap music video in his neighborhood, his mother asks him what kind of poet he will be. Gunnar replies, "The cool tantric type. Shaolin monk style. Lao Tsu, but with rhythm."[23] The statement points to the resonance the Shaolin monks have within African American culture. Several martial arts films feature monks avenging the deaths of their teachers or the destruction of their temple. African Americans identify Shaolin monks as signifiers for honorable rebellion, rebellion with historical and cultural significance. While the Indian teacher Bodhidharma gave the monks at the Shaolin monastery spiritual guidance, Shifu Tomio suggests that the martial tradition in China contributed to their reputation as fighting monks.[24] Shaolin monks became a force of defiance against the ruling Qing court, a foreign government that the masses had resented ever since the invading Manchus established it. The fighting ability and the ethical motivations of the Shaolin became their hallmark, for Ming-Dao Deng notes that "even the Qing government respected [Shaolin] temples. . . . men became monks solely to escape the Manchus and learn martial arts. The gun was nearly unknown, and people believed that the human body was the ultimate instrument of war."[25] Despite the formulaic nature of some martial arts films, the Shaolin monks who populate them remain symbols of resistance for African Americans. When Gunnar links his preferred poetic style with martial arts, he embraces a Chinese cultural style as a way to acknowledge individual African American worth.

On the other hand, Gunnar also uses misrepresentations of Chinese culture as metaphors for his own reality. When describing himself in the whitest of environments, Santa Monica, Gunnar underscores his own mediocrity by calling himself "the number-one son of a spineless color-struck son of a bitch."[26] This allusion combines the aforementioned distancing from the prestige of being a "seventh son" as well as reference to the progeny of Charlie Chan, a caricature of Asian Americans designed to highlight a passive and non-radical Asian American identity, as noted in Chin's *Gunga Din Highway*. The sons embody the same characteristics that Elaine Kim suggests make Charlie Chan popular: audiences manifest an "approval of him as a non-threatening, non-competitive, asexual ally of the white man."[27] Chan's children are so nondescript that they do not even warrant names. Gunnar views his own invisible nature in terms of the anonymity of Charlie Chan's four sons. In acknowledging both legitimate and questionable uses of Chinese culture, the novel demonstrates an awareness of the fine line between appropriation and exploitation. But the novel steers Gunnar away from perpetuating reductive stereotypes by recognizing a variety of Asian and Asian American cultures and contextualizing that interest with accurate history.

Such a chameleonlike personality comes in handy when Gunnar's kaleidoscopic world meets the harsh reality of the 1992 Los Angeles riots. Like so many young African American men and women, Gunnar is floored by the destruction of the illusion of equality and spirals into despair. His shock at the King verdicts represents the degree to which the promises of equality made by previous generations fail: "I never felt so worthless in my life. . . . my pacifist Negro chrysalis peeled away, and a glistening anger began to test its wings. A rage that couldn't be dealt with in a poem or soothed with the glass of milk and glazed doughnut offered by our kind host" (130–31). While he often looks at his experiences with blithe amusement, the King verdicts bring a cold reality to the fore. He realizes that he lives in a world where four white officers can beat a black man viciously on video and get acquitted of any wrongdoing whatsoever. He knows that society would do the same to him, no matter what kind of success he achieves in his life, or how much he overcomes. He begins to rage at a society that consistently fails to extend those principles of equality and justice to blacks. Poetry seems inadequate to interpret such events, and the violence espoused by Psycho Loco begins to look like an attractive option—a senseless act for a senseless act. While he turns away from violence and poetry as viable options, Gunnar loses faith not only in the American justice system, but the society that supports it.

To assuage Gunnar's despair, the novel turns to an unlikely source: Coach Shimimoto, a Japanese American teacher and internment camp survivor. While Shimimoto does not share Gunnar's racial background, he does share the disillusionment Gunnar experiences as a result of Japanese internment of the mid-twentieth century. Both internment and the riots were motivated in part by attempts to contain "dangerous ethnic elements" of society. Sucheng Chan notes that as early as 1918, the United States military characterized persons of Japanese ancestry within the United States as "potentially 'dangerous persons'" and by the 1940s as "enemy aliens."[28] The order to intern the Japanese population in the western United States based internment on an effort to contain a dangerous racial population:

> [General De Witt] soon drafted a statement (referred to as his "Final Recommendation") calling for the removal of all persons of Japanese ancestry on racial grounds. The Japanese were an "enemy race," declared the document, whose "racial affinities [were] not severed by migration" and whose "racial strains" remained "undiluted" even among members of the second and third generations. Therefore, because the army had no ready means to separate out the disloyal from the loyal, all persons of Japanese ancestry, regardless of their citizenship status, must be removed from the coast.[29]

Frank Wu describes internment as anything but benign: "They were sent to ten interment camps in deserts and swamps, where they lived in makeshift barracks hastily erected by the Army, behind barbed wire, in the shadow of gun towers and under armed guard. They were treated as a group. Individuals were interned without regard for due process."[30] Shimimoto's perspectives as a Japanese American internment camp survivor provide a basis of empathy between himself and Gunnar because they share the trauma resulting from arbitrary actions by those in positions of authority. Japanese Americans were treated as criminals, and second-generation Japanese Americans wondered why they were treated this way while their fellow Americans remained free. Ronald Takaki observes that "proud people before evacuation, they felt diminished, their dignity destroyed. Some were overwhelmed by their despair."[31]

Having experienced this incomprehensible event, Shimimoto is in a unique position to anticipate Gunnar's disillusionment regarding the Rodney King verdicts. To lessen the blow, Shimimoto has his players practice extra late, perhaps to make them too tired to react. Before leaving, he makes a player define concatenate ("concatenate means together. Not like all-in-the-same boat together, but like connected, like a bicycle chain") and tells them to remember it as he lets the "soon-to-be-revolutionaries" go.[32] It is this advice that helps Gunnar make sense of the verdicts for himself: "The day of the LA riots I learned that it meant nothing to be a poet. One had to be a poet and a farmer, a poet and a roustabout, a poet and a soon-to-be-revolutionary."[33] His use of Shimimoto's phrase demonstrates the lesson he learns, a lesson grounded in Shimimoto's own internment experience. Shimimoto shows Gunnar a response to racial injustice built on survival, not victimization. In this way, he acts as a practical mentor to Gunnar.

Using Shimimoto as a mentor critiques the assumption that only black men can mentor black boys in times of crisis. While slavery and post-Reconstruction did their part to disrupt black families, the absence of male figures emerges in the Moynihan Report, which described black women as the greatest threat to the development of young black men. Drafted by Daniel Moynihan and Nathan Glazer, the report establishes the notion that the rise and dominance of the black matriarchy places black masculinity in peril. If blacks are responsible for the problems in the black community, then "the 'black matriarchy' . . . was the core of the problem, imposing a 'crushing burden on the Negro male.'"[34] With their unprecedented influence in the family as head of household, black women allegedly usurp the role of black men, demoralize them, and force them to desert their families. These single-family households result in dysfunctional children, particularly boys: "Lacking male role models, they grew up sexually confused and demonstrated antisocial behavior including juvenile delinquency, crime, poor educational achievement, and welfare dependency."[35] The logic in the Moynihan report suggests that, because of this crisis, young black men need black male role models to show them how to be black men. Vera Paster echoes this sentiment: "Upwardly mobile, achieving, effective Black males reported stronger attempts to be like their fathers and felt encouraged by their mothers to identify with their fathers."[36] Those pertinent patterns and values, so the cultural narrative suggests, can only come from black men in primary caretaker roles. Clyde W. Franklin II argues that "black men "alter their instructions to

Black males" to account for "'real' practices of American values and beliefs in American society that Black males may be experiencing at a given time," based on their own experiences as black men.[37]

The Los Angeles riots help reignite this debate, for the conditions that spark the riots are tied to "dysfunctional" African American family life, particularly the absence of African American male role models. According to the ethnic conflict metaphor that emerged in the wake of the riots, shopkeepers complained about the laziness of the African American community, which prevented closer relations: "[In the inter-ethnic conflict frame] Korean American entrepreneurs personify the values of individual responsibility and family solidarity, while African Americans stand for welfare dependence and family dissolution."[38] Such family dissolution includes the perceived lack of mentorship regarding black males, for if young black men had better role models and guidance, such cultural chaos could be partly avoided.

Beatty critiques black father-son relations within the context of the riots, as Gunnar and his police chief father Rolf Kaufmann are both caught up in the melee. The novel consistently challenges the effectiveness of Gunnar's African American father. Ever since he can remember, Rolf has failed as a father figure. His extreme desire to assimilate can be traced to his own teenage years. Coming off as "a docile and meek nonthreat," he escapes some of the more harsh repercussions from *Brown v. Board* decision that required the desegregation of American schools. More importantly, he internalizes the racial insanity that makes him a second-class citizen: "My father fondly recalled the laughs and cold celebratory summer vacation Dixie beers he shared with the good ol' boy senior class after their macabre reenactment of the Schwerner, Goodman and Chaney murders."[39] By identifying with his white bullies who humiliate him and belittle the sacrifice individuals made for equal rights, he sets a bad example for Gunnar in confronting a racial world.

Rolf's decision to assimilate at all costs also plays a role in his de-emphasis of any kind of racial solidarity. As an officer in the army during Vietnam, he displays no sense of loyalty to his men or to the larger ethnic implications of the Vietnam conflict. He regales Gunnar with war stories of "how his all-black platoon used to ditch him in the middle of patrols, leaving him alone in some rice paddy having to face the entire Communist threat by his lonesome."[40] The only lessons he imparts to his son are lessons in assimilation to white dominant cultural expectations, even when they go against his self-interest. In doing so, Rolf misses an opportunity for the kind of cross-racial solidarity in which his soldiers engage. Vijay Prashad characterizes "Muhammad Ali's public stance—I ain't got no quarrel with them Vietcong" as representing a critique of having people of color fight other people of color from home and over issues unrelated to their own interests.[41] Rolf's exploits in his youth affect his later perspectives as a Los Angeles police officer: "After he joined the Los Angeles Police Department, he'd complain that he'd left the Indonesian jungle for the Inzocohesion jungle—'gone from fighting Viet Cong to King Kong.'"[42]

Rolf's personality quirks have a devastating impact on his relationship with his son. He only makes occasional appearances in Gunnar's life. Such appearances fail to instill the kind of respect one would expect to see between fathers and sons. This dysfunctional relationship reaches its climax during the riots. Instead of commiserating with his son about the racial undertones of the Rodney King verdict, or at least cutting him some slack during the riot as an LAPD officer, Rolf acts like a racist member of law enforcement: "When I turned to face my father, the hard rubber butt of the shotgun crashed into my jaw. I saw a flash of white and dropped to the pavement. My father's partner stepped on my ear, muffling his words: 'You are not a Kaufman. I refuse to let you embarrass me. You can't embarrass me with poetry and your niggerish ways. And where did you get all these damn air fresheners?'"[43] Rolf seems to reenact the King beating itself, identifying more with his identity as a police officer than that of a father. These events demonstrate that Rolf, though a black man, is not inherently the best role model for Gunnar. Rather than seeing his father as someone worthy of emulation, Gunnar views his father's behavior as embarrassing. Rolf fails to have a positive relationship with his son, resulting in Gunnar's desire to disassociate himself from him: "His weakness shadowed my shame from sun to sun."[44]

Rather than rehashing a narrative in which African American men function as the only proper role model for black boys, the novel places a Japanese American internment survivor in this role. In doing so, it posits that the similarities between the Japanese American internment and the 1992 riots provides a better basis for mentorship than assumptions about African American men's ability to mentor based solely on ethnic affiliation. With Shimimoto as a mentor, Gunnar finds fault with the cultural logic of the latter:

> The stereotype is that most successful black men raised by single mothers had a surrogate father figure who turned their lives around. A man who

"saw their potential," looked after them, taught them the value of virtuous living, and sent them out on the path to glory with a resounding slap on the butt. Coach Shimimoto didn't do any of those things. He just paid attention to me. The only time he ever told me what to do with my life was during basketball practice.... I can't say that I learned any valuable lessons from Shimimoto. He never gave me any clichéd phrases to be repeated in times of need, never showed me pictures of crippled kids to remind me how lucky I was.[45]

Shimimoto gives Gunnar what he does not get from his black father: attention. No platitudes, just the acknowledgment that Gunnar exists. Gunnar's critique of black mentorship in favor of an interethnic option challenges the ethnic conflict metaphor that emerges from the 1992 riots by challenging ethnic expectations.

While Coach Shimimoto's mentorship demonstrates the use of Japanese American experiences to interpret African American experiences, the novel also taps into Japanese culture to do the same. It uses Japanese puppet plays and postwar nihilism to explain contemporary black despair and disillusionment brought on by the riots. While Shimimoto helps lessen the initial blow, Gunnar and Scoby seem less optimistic in the novel following the riots, and a perceptible sense of depression and pessimism settles upon them.

The novel uses Japanese puppet plays to articulate the contours of Gunnar and Scoby's despair. Also known as *ningyo joruri*, Japanese puppet plays emerged in Japan in the 1680s and combined music and storytelling. One of the most frequent genres was the love-suicide play. These love-suicide plays reflected the tensions between the expectations of society and the desires of the individual. Most follow the same plot: a merchant falls in love with a courtesan, but circumstances prevent them from being together, so they resolve to commit suicide in honor of their love. Donald Shively notes that "the domestic play centers around the mental state of the main characters" and the plight of those "torn between their love and their obligations."[46] In this genre the individual, in most cases the merchant, feels pressure from society to meet certain obligations. This pressure, captured in the Japanese concept of *giri*, is no small matter, for it refers to "the obligation to conform to certain moral principles, traditions, and laws.... In its broadest sense, [it] could encompass the total social environment of the individual."[47] The suicide that punctuates these plays serves as an indictment of the social environment that forces individuals to conform to such obligations rather than fulfill their individual wishes: "The heroes suffer under the ethical system and are destroyed by it. . . . Their failure is not entirely their fault."[48] In other words, the lovers take an extreme act to critique the societal expectations that drive them to it.

The White Boy Shuffle uses the tensions between individual and society in the Japanese love-suicide plays to underscore the post-riot despair of contemporary blacks like Gunnar and Scoby. Like Gunnar, Scoby appears in the novel as a young black man with talent. Demonstrating an obsession with jazz, he also has the unexplained ability to hit every shot he takes on the basketball court. This gift starts to take its toll on him:

> Scoby's eyes reddened and he started to sniffle. He was cracking under the
> pressure. Watching his hands shake, I realized that sometimes the worst
> thing a nigger can do is perform well. Because then there is no turning back.
> We have no place to hide, no Superman Fortress of Solitude, no reclusive
> New England hermitages for xenophobic geniuses like Bobby Fischer and
> J.D. Salinger. Successful niggers can't go back home and blithely disappear
> into the local populace.[49]

The pressure comes from a society not used to seeing successful black men. Rather than translating into happiness, success only brings dread to Scoby. Gunnar notes that his inability to miss a shot completely turns the way they see the world upside down: "The philosophers are easily the most despicable of the lot. I suppose they have the most to lose. . . Nick's thrown every theory, every formula, every philosophical dogma out of whack; he's like a living disclaimer."[50] There are also the racist basketball fans who turn his love of the game into drudgery: "After Scoby hits his first basket, fights break out; it's sick, there's so much scorn in the world. Usually when you dive into the crowd for a loose ball, the fans try to catch you, help break your fall. When Nick goes headlong in the stands, the reporters scatter, picking up their coffee cups and laptops and letting Scoby crash into the table. They don't even help the nigger to his feet."[51]

The tensions between Scoby's desire to be an individual by following his dream and the obligations imposed on him through the stereotypes of the mainstream culture causes his despair, a despair made more poignant by the cultural language of the Japanese love-suicide plays. Like the lovers, Scoby has a negative response to the obligations that society places on him as a result of his phenomenal ability never to miss a shot in basketball: "Nicholas weeps with the star-crossed lovers. 'I know what it feels like to live in a world where you can't live your dreams. I'd rather die too. Why won't they leave us alone?"[52] The "they" refers to all people who have a pre-conceived notion of what he should be, including those who try to down-play his basketball talent. Prior to his own suicide, Scoby's thoughts go "back to Tokubei, the soy sauce dealer, and the unbelievably codependent courtesan Ohatsu in Chikamatsu's *Love Suicides at Sonezaki*, the doomed lovers under the fronds of a palm tree binding their wrists, preparing for noble deaths"[53] (206). He sees suicide as a way to place blame on soci-ety for making him feel worthless, like the lovers in the play: "Our lives, our lots, have not been as we wished. Never, until this very day, have we known a single night of heart's relaxation."[54] In light of the love-suicide genre, his actions appear heroic against the background of a conformist society, just like the lovers, who Donald Keene argues are used by Chika-matsu "to transform most unpromising figures into the hero and heroine of tragedy."[55] Scoby kills himself because he cannot reconcile to the absurd and ridiculous obligations of the dominant culture that insists on making blacks conform to reductive stereotypes.

In addition to Japanese love-suicide plays, Japanese nihilism points to another response to contemporary black disillusionment, namely, the honorable suicide. Remember that Gunnar exclaims, "I never felt so worthless in my life" in the wake of the riots.[56] Following the riots, Gunnar spends two weeks at basketball camp. Not surprisingly, he characterizes the camp in terms of unequal power dynamics between blacks and whites (a place where he finds white coaches "slobbering over skinny kids") and this fuels his increasing disillusionment.[57] While he likes riding the horses, he cannot help feeling more objectified and less able to control his life: "I sympathize with [the horses in the stables] 'cause this place makes me feel like a racehorse. Every morning I get up at six o'clock to get weighed, fed, and put through my paces."[58] His objectification as a basketball phe-nom leaves little room for a complex sense of self built on a foundation of appreciation for African American culture.

It is also at basketball camp that Gunnar starts to have nightmares: "I didn't know what the hell I was carrying on about. All I knew was that it had something to do with death. Like I was running through different sce-narios of how I'd like to die. So we got into a conversation about death or more specifically our demises, from which I concluded that niggers aren't afraid to die but are worried about how to die."[59] In his letter to Scoby he admits: "This death thing is for real. I can't avoid it so I might as well embrace it. Right?"[60] These pressures to conform to an identity crafted by the dominant culture contribute to his thoughts about death. Reinforced by the senselessness he feels in the wake of the riots, Gunnar's pessimism relates to the way the larger culture fails to recognize him as an individual and uses him for its own aims.

This cultural context mirrors the emergence of nihilism in post–World War II Japan in response to the erasure of cultural connections through Americanization. After the war, the victors initially sought to punish the Japanese for challenging the idea of Western superiority. Yukiko Koshiro asserts that the Allies attempted "to instill among the Japanese people a proper sense of relations between the white conqueror and the colored vanquished. . . . To American eyes, the worst Japanese war crime was the attempt to cripple the white man's prestige by sowing the seeds of racial pride under the banner of Pan-Asianism."[61] Motivated by the fear of the resurgence of Japanese racial pride, many Allied policies sought to diminish the Japanese cultural presence. The Allied occupation imposed Americanization on the Japanese without any consideration of the desires of the inhabitants of the defeated nation.

The nationalistic nihilism of Japanese writer Yukio Mishima seeks to recapture the racial pride that westernization stripped away from the Japanese. Roy Starrs observes that Mishima sees Western society, particularly in the form of the culture of the United States, as suppressing Japanese culture in the postwar period: "What he rejected was the democratic, liberal/humanitarian strain of that culture . . . [that] had become dominant in the post-war period in both Japan and the West, as a direct historical consequence of the defeat of the Axis powers in World War Two. . . . The 'decadence' or 'demoralization' of post-war Japan is, as we have seen, associated with Americanization."[62] Shuichi Kato echoes this sentiment by suggesting that Mishima viewed "a clearly expressed nostalgia for earlier days as a part of a critique of the social system."[63] While rejecting the notion of slavishly resurrecting a nostalgic past, Mishima uses Japanese culture to stave off culturally hostile forces. For him, it is entirely appropriate to insist on the presence of Japanese culture, finding certain forms of the postwar era "inimical to the 'Japanese spirit,'" including "the 'Peace Constitution,' the de-deification of the Emperor and the regulation of the military to the status of a 'self-defense force.'"[64]

Mishima couples this nationalism with suicide. Death functions not as resignation, but as an active response to an absurd situation produced by western forces and linked to survival. According to Starrs, Mishima practiced "an 'active nihilism,'" which represents "a sign of increased power of the spirit."[65] For Mishima, active nihilism can manifest itself in destruction which becomes the opportunity to free the individual "from the forces, both psychological and ontological, which have been oppressing him."[66] Moreover, Mishima viewed death in Japanese cultural terms, as part of an honorable samurai life. In his biography on Mishima, John Nathan draws attention to his fascination with Bushido, or "the way of the warrior," which "demanded that the warrior bear the prospect of his own death ever before him." For Mishima, this translated into a "consciousness of peril," a declaration "that the only solution to the lifelessness of peace was the consciousness of death, the sense of proximity to at least the possibility of death."[67]

Japanese nihilism provides the language that explains Gunnar's response to the disillusionment he feels toward his exploitation and the powerlessness he feels as a young black man. His call for suicide functions as a defiant response to an American society that continues to denigrate American blacks by degrees. Gunnar rejects the notion of suicide as an empty gesture: "So I asked myself, what am I willing to die for? The day when white people treat me with respect and see my life as equally valuable to theirs? No, I ain't willing to die for that, because if they don't know that by now, then they ain't never going to know it."[68] By stating what he is *not* willing to die for, Gunnar emphasizes that one's suicide should count for something. Like Mishima's notion of death, suicide functions as a mode whereby African Americans gain a sense of agency denied by the dominant culture. Moreover, when asked by reporters when he plans to commit suicide, his response, "When I'm good and goddamn ready," goes straight to the point. The point is to have control over one's life, and to commit suicide just because others expect him to would be to play into those controlling forces. Relying on a brand of Japanese nihilism that grants agency, Gunnar explains his motives to a reporter when asked whether he is encouraging people to give up: "That's the Western idea of suicide—the sense of the defeated self. 'Oh, the dysfunctional people couldn't adjust to our great system, so they killed themselves. . . .' It is as [Yukio] Mishima once said: 'Sometimes hara-kiri makes you win.' I just want to win one time."[69] Gunnar draws on the notion of positive nihilism from Japanese culture.

The novel uses both the Japanese puppet plays and Japanese nihilism to translate contemporary African American disillusionment in the wake of the riots. In doing so, it sheds light on the challenges that face contemporary blacks, challenges that are not adequately addressed or properly characterized by the traditional civil rights movement strategies of the mid-twentieth century. The experiences of African Americans born in the late 1960s and early 1970s (the post-integration generation) are distinct from the civil rights movement generation that precedes it. The fault lines between them can be traced to a significant shift during the 1960s movement. While passage of society-altering legislation like the Civil Rights Act of 1964 and Voting Rights Act of 1965 held the promise of full and equal participation by blacks in the society, those promises had yet to be realized by the late 1960s. Harvard Sitkoff points to urban riots, anti-white rhetoric of the Black Power movement, and suspicions of working-class whites as evidence of a retreat from ideals of equality. He concludes: "Prejudice and discrimination, both subtle and blatant, continued to poison race relations. . . . Whatever the movement had accomplished, the hardest and most paramount tasks still lay ahead."[70] Given that the United States had not seen widespread racial violence since the Watts riots of 1965, many assumed that such progress was indeed under way. Some voices from that earlier generation criticize the contemporary generation for this sense of despair in the face of such progress against outright racism. Bakari Kitwana observes that such criticism "is rooted in the unwillingness among the older generation to adjust to the social transformations that have shaped the hip-hop generation," and notes that "the older generation fails to understand the new Black youth culture in all of its complexities."[71] Some of this misunderstanding occurs around the kind of despair and disillusionment we see in Gunnar and Scoby. Cornel West describes this nihilism among blacks as "the lived experience of coping with a life of horrifying meaninglessness, hopelessness, and (most important) lovelessness" that results in "a numbing detachment from others and a self-destructive disposition toward the world."[72]

However, by using Japanese nihilism to describe contemporary black disillusionment, the novel demonstrates that Gunnar's generation reacts to a different kind of environment. Individuals of Gunnar's generation may enjoy more open doors, but that access creates a whole new set of issues. This retreat from the promises of civil rights continued up through the 1980s, when the post-integration generation inherited the realities of its failure. Kitwana identifies a particularly salient worldview that questions the success of integration because "continuing segregation and inequality have made [equality] especially illusory for many young Blacks."[73] Neal refers to people who come of age during the same time period as individuals who "experienced the change from urban industrialism to deindustrialism, from segregation to desegregation . . . without any nostalgic allegiance to the past . . . , but firmly in grasp of the existential concerns of this brave new world."[74] Both Neal and Kitwana point to the different experience of this generation, one that is more complex given the different cultural context. Kitwana further observes that this generation "is the first generation of African Americans to come of age outside the confines of legal segregation."[75] They are the first generation to encounter a society without codified inequality. Moreover,

> in that time of national political movements and youth radicalism, fighting the power was a given, and the lines of battle were more clearly drawn—mostly in Black and white. The 1950s and 1960s brought many changes in law, and the early 1970s ushered in an age of black elected officials, but the 1980s and 1990s were void of any significant movement around which young Blacks could organize at the notional level. For us, in part due to the previous generation's victories, today's "enemy" is not simply white supremacy or capitalism.[76]

Such progress comes with a price. The post-integration generation faces a different set of obstacles from that of the civil rights movement generation. Whereas the civil rights movement generation would suggest that the popularity that Gunnar and Scoby experience in the mainstream culture represents the success of integration, Gunnar describes it as a burden. Society uses their talents to pigeonhole them and rob them of control over their lives. Success translates into a duty, an obligation they cannot escape: "American society reels you back to the fold. 'Tote that barge, shoot that basketball, lift that bale, nigger ain't you ever heard of Dred Scott?'"[77] Scoby and Gunnar's generation have been told all their lives that doors have been opened for them and all they have to do is work hard. When asked by Gunnar why he doesn't quit, Scoby reasons, "Do what you do best. That's what I've heard my whole life. First it was hopscotch and now it's basketball."[78] Kitwana describes the gains of the civil rights movement generation as a double-edged sword: "We don't mythologize the social gains of the 1950s, 1960s and 1970s because having experienced the benefits of these gains firsthand we know they weren't panaceas. At the same time, we do romanticize them. They, along with other so-called civil rights gains, have been institutionalized in the present as part of America's glorious history. They stand in our collective memory as historical wrongs corrected."[79]

At the same time, Gunnar and Scoby face a world that operates as if equality holds sway, but in fact it is still filled with inequality and proliferates with the same reductive stereotypes about blacks. Instead of facing assumptions about black inferiority, as earlier generations of blacks did, Gunnar, Scoby, and Yoshiko encounter a different kind of stereotyping when admitted to Boston University. In his creative writing class, Gunnar encounters white, privileged students who have a condescending view of people of color and paint themselves as liberal saviors who introduce themselves "with bohemian haughtiness." Peyote Chandler, who makes a point to identify herself with "the Greenwich, Connecticut, Chandlers" and references her education at Londonderry Academy, makes sure the class knows about her mother's ambassadorship to Pakistan and her father's ownership of a factory in Asia. In order to compensate for her upper-class background, Peyote reassures everyone that "the factory employs hundreds of starving children at what I believe is a respectable living wage of seven rupees a week."[80] Another classmate, Chadwick Osterdorf III, "graduated from Choate with high honors" and "spent this past summer selling guns to downtrodden ghetto youth to defend themselves against the oppressive system."[81] Like Peyote, Chadwick rationalizes an elite background with ostensible gestures toward those outside his class. However, Gunnar recognizes such gestures as empty and superficial, finding himself "bored with [Peyote's] Mayflower pedigree" and criticizing Chadwick's supposed emulation of Rimbaud the poet: "Come on, Rimbaud wasn't no gun-running revolutionary. What he really wanted to sell was slaves, black African niggers, but he was too stupid to catch any, so he sold weapons to some king who ripped him off."[82] Gunnar encounters not a cross-burning Klan but something more subtle, and perhaps more sinister: white liberalism disguised as solidarity. Peyote and Chadwick have no real-world experience with the lives of the people they claim to care about, nor do they recognize their own complicity in the system that keeps them oppressed, for they continue to identify with their elite backgrounds with no sense of irony. It is these very superficial relations that Gunnar critiques in the white activist campus group SWAPO, which can't understand why they do not have any black members. Gunnar explains: "See, it's like this—no one could possibly care enough to be treated like a baby seal. Colored people aren't mascots for your political attitudes."[83]

Gunnar and crew also face a mode of diversity that is equally superficial when they search for an extracurricular club on campus. Concoction, which consists of mixed-race individuals who feel marginalized by both blacks and whites, actually rejects Gunnar. Ostensibly there to celebrate diversity, Concoction actually seeks to erase diversity altogether. Discussion topics such as "how to check African-American/Latino/Asian on your job application and rise above your employer's stereotypes by asserting your biraciality in the workplace in a nonethnic manner" actually focuses on how to assert a multiethnic background without the negative side effects of stereotypes, depleting it of any negative connotations. They invite guests to learn how to use diversity from "Jane Paleface, renowned Indian rights activist, [who] explains how to claim one sixty-fourth Native American heritage and get your oil and casino kickback checks without having to live on the reservation."[84] Jane does not represent an activist trying to right a historical wrong, but an opportunist who shares how to use ethnicity to benefit economically. Angela Y. Davis explains the corporate benefit of this type of diversity: "This leads us back to the corporate multicultural strategies, wherein the purpose of acknowledging difference is to guarantee that the enterprise functions as efficiently as it would if there were no cultural differences at all. . . . Although you are permitted to be an 'other,' you must work 'as if' you were not a member of a marginalized group."[85] Once again, such nuanced perceptions have great impact on how people who are different are treated.

These subtle yet important dynamics of difference differ from those that confronted civil rights predecessors. The post-integration generation faces issues based on the diversity of identity rather that the establishment of a single black identity, which was a call emerging from a more nationalistic wing of traditional civil rights. Education, promoted as the cure for racial intolerance, simply creates another mode of racial tension:

> "Generation Hip Hop" was endowed with a hope that eluded blacks before them. The most visible barriers to success were supposedly removed, and a more level terrain would allow them to flourish on a par with their white peers. . . . As a result, a post-*Bakke* generation of blacks moves about mixed campuses aware of white scrutiny and the negative imagery of blacks in the popular media and white people's minds.[86]

Moreover, individuals like Gunnar encounter "legitimacy" tests from other blacks, perhaps to a greater extent than their civil rights movement forebears. Ambrosia, an Afro-centric black student union, focuses on the outer trappings of ethnic culture, arriving "wearing loud African garb over their Oxford shirts and red suspenders, drinking ginger beer, and using their advertising skills to plan how best to package the white man's burden."[87] They also embrace some of the reductive rhetoric of more nationalistic voices of prior generations of civil rights. Members argue over "about how brave they'd be fighting on the front lines of America's race war."[88] But it is not just their pretenses and superficial attachment to an oppositional political stance that Gunnar finds disturbing. It is also their tendency to ostracize those who do not agree with the party line. When Gunnar questions whether an Afro-chic fashion show can seriously solve the problems black people face, he is insulted by other members: "'Nigger crazy, he trying to confuse the youth.' 'Smart-alecky fool need to be playing basketball, that's what he need to be doing.'"[89] These episodes relate the pressure for Gunnar to conform, despite the options and opportunities that face him as a post-integration generation member and echo some of the pressures of contemporary blacks noted by Neal: "The activists are most aware of their racial heritage, generally as a response to their campus environment, the influence of their parents, or a genuine desire to know more about themselves. . . . Students in these categories often play their self-assigned role of enforcing blackness, often in the most limiting ways."[90]

The civil rights movement generation has no weapons in its arsenal to combat the emotional toll that social progress brings. The post-integration generation constructs other strategies, strategies that include ones informed by Japanese culture, like nihilism. Gunnar's suicide movement, inspired by Japanese nihilism, is poised against traditional civil rights movement strategies. Beatty captures this sentiment in the prologue of the novel, when the suicide craze is in full swing: "In the quest for equality, black folks have tried everything. . . . Nothing works, so why suffer the slow deaths of toxic addiction and the American work ethic when the immediate gratification of suicide awaits? . . . It will be the Emancipation Disintegration. Lunch counters, bus seats and executive washrooms be damned: our mass suicide will be the ultimate sit-in."[91] Using the language of the civil rights movement, Gunnar characterizes suicide less as an act of protest aimed at social change and more as the last action people can make on their own behalf.

While Beatty's novel uses Japanese cultural production to explain the post-riots mindset of young African Americans, it also uses African American culture to translate Asian immigrant experiences impacted by the ethnic conflict metaphor that emerges from the Los Angeles riots. This metaphor paints Korean merchants as successful immigrants who attain the American dream and victims of violent African American unrest. Abelmann and Lie note the connection between the media perception of Korean Americans and the traditional immigration narrative: "In accounts decrying the mob violence, Korean Americans emerged as the model minority, immigrant entrepreneur who had realized the American dream."[92] The American dream implies a particular kind of promise to immigrants: "[It] denotes a belief in the United States as a land of opportunity in which no major obstacles exist to individual success. . . . Inequalities and divides of class, gender and race are ultimately meaningless; rugged individualism reigns supreme in this social view. Put simply, people with talent and who work hard succeed, while others do not. Those who fail, then, have no one to blame but themselves."[93] However, Asian immigrants pursue the American dream within a context that includes other ethnic groups that the majority culture may view as victims, threats, or burdens. Asian immigrant success may be defined by the "failure" of other ethnic groups, especially in relation to the model minority stereotype.

The idea of the model minority emerged from a 1966 *U.S. News and World Report* article, which immediately set up a contrast between Chinese immigrants and blacks. It cites Chinatowns where one finds "an important racial minority pulling itself up from hardship and discrimination to become a model of self-respect and achievement in today's America . . . at a time when it is being proposed that hundreds of billions be spent to uplift Negroes and other minorities."[94] The article extols the virtues of Chinese Americans, and by extension, other Asian American groups: "Not all Chinese-Americans are rich. Many, especially recent arrivals from Hong Kong, are poor and cannot speak English. But the large majority are moving ahead by applying the traditional virtues of hard work, thrift and morality."[95] The model minority stereotype reflects assimilation, often associated with a one-way cultural transfer, from ethnic to dominant culture. During the assimilation process, most immigrants are subject to pressures by the dominant American culture to erase all traces of ethnic culture. John Higham asserts that, in exerting such pressures, American society historically "opened a frontal assault on foreign influence in American life. They set about to stampede immigrants into citizenship, into adoption of the English language, and into an unquestioning reverence for existing American institutions. They bade them abandon entirely their Old World loyalties, customs, and memories."[96]

The White Boy Shuffle recognizes the tendency for assimilation to erase ethnic differences at Mestizo Mulatto Mongrel Elementary, Gunnar's first school. At first glance, it appears that MMME would be a site of healthy respect for diversity, but the illusion quickly fades when Gunnar describes it as "Santa Monica's all-white multicultural school." Even as a young boy, Gunner recognizes that Ms. Cegeny, his teacher, reduces "race, sexual orientation, and gender to inconsequence."[97] She wears a T-shirt that crosses out all words of racial designation in favor of the purportedly all-inclusive "human" category. The motto posted above the blackboard echoes the erasure: "Eracism—The sun doesn't care what color you are."[98] Even her name suggests a kind of racial erasure as a result of racial mixture as it plays on the word "miscegenation." Such cues deemphasize difference in the service of assimilation and a common culture: "Common or core culture *transcends* cultural difference. It manages diversity via a set of principles that is neutral to the distinctive qualities of the various cultures it manages."[99] Appealing to the largest common denominator subsumes the value of difference rather than embracing it. For example, when working on math problems in Ms. Cegeny's class, Gunnar notices that the Japanese do not fare well:

> Everything was multicultural, but nothing was multicultural. The class studied Asian styles of calculation by learning to add and subtract on an abacus and then we applied the same mathematical principles on Seiko calculators. Prompting my hand to go up and me to ask naively, "Isn't the Seiko XL-126 from the same culture as the abacus?" Ms. Cegeny's response was, "No we *gave* this technology to the Japanese after WWII. Modern technology is a Western construct."[100]

Ms. Cegeny meets Gunnar's attempts to assign value to the Japanese culture that in both ancient and modern times supplied advanced methods of calculation with resistance. She assigns technological superiority to the West and condescendingly suggests that such an exchange represents an act of pity by the victor nation over the vanquished Japanese at the end of World War II.

This rhetorical smackdown has repercussions and significance for Sheila, Gunnar's Japanese American classmate, for it demonstrates how assimilating to the dominant culture results in ethnic cultural erasure. Gunnar explains further: "Oh. To put me in my place further, Sheila Watanabe hummed, 'My country 'tis of thee, sweet land of liberty' loud enough for the whole class to hear."[101] Sheila's humming of the patriotic song aligns her with Ms. Cegeny's correction of Gunnar, suggesting that she emulates the norms of American society to her own detriment. Ms.

Cegeny's silence on this interchange could be read as approval. She does not chastise Sheila for humming. She validates her as the "model minority," enacting a dynamic where "whites were the elders telling the older siblings, African Americans, that they should be more like the younger ones, Asian Americans."[102]

Such appeals to common culture have particular consequences for Sheila that she fails to realize. In attempting to ingratiate herself with the majority at Gunnar's expense, she overlooks the fact that Ms. Cegeny's appeal to a common, homogenizing culture distorts her ethnic history. Japanese Americans experienced similar denigration during Japanese internment. The Japanese were placed in camps during World War II because they failed to be perceived as part of the common culture. Wu sees Japanese internment as just one way that "the perpetual foreigner syndrome works to deprive Asian Americans of civil rights and transform us into a racial threat."[103] Sheila's response demonstrates her eagerness to play along and assimilate, a move that "sets the fundamental conditions for full economic and social citizenship in the United States" by requiring "adherence to core principles and behaviors," rejecting "racialized group consciousness" and repudiating cultural equity among groups.[104] Sheila does not see that, by making fun of Gunnar, she fails to acknowledge herself as a Japanese American.

The ethnic conflict metaphor that emerges from the Los Angeles riots depends on a depiction of Koreans and Korean Americans as members of the "good" ethnic immigrant group who become victims because of their successful pursuit of the American dream, much like Japanese Americans. However, the novel challenges this notion by suggesting that Korean and other Asian immigrant groups ally themselves not with the majority culture but with other ethnic American cultures. Indeed, in the actual story of Asian immigration, Koreans and others have reason not to view themselves as model minorities. Edward T. Chang notes that "Korean Americans have never been part of the so-called [WASP] 'establishment' that has dominated the African American community for the past two hundred years."[105] Citing policies that barred Koreans from becoming naturalized citizens until 1952, Chang concludes, "Korean Americans can never claim to be part of white America because of the physical appearance that distinguishes them apart from Whites."[106] The novel takes advantage of this dynamic, envisioning the acculturation of Korean and other Asian immigrants to African American culture, based on similar experiences and struggles, a move that challenges the ethnic conflict metaphor.

Acculturation suggests that immigrants may retain elements of their ethnic cultures even as they take on aspects of other cultures. The novel uses African American culture as an alternative acculturative destination for Korean immigrants. The character of Ms. Kim reflects sympathies that develop with Korean immigrants in black neighborhoods. A fixture in Hillside, her presence forces the reader to see how Korean Americans build productive lives with African Americans. She is half-black and half-Korean, a biraciality that Beatty maintains in her behavior: "To us, when she was behind the counter in her store, Ms. Kim was Korean. When she was out on the streets walking her dogs, she was black."[107] Embraced by the black community without having to give up ties to her ethnic culture, Ms. Kim also reflects bicultural identity in her speech, for Joe Shenanigans reports that "she be talking Korean and black broken English at the same time."[108]

Such sentiments are reciprocated when the Gun Totin' Hooligans plan revenge for the death of their comrade, Pumpkin. They ultimately refuse to consider Ms. Kim a target because "the families of every fool in the room would starve to death, because Ms. Kim carried them on credit for two weeks out of the month."[109] Rather than being their enemy, they recognize that Ms. Kim helps them. Furthermore, the residents refuse to burn and loot her store during the riots, so she does it herself: "Holding one of her makeshift grenades, Ms. Kim lit the oil-rag fuse and strode to the front of the store. . . . Ms. Kim silently hook-shot another cocktail onto the roof and watched her store burn with a satisfied smile. A few folks tried to douse the flames with garden hoses, but Ms. Kim cut their hoses in half with a Swiss Army knife, then went looking for the police to place herself under arrest."[110] The neighborhood refuses to destroy her store because they see her as part of the community. At the same time, Ms. Kim recognizes the injustice of the verdicts. With Ms. Kim, Beatty envisions black–Korean cooperation and provides a model for Korean acculturation to African American culture.

In addition to Korean immigrants, Japanese immigrants also successfully assimilate to African American culture in the novel. Yoshiko, Gunnar's Japanese mail-order bride, becomes a fixture in Gunnar's life. As a birthday present, Psycho Loco procures "a mail-order bride through the services of Hot Mama-san's of the Orient."[111] She arrives via UPS, and the driver describes her fate if she is "refused delivery": "She goes back to the warehouse and collects dust for three days till we send her back to Japan fourth class, which probably will mean three weeks in the hot cargo bay of a transport ship. . . . She's just like a package. She came with instructions, but it's all in Japanese."[112] The UPS driver articulates a mindset that treats Asians as things. His objectification of Yoshiko causes Gunnar to unceremoniously throw him out. But later Gunnar surmises that she chooses him over "an Iowa grad student named Stanley" as a result of reading his poetry in a magazine, suggesting that she believed she would have more in common with Gunnar. At the wedding ceremony, Gunnar's mother deems Yoshiko "black at heart" and she seems to prove it when she demonstrates her facility with English:

> "English?" Yoshiko stood up sharply, a little redfaced and wobbly from all the beer she'd drunk. "Me speak English." To wild applause, Yoshiko pecked me on the lips, then climbed onto the tabletop, chugging her beer until she reached the summit. My bride, literally on a pedestal, was going to pledge her life to me. You couldn't wipe the smile off my face with a blowtorch. Yoshiko cleared her throat and threw her hands in the air. "Brummph boomp ba-boom bip. I'm the king of rock—there is none higher! Sucker MC's must call me sire!"[113]

In addition to its comedic value, the incident describes Yoshiko's acculturative destination as distinctly African American. As quintessentially American as jazz, hip-hop also represents a distinctive mode of African American cultural production, as previous chapters demonstrate. By singing the lyrics by Run-DMC, one of the most iconic hip-hop groups, Yoshiko aligns herself with African American culture. Her acculturation to African American culture allows her to maintain ties to her ethnic culture. To make Yoshiko feel welcome, Psycho Loco prepares a menu of ribs and udon noodle soup. Even the terrible duo, Betty and Veronica, get excited by the prospect of Yoshiko sharing "those crazy Japanese hairstyles."[114]

The novel uses Yoshiko to highlight the options available to Japanese immigrants in African American culture. It places more value on cultural exchange than on cultural erasure. Yoshiko readily participates in African American culture. She shows her familiarity when she and Gunnar decide how best to pursue their educations after they leave Boston University:

> Yoshiko and I engaged in our own great debates. I was Du Bois arguing vociferously for a continuation of our comprehensive overpriced Ivy League educations. I suggested that we attend each Ivy League school for one

semester, gleaning the best bullshit from the best bullshitters, and emerge as learned scholars prepared to unravel the intricacies of the world or at least work as Wall Street market analysts. Yoshiko was Booker T. Washington fighting passionately for a more proletarian edification, one involving a practicum in the crafts and technical vocations. And what better tutelage than that offered by America's renowned correspondence colleges?[115]

Yoshiko's ability to participate in the age-old debate in African American intellectual tradition demonstrates her facility with African American culture.

"Not Quite What You Were Expecting": Afro-Asian Gender and Solidarity in *The Matrix* Trilogy

While Beatty's novel echoes the complex examination of dynamics within and between ethnic groups, *The Matrix* trilogy addresses a void in both Beatty's novel and Lee's film. Women do make appearances as characters in *The Big Boss* but in small, supporting roles. Thai women are maids in the big boss's compound and prostitutes in the brothels he controls. However, it is a Thai woman who tips off Lee's character about the illegal drug trafficking at the ice factory. While the potential for gender cooperation is never fully explored, it does allude to the way *The Matrix* trilogy engages the metaphor of ethnic conflict that emerges from the Los Angeles riots. The films respond to ethnic antagonisms created by an urban environment that pits blacks and Asians against a white power structure. While the narratives surrounding the Los Angeles riots construct tensions between African Americans and Korean immigrants in an urban area, *The Matrix* trilogy presents interethnic cooperation against forces represented as white and male. The films use African American womanism to explore Afro-Asian solidarity between men and women, which represents a mode of cultural translation. Featuring multiple Afro-Asian pairings between men and women, *The Matrix* trilogy invests transgressive power in the relationship between the Asian and African American characters, who model Afro-Asian solidarity as an alternative to the white power structure based solely on ethnicity or gender. Their relationship envisions an alternative within the ethnic conflict metaphor by centralizing gender.

The Matrix trilogy brings a new twist to a common science fiction theme, namely, the fate of a society that becomes increasingly dependent on the technology it creates. In *The Matrix*, the first film of the trilogy, Mr. Anderson, portrayed by Keanu Reeves, appears to be an unassuming worker bee, a programmer for a large computer company, Metacortex. However, in his off-time, Anderson is Neo, a hacker who searches the Internet for signs of Morpheus, a legendary hacker wanted by law enforcement. Neo's search for Morpheus places him at a crossroads: help the Agents, clad in black suits and led by Agent Smith, to capture Morpheus; or throw his lot in with Morpheus, Trinity, and others to discover the truth about the world in which he lives. By taking the red pill, Neo discovers that his life is a virtual construct created by machines to control the human population and feed off their bio-electric energy. Initially created by humans, the machines win the war that breaks out between them and humans. Machines now control the matrix, where most humans are blissfully unaware of their imprisonment, and hunt the handful of human rebels, who, freed from the matrix, voluntarily jack in to wreak havoc on the system and free humans. Neo has been freed because Morpheus believes he is the One, that individual destined to end the war with the machines. After initially rejecting his destiny, Neo begins to accept the mantle of the responsibility when he mounts an assault on the Agents in order to free a captured Morpheus. As a result of Morpheus's faith and Trinity's love and devotion, Neo fully realizes his power as the One and defeats the Agents.

In *The Matrix: Reloaded*, the second installment of the trilogy, Neo, Morpheus, Trinity, and other leaders of the human resistance work together to defend Zion, the last human city outside of the matrix, from the machines' retaliation in response to the havoc caused by Neo in the first film. While one ship remains behind to hear word from the Oracle, an ally in their fight, Morpheus and his crew return to Zion. This provides a glimpse of their defenses, their domestic lives, and celebrations by the humans outside the matrix. When the human rebels establish contact with the Oracle, she instructs Neo to go to the Source, the mainframe. This act would stop the war between humans and machines. Neo also encounters his nemesis, Agent Smith, who rather than being deleted after losing to Neo in the first film, replicates himself in order to take over the matrix. Yet, Neo's primary adversaries are the machines themselves, and with the aid of the Keymaker, who the humans stole from the Merovingian, an old and power-hungry program, Neo returns to the Source. From the Architect, a program largely responsible for the creation of the matrix, he learns that the One is an anomaly of the system who was never intended to end the war. When presented with the choice to save humanity, or save Trinity,

Neo elects to save Trinity, but returns to the human rebels to figure how to save them. At the end of this installment, he falls into a coma after an encounter with sentinels outside the matrix.

The fate of both machines and humans is determined in *The Matrix: Revolutions*, the third installment of the trilogy. Rescued from limbo, Neo discovers that the resolution of the war between humans and machines will be reached in the final confrontation between himself and Agent Smith, who now threatens to destroy the machines as well. As the humans hold off the machines' onslaught of Zion, Neo and Trinity travel to Machine City. While Trinity is killed in the process, Neo strikes a truce with the machines, who stop their assault on Zion while he fights their common enemy, Agent Smith. Neo's destruction of Smith restores the matrix and ends the machines' attack. Apparently dead, the machines take Neo's body, and the Oracle gets an assurance from the Architect that "all who want out" of the matrix will be released.

Wowing audiences with innovative special effects and spectacular fight scenes, *The Matrix* films diverge from typical science fiction fare by making ethnic difference central to their meaning. Daniel Bernardi notes that sci-fi mirrors the frontier myth in that they retell "the story of a white hero who domesticates or obliterates 'wild' Indians, 'dirty' Mexicans, and 'heathen' Chinese in his quest to tame the West. . . . Since the all-white world of Fritz Lang's *Metropolis* (1926), the story of a white future has reigned supreme."[116] Many significant sci-fi films, including *2001* (1968), *Star Wars* (1977), and *Blade Runner* (1982) posit a white future, signaling links between progress and whiteness. Initial notions of progress derived from Enlightenment ideals exclude people of color from the march. By establishing that groups of people, like Africans, did not possess reason, and that others, like Asians, possessed less reason than white men, the Enlightenment project fails to include them as active agents in the development of civilization. Paul Gilroy describes the narrative of progress, implicit in many science fiction films, as an "innocent modernity" that purges "any traces of the people without history whose degraded lives might raise awkward questions about the limits of bourgeois humanism."[117] Because science fiction films rely on the assumption that the future represents progress of civilization, they replicate the exclusion of people of color from that kind of future.

The failure of many mainstream science fiction films to engage ethnic discourses reflects contemporary society's failure to do so. De Witt Douglas Kilgore reminds us that "science fiction is marked by the racial logic of its surrounding society."[118] While American society may be one of the most diverse, appeals to a common culture tend to erase the differences represented by people of color. Such appeals suggest that there are "common values, shared principles, core beliefs, national purpose, bringing people together."[119] Newfield and Gordon argue that common culture "*transcends* cultural difference" and "manages diversity via a set of principles that is neutral to the distinctive qualities of the various cultures it manages."[120] In other words, appeals to common culture act as a bulwark against difference. When science fiction films posit a future devoid of people of color, it simply mirrors perceptions of existing society where diversity is subsumed under calls for a homogeneous culture.

In those unusual cases when mainstream science fiction films engage in difference, stereotypical modes can come into play. For example, the *Star Trek* franchise consciously challenges the notion of a white future by creating a context where "racial harmony and tolerance were to be the norm rather than the exception in the ongoing *Star Trek* diegesis. . . . [Roddenberry] called for a multicultural future."[121] Despite the attention to diversity, *Star Trek* to a certain extent reinforces normative ways of looking at ethnicity. Bernardi explains that creator Gene Roddenberry originally envisioned Spock as a biracial Latino navigator, "one part is brilliant, a trait that comes from his Boston (presumably European) paternal line; the other part is irrational, a failed Latin lover, a trait that comes from his Brazilian maternal line. This dichotomy is a familiar one, playing on common racial essentialisms and stereotypes about Latinos."[122] Spock's recurrent struggles between his Vulcan heritage and his human one mirror the struggles of mulattos, or mixed-race individuals, in American culture. Late-nineteenth- and early-twentieth-century novels routinely depict mulattos as erratic, unstable, and unable to blend into either culture. Thus, such attempts to infuse the science fiction genre with ethnic difference can fall back on earlier essentialist assumptions about races.

A film series like *Planet of the Apes* (1968–73) also invokes stereotypical ethnic discourses even as it tries to move beyond them. Eric Greene notes, "The filmmakers made a deliberate choice to veer away from the direction of [Pierre] Boulle [author of the 1963 French novel *La Planète des Singes*, the basis for the film] and [Rod] Serling's original conceptions and to construct an ape society based on racial hierarchy in which the darkest apes were at the bottom."[123] At the bottom of the social ladder, gorillas make up the majority of the military and are completely excluded from intellectual and political circles, which are inhabited by lighter-colored chimpanzees and orangutans. That choice evokes historic links between apes and African Americans as evidence of their inferiority: "Because apes and monkeys resemble humans but are still animals, 'ape,' 'gorilla,' 'monkey' and related terms became favorite epithets to degrade those whose otherness and inferiority were believed to be manifested by and *inscribed* upon their bodies, people who, while they appeared human, were seen as less than human."[124] Such epithets also serve to dehumanize blacks by defining them by emotion rather than by reason. Ron Eglash notes that such a "primitive racism" renders African Americans "'closer to nature'— not really a culture of all but rather beings of uncontrolled emotion and direct bodily sensation, rooted in the soil of sensuality."[125] While the ape– human dynamic in the *Planet of the Apes* series sheds a spotlight on late-1960s black–white relations, it also reinforces stereotypical notions about African Americans in its depiction of ape society.

One of the reasons why *The Matrix* trilogy created such a splash can be traced to its divergence from these landmarks of futuristic terrain in mainstream science fiction film. These films foreground not just ethnicity, but also complex racial dynamics of our day. While critics like C. Richard King and David Leonard argue that the films are "little more than surface color, detached from racialized communities and histories, so that race no longer matters,"[126] I argue that representations of African American, Asian, and Asian American ethnicities are key to understanding the trilogy. The directors cast Keanu Reeves in the principal role of Neo. Not only is Reeves of Asian ancestry, he has also starred in several films that link Asians and science fiction, the implications of which will be discussed later. In addition to Reeves, the films are replete with African American, Asian, and Asian American actors in pivotal roles. Prior to taking up the role of Morpheus, Laurence Fishburne earned a reputation in films that centralize blackness, including *Othello* (1995), *School Daze* (1988), and *Boyz N the Hood* (1991). Morpheus's crew is also multiracial as well, featuring Marcus Chong and Anthony Ray Parker, as Tank and Dozer respectively, in *The Matrix* and later Harold Perrineau as Link in the two sequels. The all-powerful Oracle is portrayed by black women, Gloria Foster in the first film and Mary Alice in the sequels. Jada Pinkett Smith plays Niobe, former love interest of Morpheus who displays impressive piloting skills in *Revolutions*. Harry Lennix plays Commander Locke, military leader of Zion. Randall Duk Kim plays the Keymaker, exiled program rescued by the human rebels who helps Neo in his quest. Collin Chou plays Seraph, protector of the Oracle; Nona Gaye plays Zee, sister of Dozer and Tank from *The Matrix* who helps defend Zion in the final assault in *Revolutions*. Cornel West, noted professor of African American studies at Princeton, plays a councilor. Such a list not only shows the multitude of characters of color, but also reveals a pattern of power relations. Often, the characters of color align together against more oppressive forces in the film, generally characterized as white and male. Hugo Weaving plays Agent Smith (in fact, all of the agents are white men). Lambert Wilson plays the Merovingian, a powerful program that only wants more power. Helmut Bakaitis plays the Architect, a program responsible for creating and maintaining the matrix. By establishing this dichotomy, the trilogy highlights the dynamics between groups identified by their difference, differences that resonate with ethnic dynamics in American society.

This dichotomy between representations of people of color and representations of whites points to an alternative to the urban struggle encapsulated by the metaphor of ethnic conflict that emerges from the Los Angeles riots. As previously discussed, this metaphor constructs African Americans as antagonists poised against Korean shopkeepers. However, *The Matrix* trilogy provides an alternative vision of urban dynamics by making whiteness central to the antagonism. In the film series, white characters consistently portray villains who seek to destroy characters of color. The Merovingian, the Architect, Agent Smith and his fellow agents, and the Trainman are all white men who seek to thwart characters of color. The traitors found among the humans, such as Bane and Cypher, are both white. People of color are not betrayed by people of color in the film, nor do they have their bodies invaded by Agents, something that happens to individuals still hardwired to the system. Conversely, characters of color consistently cooperate with one another. The Oracle, the Keymaker, Seraph, Rama-Kandra, and Sati, programs represented by people of color, all help the humans in their struggle.

More than just aligning people of color against white men, the trilogy specifically creates Afro-Asian pairings, particularly those that involve men and women. One type can be seen in *The Animatrix*, a collection of short animated films released between *The Matrix: Reloaded* and *The Matrix: Revolutions*. "Final Flight of the Osiris" bases the interaction between black men and Asian women on desire. The animated short opens with a spinning overhead shot that shows the audience a dojo lighted from above, alluding to the dojo scene between Neo and Morpheus in *The Matrix*, another instance of an Afro-Asian pairing. An African American man, blindfolded and with a sword, enters the shot. In the next shot, a woman, dressed in red, also blindfolded and with a sword, enters behind the man. His shirt is open; she wears a short, kimono-styled garment that reveals red underwear when she jumps and does acrobatics. As they fight, swords rip away pieces of the opponents' clothing. We realize that this is the point of this "combat," as the man peeks from under his blindfold and gives a smirk as the woman eventually ends up with only a red bandeau top and thong underwear. Eventually, the woman cuts away his pants, and mirrors the peeking and smirking. Just when they are about to kiss, they are interrupted by an alarm. We realize that this is merely a computer simulation. In the real world, the *Osiris* happens upon machines massing for an attack on Zion. Our battling couple, Thadeus and Jue, realize that Zion needs to be warned. Jue volunteers to deliver the message while Thadeus stays behind to command the ship, ensuring that the machines do not destroy them before Jue can accomplish her mission. Jue enters the matrix and delivers the message. Soon after, the sentinels overtake the *Osiris* and kill everyone on board.[127] The interaction between Thadeus and Jue is based on an intimate relationship, and uses visuals that focus on their bodies to elucidate this particular mode of Afro-Asian pairing. The majority of the film is devoted to this erotic dance they perform, a dance that depends on the objectification of Jue in ways common to Asian women. Andy Jones, the director, explains that the creators knew Jue was Asian and wanted her character to be "sexy and erotic" and accomplished this through her outfits and movements.[128] Casting Jue as the sensual Asian women hearkens back to stereotypes of Asian women that centralize their characters around their bodies to the exclusion of other character development.

However, in the films proper, relationships between Asian men and African American women conform to a pattern of mutual respect and duty to the larger cause. For example, Niobe has Ghost as her second-in-command, who proves to be reliable and supportive of his strong black female captain. They are introduced in the meeting at the beginning of *The Matrix Reloaded*, where the ships' captains and their first officers meet to decide who will wait to hear word from the Oracle. Niobe and Ghost later work well together with Neo on his desperate mission to shut down the power plant. In tense moments before the final onslaught of the machines in *The Matrix Revolutions*, Niobe believes she has the skills to navigate a ship not her own back to Zion. Roland, the prime naysayer, comes off as a crotchety older white man who questions her abilities. Ghost, meanwhile, does not question, but makes preparation. On most of the journey, Roland's tone questions the ability of Niobe, but even in the thick of battle,

Ghost takes orders and diligently does his job. As Niobe successfully navigates the mechanical line with his ship, doing turns and flips that he did not think it could do, Roland reluctantly gives Niobe credit for her skills. His dynamic with Niobe contrasts starkly with her relationship with her second-in-command.

The Matrix Reloaded also introduces Seraph to audiences as the protector of the Oracle, another African American female character. Consumers of Asian film may recognize Collin Chou, the actor who portrays the Seraph, as a regular in Hong Kong films, including Jet Li's Hong Kong offerings like The Enforcer (1995) and The Bodyguard from Beijing (1994), and films in the triad genre like Return to a Better Tomorrow (1994). In addition to this prior association with martial arts, Chou's character enters the trilogy in a space overdetermined as Asian: a spare room with Asian-inspired décor and few amenities, located in Chinatown with wood accents, looking more like a rural teahouse than something found in the center of a city. King and Richardson describe him as "Kung Fu master turned escort" who "reflects the mysterious wisdom of Asian characters."[129] While many have recognized the spiritual connotations of his name, few have explored the meaning of his position as bodyguard of the Oracle. Seraph and the Oracle have a long-standing relationship, for he has protected her for years. Highly trustworthy and a fierce fighter, he has even beaten Agent Smith on a prior occasion. The relationship between Seraph and the Oracle is one of cooperation in a common cause. Although the Oracle has more power, she sends Seraph to accomplish important tasks, such as bringing Neo to her, protecting Sati, and retrieving Neo from limbo.

It is significant that Seraph chooses to serve in the sometimes unpopular role of the Oracle's protector, unlike other programs who are forced into servitude by other more powerful programs. His decision to be the Oracle's protector puts him out of favor with programs like the Merovingian and Agent Smith. In The Matrix Revolutions, Seraph accompanies Morpheus and Trinity to secure the release of Neo. This necessitates a visit to the Merovingian's club, for the Train Man, the program who controls passage to and from limbo, works for the Merovingian. Entering with their backs to each other and guns drawn, Seraph, Morpheus, and Trinity move through this clearly hostile environment. When they enter, the Merovingian yells, "The prodigal son returns!" and asks Seraph if he is here for the bounty. Once they reach the balcony, he greets Seraph: "And since you, my little Judas, have walked in here I can only surmise that the fortune teller has found herself another shell."[130] This interchange suggests a prior event where Seraph's decision to ally himself with the Oracle resulted in enmity with white power forces. Because the Oracle is someone to whom the Merovingian considers himself superior, he takes a condescending tone with Seraph. Like the Architect, he never calls the Oracle by her name, and denigrates her even further by characterizing her abilities as some kind of magic trick, a mere illusion compared to his power.

The relationships between Seraph and the Oracle and Niobe and Ghost prefigure the most complex Afro-Asian pairing between men and women in the trilogy: Neo and the Oracle. Their interaction culminates in solidarity in part because each acts as nontraditional representations of Asian men and African American women. Prior to being designated as the One, Neo leads a marginalized life. His boss views him as a cog in the technology company, Metacortex, and he does not fit in. He is not the worker bee that his boss wants him to be. The reasons for his failure to become part of the Metacortex way of doing things stems from an inherent divergence of perspectives, revealed in Mr. Rinehart's chastisement of Neo upon his latest tardiness to work: "You have a problem with authority, Mr. Anderson. You believe that you are special, that somehow the rules do not apply to you. Obviously you are mistaken."[131] From Mr. Rinehart's perspective, one individual is not distinguished from another. Conformity replaces individualization, and Neo does not fit into those expectations. When away from work, Neo's extracurricular activities also place him in a marginalized world. He is a respectable computer programmer by day and hacker by night. He seems to have a reputation for getting illegal technology for those in-the-know, such as Choi, who shows up at his apartment late at night.

This marginalization is linked to Neo's nonwhite, Asian identity. Once again, the casting of Reeves plays a role, for Peter Feng suggests that some spectators "label Reeves as Asian Pacific passing as white," relying on the assumption that they act in the role of "an insider who registers that the dupe has failed to read the passer 'correctly.' . . . the insiders believe that there is a true (Asian Pacific) identity behind the appearance."[132] Some of his previous roles set him up for this, including the title role in *Johnny Mnemonic*, where Reeves plays a walking computer who acts as a courier for information. Within *The Matrix* trilogy, Neo's facility with technology links him to an Asian identity. He participates in the discourse of "techno-orientalism," a term coined by Greta Niu that reflects "a way of viewing (of making an object of knowledge) Asian American without attending to the relationship between Asian bodies and technology."[133] This association is bolstered in cyberpunk novels like *Neuromancer*, in which "Asian characters install, manufacture and maintain the body modifications that make heavy duty hacking possible for console cowboys."[134]

When Asians appear in the science fiction genre, they frequently are associated with technology. Neo performs this function for Choi, who comes to him for bootleg technology. This scene begins with Anderson literally surrounded by technology. As a computer programmer for Metacortex, Jason Haslam suggests he is "literally encircled by the detritus of the technological world."[135] After taking the red pill, Neo's abilities manifest themselves in ways associated with technology, enabling him to do what other humans cannot, such as see the code of the matrix or successfully battle Agents. The Architect measures Neo's responses to his questions as if Neo was a machine processing a request. In addition to Asian associations with technology, the films continue to gesture toward Neo's Asian identity by pairing him with Morpheus, making him a member of another black-Asian pairing in the film.

While audience members may see Neo as vaguely Asian, the film never overtly articulates the ethnic identity of his or any other character of color. Indeed, the topic never comes up. However, Morpheus tells Neo that the world inside the matrix is "the world we know."[136] Just as it adheres to the physical properties of the world we know, like the laws of gravity, it also adheres to the power dynamics of the world we know. For example, mainstream American culture often fails to make distinctions among Asian ethnic groups. In the world we know, Asian panethnicity draws on the similar experiences of people of Asian descent across the different subgroups and suggests power in such an orientation. Yen Le Espiritu admits that "Although the pan-Asian concept may have originated in the minds of non-Asians. . . [Asian Americans] transformed it to conform to their ideological and political needs. . . . Not only did Asian Americans consolidate, but they also politicized, using the very pan-Asian concept imposed from the outside as their political instrument."[137] Seeing the identities of the Asian characters in a panethnic way allows the film to allude to ethnic cultural dynamics.

While Neo represents an Asian hero, the Oracle reflects a womanist point of view, one concerned with the survival of an entire people, male and female, across ethnic lines. Played by African American actresses, the Oracle participates in the survival of humans who are overwhelmingly black and Asian. Womanism sheds light on various ethnic inquiries. Alice

Walker coined the term, which she constructs with several layers. Many scholars have found relevance in the way "womanist" centralizes agency in relation to both ethnicity and gender: "Committed to survival and wholeness of entire people, male *and* female. Not a separatist, except periodically, for health. Traditionally a universalist. . . . Traditionally capable."[138]

While literary and cultural studies scholars frequently cite the term, it receives the most exploration in the realm of feminist theology. Those explorations focus on the agency of women to envision the world through their own experiences. Stacy M. Floyd-Thomas focuses on ethnicity within a female context: "To be a womanist, in turn, is to be a 'Blackwoman—one among the dispossessed, no matter whose house one may work in or visit."[139] Karen Baker-Fletcher describes womanism as "the communal, cultural, activist thought and practice of ordinary black women or women of color in response to socio-historical experiences of slavery, colonization, genocide, apartheid, racism, sexism, classism, heterosexism, and globalization."[140] This female perspective dominates here, but scholars of womanism also look to issues of ethnicity. Pui-Lan Kwok seeks to diversify the voices of women of color, hoping that "womanist scholars would pay closer attention to the struggles of Third World feminists, so that new dialogues and coalition work can flourish. . . . women in the Third World can broaden the scope of womanist analysis, so that it can make concrete connections between racism in the American domestic situation and America's dominance in the world."[141] Difference becomes contextualized by the experiences of women. When Walker coins the term womanism, she describes a person who is "committed to survival and wholeness of entire people, male *and* female. Not a separatist."[142] Floyd-Thomas describes this tenet of Walker's definition as "Black women's ability to create, re-member, nurture, protect, sustain, and liberate communities which are marked and measured not by those outside of one's own community but by the acts of inclusivity, mutuality, reciprocity, and self-care practiced within it (opposite of the biological deterministic assumption that a woman's role is to serve as nurturer and protector)."[143] Valerie Smith alludes to the cross-cultural and intergender potential of this mode of black feminist thought as a way "to refer not only to theory written (or practiced) by black feminists, but also to a way of reading inscriptions of race (particularly but not exclusively blackness), gender (particularly but not exclusively womanhood), and class in modes of cultural expression."[144] The ethnic concerns of black feminism need not be confined to African American experiences. It can be expanded to other ethnic cultures by using black feminism as a lens to "read" other racial experiences. Yet womanist and black feminist scholars do not articulate how womanism is to engage other ethnicities, nor do they present a vision of engaging the men of other ethnic communities.

However, *The Matrix* films broach this largely unexplored territory by centralizing the Oracle as part of an Afro-Asian pairing. Such a reading requires that we view the Oracle as something more than a postmodern mammy. Lisa Nakamura calls the Oracle "a glorified child-care worker" and suggests her acceptance of the traditional role "represents the limits of this multiculturalist fantasy of interhuman democracy."[145] Patricia Hill Collins describes the mammy figure as a major controlling image that represents the idealized black woman as perceived by the white patriarchy "by loving, nurturing, and caring for her white children and 'family' better than her own." No threat to the power structure, she "still knows her place as an obedient servant" who "has accepted her subordination."[146] Child care also figures prominently into Isiah Lavender's assessment, which identifies the Oracle as "a Mammy figure because she keeps a mindful eye on a group of children of varying ethnicities and races," whom "she nurtures in true mammy fashion."[147] Because a zaftig, older black woman lives in a dilapidated urban building reminiscent of contemporary ghettos, taking care of children and engaging in the domestic activity of baking, she becomes linked to the mammy figure. Some critics cite her as evidence of the film's failure to secure a place for updated roles for African American women.

However, the Oracle fails to conform to the mammy stereotype in several key ways. She does not have the quintessential relationship with white womanhood central to the mammy. The mammy figure initially served to define relationships between black and white women in the antebellum era. Patricia Morton writes that both cinematic mammies and their literary counterparts operate as foils for white womanhood, "cast as jolly and warm" and characterized "as huge, tough, and masculinized enough to emphasize the ultrafemininity of the white female stars."[148] Collins adds that "juxtaposed against the image of white women promulgated through the cult of true womanhood, the mammy image as the Other symbolizes the oppositional difference of mind/body and culture/nature thought to distinguish Black women from everyone else." Not limited to the antebellum era, the modern-day mammy "buttresses the racial superiority of white women employers."[149]

Yet, the Oracle's presence does not function in this way in relation to Trinity, the other major white female character. The Oracle is not taking care of her children; she is not cleaning her house. The Oracle does not function as a servant to Trinity. Quite the contrary. Trinity treats the Oracle with awe, and frequently seeks her guidance as an authority figure. Rather than buttressing the white female character, the Oracle subverts the stereotypical mammy by possessing agency. She possesses knowledge that others do not, which grants her a great degree of power. Haslam observes that the Oracle functions as the rebellion's agent "signifyin' on dominant sexist and racist discourse, hiding the rebellion against the white matrix until it is too late."[150] Moreover, the Oracle may be defined more by her interaction with the film's male characters than with the female ones, providing more interaction with the power dynamics in the films. As a powerful program who is the "mother" of the matrix itself, she grapples mostly with the male representatives of power. Her location in the heart of the inner city, distant from centralized locations of power, should not be mistaken for powerlessness. Haslam suggests that the Oracle's "support of Neo in effect shows his lack of power."[151] She may not be the One, but the One needs her, making her more significant than merely someone's chain-smoking, cookie-baking grandma.

The Oracle's interaction with Neo represents a womanist strategy that underscores Afro-Asian solidarity against dominant white forces. In their initial encounter, the Oracle uses womanist misdirection to get Neo to move past his own assumptions. Clearly uncomfortable in her kitchen, Neo initially rejects his role as savior. In contrast, he immediately accepts what Morpheus tells him about being enslaved to the matrix, abandons the world as he knows it, and takes the red pill. Part of his motivation can be traced to his admiration of Morpehus established earlier in the film in the male-dominated world of hacking. Yet, Neo resists the authority of the Oracle, in part because she is a black woman. She relates an equally unbelievable scenario of his identity as the One, but his skeptical demeanor in the form of crossed arms and stiff body language reflects his resistance to anything she has to say.

In response to Neo's resistance, the Oracle employs a version of signifying that plays on her knowledge of Neo's assumptions. A womanist perspective understands the construction of knowledge and the ways that whites, especially males, inform norms. The Oracle's womanist perspective seeks to unpack Neo's unacknowledged assumptions using a form of signification, saying one thing while trying to convince someone of something else. She works with Neo's assumptions about her as a black woman to draw his attention away from belief in her, something he is less comfortable with, to his interaction with Morpheus, something he is more comfortable with. By telling Neo that he "looks like he is waiting for something," she shifts the conversation from Neo's belief to Morpheus's obsession: "Morpheus believes [that you are the One] so blindly that he's going to sacrifice his life to save yours. . . . Neo, you are going to have to make a choice. . . . one of you is going to die."[152] The Oracle shifts the nature of the choice Neo needs to make. Instead of accepting that he is the One, Neo needs to attend to his respect for Morpheus and his desire to assure his safety.

The Oracle also uses womanist strategies to teach Neo about the nature of choice. Even by their second meeting in *Reloaded*, Neo continues to doubt the Oracle. Having realized that she is a program rather than a person, he suspects that she also is designed to control humans. Again, she uses strategies of signifying and his assumptions regarding black women to make him more comfortable with the flux that choice represents. With its subversive motives, womanism seeks to open up possibilities beyond the binaries and relies on uncertainty. It emphasizes ambiguity and options. The Oracle reflects such womanist concepts by meeting Neo's resistance with a choice. She acknowledges his uncertainty by telling him, "there is no way for you to know whether I'm really here to help you or not," and encourages him to make up his "own damn mind."[153] The candy she offers him is a metaphor for choice and the fluidity it represents, a fluidity she accepts. Her view of the world looks forward to change but does not devolve into moral relativism. Idris Samawi Hamid reminds us that "despite being the torch-bearer of choice, she is no nihilist or anarchist. While she subverts order locally, she seeks to preserve order globally."[154] Here, the Oracle seeks to allay Neo's fear of change by having him embrace the results of the choices he makes: "You didn't come here to make a choice, you've already made it. You're here to try to understand why you made it."[155] Neo is afraid because he is uncomfortable with making the choices based on unacknowledged motives. Choice represents the unknown. His decision to sit down next to the Oracle and accept the candy is indicative of his acceptance of the Oracle's more flexible way of thinking.

The Oracle's womanist strategies foster solidarity and encourage Neo to work with her against a larger threat. Womanism utilizes the energies of men and women for the benefit of all. At the playground the Oracle uses plural pronouns like "we," which links her fate to Neo's. She tells him that the only way to get to the future is together, and that "we are all here to do what we are all here to do." She disparages programs that "are doing something they aren't supposed to be doing," interfering with the humans and appearing in "every story you've ever heard about werewolves, vampires, or aliens."[156] She thinks everyone (programs, machines, humans) should coexist. In her kitchen in *Revolutions*, she uses language of commonality, telling Neo, "I want what you want," and suggesting that if they can't find an answer, then "there may be no tomorrow for any of us."[157]

The Oracle deploys solidarity spurred by womanist strategies against dominant white forces. The relationship between the Oracle and Neo represents a coalition between black women and Asian men as a defense against such forces. The Merovingian sows seeds of doubt when he refers to the Oracle as a "fortune teller" and questions Neo's own agency when he follows her directions without question.[158] This posture against any such coalition accounts for the condescension expressed by the Architect for the Oracle. When Neo encounters the Architect, he wastes no time suggesting his relationship with the Oracle is questionable because she is questionable. Neo refers to her by the title Oracle, but the Architect refuses to and describes her as a "lesser mind," despite the fact that it was her solution that made the matrix work.[159]

The Oracle and Neo are also poised together against white dominant power forces represented by Agents like Smith. He represents a rogue whiteness that threatens machines as well as the humans seeking freedom, represented by blacks and Asian actors. He has always possessed the seeds of his own rebellion against the very system he serves. When he captures Morpheus, his monologue belies a frustration with his role within the matrix. Taking off his glasses and removing his earpiece which links him to the other Agents and presumably the information network of the matrix, Smith tells Morpheus his true feelings: "I hate this place. This zoo, this prison, this reality, whatever you want to call it. I can't stand it any longer. . . . I must get out of here. I must get free and in this mind is the key, my key. Once Zion is destroyed there is no need for me to be here. Don't you understand? I need the codes. I have to get inside Zion and you have to tell me how. You're going to tell me or you're going to die."[160] Smith's cool self-satisfied demeanor is replaced by a sense of desperation. The matrix acts as a means of control for him as well, locking him into never-ending pursuit of rebelling humans. In contrast to the dissent of humans, Smith's rebellion focuses on his own needs and desires. The other Agents seem content, but Smith wants to be free.

Reborn, Smith echoes this mantra of freedom when he meets Neo on the urban playground. While he speculates, "perhaps some part of you imprinted on to me, something overwritten or copied," it is more accurate to say that his encounter with Neo provides an opportunity for him to act on his desire to be free: "You destroyed me, Mr. Anderson. Afterward, I knew the rules, I understood what I was supposed to do, but I didn't. I couldn't. I was compelled to stay, compelled to disobey. And now here I stand because of you, Mr. Anderson, because of you I am no longer an agent of the system, because of you I've changed. I'm unplugged."[161] Rather than hiding in the matrix or returning to the Source, Smith multiplies and schemes to take over the matrix. Clearly, he is one of those programs "doing things they are not supposed to be doing." A roving entity not beholden to the system or the humans, Smith constitutes a threat to both: "There is no escaping reason, no denying purpose, because as we both know, without purpose we would not exist. . . . We are here because of you. We are here to take from you what you tried to take from us—purpose."[162] Smith is a threat because he is bent on destruction, a desire that is all the more dangerous because it is propelled by the same dogged determination he uses to hunt down the rebel humans.

Neo and the Oracle, along with other programs of color, challenge Smith's rampant assimilation as a rogue white force. The seeds for such cooperation are subtly foreshadowed in earlier scenes. When the Oracle pronounces that "everything that has a beginning has an end," it seems solely for dramatic effect.[163] When Smith literally assimilates the Oracle, she does little to prevent it. She does not engage him in conversation and does not try to persuade him of the error of his ways. She almost eggs him on by insulting him. By the time of the climatic battle between Neo and Smith, Smith believes he has foreseen this moment: "Wait. I've seen this. This is it, this is the end. You, you were laying right there, just like that and I, I, I stand here, right here. I'm supposed to say something. I say, everything that has a beginning has an end, Neo."[164] Smith does not realize what he has just said. It may be the Oracle rather than Smith speaking. Smith never refers to Neo as Neo in the entire trilogy; he always calls him Mr. Anderson. This is the exact phrase that the Oracle shared with Neo the last time they met. It functions as a signal, a signal for Neo to allow Smith to infect him. By doing so, Neo joins all the other programs that have been assimilated by Smith, including the Oracle. This is the moment where "we" work together, programs and humans, to defeat Smith from the inside. This is the ultimate act of solidarity, a solidarity that destroys rogue whiteness and restores order.

Neo's later interaction with the Oracle constitutes an alternative Afro-Asian dynamic to the ethnic conflict metaphor that emerges from the Los Angeles riots. Dynamics between ethnicities and genders tend to focus on a white/nonwhite binary. Examples include interracial dynamics between black men and white women or black women and white men. Even discussions surrounding the large percentage of outmarriage by Asian groups often focus on unions involving whites. When the focus shifts to gender dynamics between two ethnic groups, it tends to centralize tensions between the two groups. When women of color engage ethnicity in relation to gender, they seek to do so in contrast to the reductive models presented by white feminism and oppressive racial ideologies. Sandra Kumamoto Stanley ascribes a "multiple consciousness" to women of color in the United States, one that "involves a recognition of their hybrid existence—of the ways they are multiply inflected—and a challenge of paradigms based on binary oppositions."[165] However, that hybridity often includes whiteness as one of its terms among women. It rarely includes their male counterparts, and rarely extends beyond the black–white binary. Gender becomes synonymous with women, and oftentimes the work of theorists of women of color focuses on women of color, distinct from men.

Neo and the Oracle's brand of Afro-Asian dynamic challenges the assumptions raised by the metaphor of ethnic conflict in relation to gender. The Los Angeles riots encouraged the view that ethnic groups were antagonistic and beyond reconciliation, and ignored other factors that affected their interaction, including immigration, urban environment, history of race and ethnicity, and mainstream, white America. Recognizing the intra- and interethnic dynamics initially suggested by *The Big Boss*, *The Matrix* trilogy takes an Afro-pan-Asian approach, namely allying Afro-Asian pairings against a larger, more powerful white power structure. The films explore new territory by making the pairings mixed-gender, and using the African American discourse of womanism through which to read the dynamics of this Afro-Asian alliance.

While *The Matrix* trilogy uses an Afro-pan-Asian approach to challenge inter-ethnic conflict, Beatty's *The White Boy Shuffle* uses an Afro-multi-Asian approach. The novel disrupts the homogenizing impulses of ethnic conflict by demonstrating how various Asian cultures can be used to interpret African American experiences, and vice versa. Rescuing

African American culture from a particular brand of insularity, Beatty's novel embodies cultural exchange, recognizing how multiple ethnicities factor into such cross-cultural dynamics. African American despair in the wake of the riots highlights acculturation and changes in interpretations of Asian immigration. This emphasis on interethnic dynamics echoes *The Big Boss*'s focus on the exploits on Chinese immigrants in Thailand.

Notes

CHAPTER 1

1. Blake Bradford et al., "Roundtable Conversation," in *Black Belt*, ed. Christine Y. Kim (New York: Studio Museum of Harlem, 2003), 11.

2. Christine Y. Kim, "Artists," in *Black Belt*, ed. Christine Y. Kim (New York: Studio Museum of Harlem, 2003), 33.

3. Kim, "Artists," 36.

4. *Ibid.*, 42.

5. Bradford et al., "Roundtable Conversation," 13.

6. *Ibid.*, 16.

7. Robert G. Lee, *Orientals: Asian Americans in Popular Culture* (Philadelphia: Temple University Press, 1999), 2, 5.

8. Vijay Prashad, *Everybody Was Kung Fu Fighting: The Myth of Cultural Purity* (Boston: Beacon Press, 2002), 128.

9. Kwai-Cheung Lo, *Chinese Face/Off: The Transnational Popular Culture of Hong Kong* (Urbana and Chicago: University of Illinois Press, 2005), 87.

10. David Bordwell, *Planet Hong Kong: Popular Cinema and the Art of Entertainment* (Cambridge: Harvard University Press, 2000), 50.

11. Lizbieta Foeller-Pituch, "Henry James's Cosmopolitan Spaces: Rome as Global City," *Henry James Review* 24.3 (2003): 292.

12. Jachinson Chan, *Chinese American Masculinities: From Fu Manchu to Bruce Lee* (New York and London: Routledge, 2001), 83.

13. Sucheng Chan, *Asian Americans: An Interpretative History* (New York: Twayne, 1991), 54.

14. Chan, *Chinese American Masculinities*, 76.

15. Stephen Teo, *Hong Kong Cinema: The Extra Dimension* (New York: BFI, 1998), 117.

16. Bordwell, *Planet Hong Kong*, 53.

17. Teo, *Hong Kong Cinema*, 116.

18. *Ibid.*, 116.

19. *Ibid.*

20. *Ibid.*, 110.

21. *Ibid.*

22. *Ibid.*, 114.

23. Bordwell, *Planet Hollywood*, 53.

24. *Ibid.*, 51.

25. Teo, *Hong Kong Cinema*, 13.

26. Farah Griffin, *Who Set You Flowin'? The African-American Migration Narrative* (Oxford: Oxford University Press, 1996), 51.

27. John Hope Franklin and Alfred A. Moss Jr., *From Slavery to Freedom: A History of Negro Americans*, 6th ed. (New York: Alfred A. Knopf, 1988), 420.

28. Harvard Sitkoff, *The Struggle for Black Equality, 1954–1992*, rev. ed. (New York: Hill and Wang, 1994), 188.

29. Stevie Wonder, "Living for the City," *At the Close of a Century* (New York: Motown, 1999), compact disc.

30. David Wilson, *Cities and Race: America's New Black Ghetto* (London and New York: Routledge, 2007), 29.

31. Barney Warf and Brian Holly, "The Rise and Fall of Rise of Cleveland," *Annals of the American Academy of Political and Social Science* 551 (1997): 211.

32. Fred Ho, "Kickin' the White Man's Ass: Black Power, Aesthetics and the Asian Martial Arts," in *AfroAsian Encounters: Culture, History, Politics*, ed. Heike Raphael-Hernandez and Shannon Steen (New York: New York University Press, 2006), 297–98.

33. *Ibid.*, 298.

34. *Ibid.*, 300.

35. Bordwell, *Planet Hong Kong*, 51.

36. Teo, *Hong Kong Cinema*, 116.

37. R. H. Hughes, "Hong Kong-Far Eastern Meeting Point," *Geographical Journal* 129.4 (1963): 450.

38. Irene Taeuber, "Hong Kong: Migrants and Metropolis," *Population Index* 29.1 (1963): 4.

39. *Ibid.*, 17.

40. Siu-lun Wong, "Modernization and Chinese Culture in Hong Kong," *China Quarterly* 106 (1986): 309.

41. Teo, *Hong Kong Cinema*, 111.

42. Lo, *Chinese Face/Off*, 87.

43. Teo, *Hong Kong Cinema*, 88.

44. Bordwell, *Planet Hong Kong*, 52, 53.

45. Gordon Mathews, Eric Kit wai Ma and Tai-lok Lui, *Hong Kong, China: Learning to Belong to a Nation* (London: Routledge, 2008), 32.

46. *Ibid.*, 33.

47. *Ibid.*, 36.

48. Gary McDonogh and Cindy Wong, *Global Hong Kong* (New York: Routledge, 2005), 89.

49. R. H. Hughes, "Hong Kong: An Urban Study," *Geographical Journal* 117.1 (1951): 4.

50. Prashad, *Kung Fu Fighting*, 130–31.

51. William Wei, *The Asian American Movement* (Philadelphia: Temple University Press, 1993), 38–39.

52. *Ibid.*, 42.

53. James Chapman, *Licence to Thrill: A Cultural History of the James Bond Films* (New York: Columbia University Press, 2000), 77.

54. *Goldfinger*, DVD, directed by Guy Hamilton (Los Angeles: MGM, 2007).

55. Simon Winder, *The Man Who Saved Britain: A Personal Journey into the Disturbing World of James Bond* (New York: Farrar, Straus and Giroux, 2006), 152.

56. Lee, *Orientals*, 116.

57. Chapman, *Licence to Thrill*, 102.

58. Lane Crothers, *Globalization and American Popular Culture* (Plymouth: Rowan and Littlefield, 2007), 18.

59. Robin D. G. Kelley, *Yo Mama's Disfunktional!: Fighting the Culture Wars in Urban America* (Boston: Beacon Press, 1997), 7.

60. Lisa Lowe, *Immigrant Acts: On Asian American Cultural Politics* (Durham and London: Duke University Press, 1996), 15–16.

61. David Palumbo-Liu, *Asian/American: Historical Crossings of a Racial Frontier* (Stanford: Stanford University Press, 1999), 268.

62. Crothers, *Globalization*, 5.

63. Katrina Hazzard-Donald, "Dance in Hip Hop Culture," in *Dropping Science: Critical Essays on Rap and Music and Hip Hop Culture*, ed. William Eric Perkins (Philadelphia: Temple University Press, 1996), 228.

64. *Ibid.*, 228.

65. Ian Condry, "A History of Japanese Hip-Hop," in *Global Noise: Rap and Hip-Hop Outside the USA*, ed. Tony Mitchell (Middletown: Wesleyan University Press, 2001), 228.

66. *Ibid.*, 223.

67. *Ibid.*, 222.

68. Mimi Thi Nguyen and Thuy Linh Nguyen, introduction to *Alien Encounters: Popular Culture in Asian America*, ed. Mimi Thi Nguyen and Thuy Linh Nguyen (Durham: Duke University Press, 2007), 28.

69. Lee, *Orientals*, 209, 211.

70. *Ibid.*, 214.

71. Michael Omi and Howard Winant, "Racial Formations," in *Race, Class, Gender: An Integrated Study*, 6th ed., ed. Paula S. Rothberg (New York: Worth, 2001), 22.

72. Lee, *Orientals*, 214, 215.

73. Homi Bhabha, *Location of Culture* (London: Routledge, 1994), 219.

74. *Ibid.*, 317.

75. *Ibid.*, 224.

76. Stuart Hall, "Cultural Identity and Diaspora," in *Everyday Theory: A Contemporary Reader*, ed. Becky McLaughlin and Bob Coleman (New York: Pearson Longman, 2005), 297, 298, 301.

77. Bhabha, *Culture*, 219.

78. *Ibid.*, 26.

79. Inderpal Grewal, *Transnational America: Feminisms, Diasporas, Neoliberalisms* (Durham: Duke University Press, 2005), 36–37.

80. *Ibid.*, 60.

81. *Ibid.*, 28.

82. Prashad, *Kung Fu Fighting*, ix.

83. *Ibid.*, x.

84. *Ibid.*, xii.

85. *Ibid.*, xii.

86. *Ibid.*, 127.

87. Bill Mullen, *Afro-Orientalism* (Minneapolis: University of Minnesota Press, 2004), xvii.

88. *Ibid.*, xxiii.

89. *Ibid.*, xxv.

90. Heike Raphael-Hernandez and Shannon Steen, Introduction, *AfroAsian Encounters: Culture, History, Politics*, ed. Heike Raphael-Hernandez and Shannon Steen (New York: New York University Press, 2006), 8.

CHAPTER 2

1. "Bruce Lee: In His Own Words," *Enter the Dragon*, DVD, directed by Robert Clouse (Los Angeles: Warner Brothers, 1998).

2. *Enter the Dragon*, directed by Robert Clouse (Los Angeles: Warner Brothers, 1998).

3. Jachinson Chan, *Chinese American Masculinities: From Fu Manchu to Bruce Lee* (New York and London: Routledge, 2001), 87, 89.

4. *Enter the Dragon*.

5. *Ibid.*

6. *Ibid.*

7. "Bruce Lee: In His Own Words."

8. Chan, *Chinese American Masculinities*, 77.

9. Richard Majors and Janet Mancini Billson, *Cool Pose: The Dilemmas of Black Manhood in America* (New York: Lexington, 1992), 4.

10. Majors and Billson, *Cool Pose*, 4.

11. "Bruce Lee: In His Own Words."

12. William Wei, *The Asian American Movement* (Philadelphia: Temple University Press, 1993), 48–49.

13. Chan, *Chinese American Masculinities*, 90.

14. Melvin Donalson, *Masculinity in the Interracial Buddy Film* (Jefferson: McFarland, 2006), 9.

15. Frank Chin, *Gunga Din Highway* (Minneapolis: Coffee House Press, 1994), 51.

16. *Ibid.*, 59.

17. *Ibid.*, 55.

18. *Ibid.*, 178.

19. *Ibid.*, 140.

20. Ronald Takaki, *Strangers from a Different Shore* (New York: Penguin, 1990), 85.

21. Sucheng Chan, *Asian Americans: An Interpretative History* (New York: Twayne, 1991), 32.

22. Robert G. Lee, *Orientals: Asian Americans in Popular Culture* (Philadelphia: Temple University Press, 1999), 59.

23. Chin, *Gunga Din Highway*, 116.

24. *Ibid.*, 117–18.

25. *Ibid.*, 116.

26. Ruth Frankenberg, "Local Whitenesses, Localizing Whiteness," in *Displacing Whiteness: Essays in Social and Cultural Criticism*, ed. Ruth Frankenberg (Durham and London: Duke University Press, 1997), 11, 13.

27. *Ibid.*, 12.

28. *Ibid.*, 14.

29. Hazel Carby, introduction to *Race Men: The W. E. B. Du Bois Lectures*, in *African American Literary Theory: A Reader*, ed. Winston Napier (New York: New York University Press, 2000), 660.

30. Chin, *Gunga Din Highway*, 117.

31. *Ibid.*, 284.

32. Sitkoff, *The Struggle for Black Equality*, 195, 202.

33. William Wei, *The Asian American Movement* (Philadelphia: Temple University Press, 1993), 25.

34. *Ibid.*, 42.

35. Chin, *Gunga Din Highway*, 261.

36. *Ibid.*

37. *Ibid.*

38. Luo Guanzhong, *Three Kingdoms*, transl. Moss Roberts (Beijing: Foreign Languages Press, 2007), 11.

39. King-kok Cheung, "Warrior Woman Versus the Chinaman Pacific: Must a Chinese American Critic Choose Between Feminism and Heroism?" in *Asian American Studies: A Reader*, ed. Jean Yu-Wen Shen Wu and Min Song (New Brunswick: Rutgers University Press, 2000), 317.

40. Charles E. Jones and Judson L. Jeffries, "'Don't Believe the Hype': Debunking the Panther Mythology," in *Black Panther Party Reconsidered*, ed. Charles E. Jones (Baltimore: Black Classic Press, 1998), 33.

41. Tracye Matthews, "'No One Ever Asks, What a Man's Role in the Revolution Is': Gender and the Politics of the Black Panther Party, 1966–1971," in *Black Panther Party Reconsidered*, ed. Charles E. Jones (Baltimore: Black Classic Press, 1998), 278.

42. Robin Kelley, *Freedom Dreams: The Black Radical Imagination* (Boston: Beacon Press, 2003), 96.

43. Larry Neal, "The Black Arts Movement," in *Within the Circle: An Anthology of African American Literary Criticism from the Harlem Renaissance to the Present*, ed. Angelyn Mitchell (Durham: Duke University Press, 1994), 184.

44. *Ibid.*, 191.

45. *Ibid.*, 195.

46. Chin, *Gunga Din Highway*, 257.

47. Larry Neal, "Black Writers Role I," in *Visions of a Liberated Future: Black Arts Movement Writings* (New York: Thunder's Mouth Press, 1989), 25.

48. Jiton Sharmayne Davidson, "Sometimes Funny, But Most Times Deadly Serious: Amiri Baraka as Political Satirist," *African American Review* 37 (2003): 403.

49. Frank Chin, "Confessions of a Chinatown Cowboy," *Bulletin of Concerned Asian Scholars* 4 (1972): 64.

50. *Ibid.*, 67.

51. Chin, *Gunga Din Highway*, 258.

52. Lee, *Orientals: Asian Americans in Popular Culture*, 116.

53. Amiri Baraka, "The Revolutionary Theater," in *Home: Social Essays* (New York: William Morrow, 1966), 211.

54. Neal, "Black Arts," 190.

55. Hoyt Fuller, "Toward a Black Aesthetic," in *Within the Circle: An Anthology of African American Literary Criticism from the Harlem Renaissance to the Present*, ed. Angelyn Mitchell (Durham: Duke University Press, 1994), 201–2.

56. Chin, *Gunga Din Highway*, 270.

57. *Ibid.*, 278.

58. Elaine Kim, *Asian American Literature: An Introduction to the Writings and their Social Context* (Philadelphia: Temple University Press, 1982), 187.

59. Patricia Chu, *Assimilating Asians: Gendered Strategies of Authorship in Asian America* (Durham: Duke University Press, 2000), 73.

60. Chin, *Gunga Din Highway*, 119.

61. *Ibid.*, 176–77.

62. *Ibid.*, 172.

63. *Ibid.*, 173.

64. *Ibid.*, 142.

65. *Ibid.*, 179.

66. *Ibid.*, 169.

67. *Ibid.*, 169, 170.

68. *Ibid.*, 304.

69. *Ibid.*, 305.

70. Prashad, *Everybody Was Kung Fu Fighting*, 127.

71. Kelley, *Freedom Dreams*, 93.

72. *Ibid.*, 68.

73. Prashad, *Everybody Was Kung Fu Fighting*, 139.

74. Chin, *Gunga Din Highway*, 75.

75. *Ibid.*, 59.

76. *Ibid.*, 93.

77. *Ibid.*, 93.

78. Frank Chin, "Come All Ye Asian American Writers of the Real and the Fake," in *The Big Aiiieeeee!: An Anthology of Chinese American and Japanese American Literature*, ed. Jefferey Paul Chan et al. (New York: Meridian, 1991), 39.

79. Chin, *Gunga Din Highway*, 92.

80. Lee, *Orientals*, 12.

81. Chin, *Gunga Din Highway*, 7.

82. *Ibid.*, 43–44.

83. Kim, *Asian American Literature*, 18.

84. Laura Uba, *Asian Americans: Personality Patterns, Identity and Mental Health* (New York: Guilford Press, 1994), 92.

85. Chin, *Gunga Din Highway*, 376.

86. *Ibid.*, 54.

87. *Ibid.*, 346.

88. *Ibid.*

89. *Ibid.*

90. Chin, "Come All Ye," 2.

91. *Ibid.*, 3–4.

92. Frank Chin, "A Chinaman Meets His Chinese Critics: Frank Chin Responds to Detractors in Asia," *Kui Xing: The Journal of Asian/Diasporic and Aboriginal Literature* 1.2 (2005): 9.

93. Najia Aarim-Heriot, *Chinese Immigrants, African Americans, and Racial Anxiety in the United States, 1848–82* (Urbana: University of Illinois Press, 2003), 113.

94. Wei, *Asian American Movement*, 50.

95. Frank H. Wu, *Yellow: Race in America Beyond Black and White* (New York: Basic, 2002), 187.

96. Sau-ling Wong, "Denationalization Reconsidered: Asian American Cultural Criticism at a Theoretical Crossroads," *Amerasia* 21.1-2 (1995): 5, 6.

97. David Palumbo-Liu, *Asian/American: Historical Crossings of a Racial Frontier* (Stanford: Stanford University Press, 1999), 310.

98. Prashad, *Everybody Was Kung Fu Fighting*, 132.

99. Donalson, *Masculinity in the Interracial Buddy Film*, 10.

100. *Ibid.*, 9.

101. Michael Kaplan, "New York City Tavern Violence and the Creation of a Working-Class Male Identity," *Journal of the Early Republic* 15.4 (1995): 605.

102. Eric Lott, *Love and Theft: Blackface Minstrelsy and the American Working Class* (New York and Oxford: Oxford University Press, 1995), 49.

103. Donalson, *Masculinity in the Interracial Buddy Film*, 143.

104. Aarim-Heriot, *Chinese Immigrants*, 113.

105. Stephen Teo, *Hong Kong Cinema: The Extra Dimensions* (London: BFI, 1997), 124.

106. Lisa Oldham Stokes and Michael Hoover, *City on Fire: Hong Kong Cinema* (London: Verso, 1999), 115.

107. Jackie Chan (with Jeff Yang), *I Am Jackie Chan: My Life in Action* (New York: Ballantine, 1998), 235.

108. *Rush Hour*, DVD, directed by Brett Ratner (New Line Productions, 2001).

109. Ji Hoon Park, Nadine G. Gabbadon, and Ariel R. Chernin, "Naturalizing Racial Differences Through Comedy: Asian, Black and White Views on Racial Stereotypes in *Rush Hour 2*," *Journal of Communication* 56 (2006): 164.

110. *Rush Hour 2*.

111. Lo, *Chinese Face/Off*, 144.

112. *Rush Hour 2*.

113. Lo, *Chinese Face/Off*, 137.

114. Wu, *Yellow*, 92.

115. Min-Ha T. Pham, "The Asian Invasion (of Multiculturalism) in Hollywood," *Journal of Popular Film and Television* 32.3 (2004): 122.

116. *Rush Hour 2*.

117. Park et al., "Naturalizing Racial Differences," 163.

118. *Rush Hour 2*.

119. Park et al., "Naturalizing Racial Differences," 164.

120. *Ibid.*

121. Claire Conceison, *Significant Other: Staging the American in China* (Honolulu: University of Hawaii Press, 2004), 3.

122. Park et al., "Naturalizing Racial Differences," 164.

123. *Rush Hour 2*.

124. John S. Gregory, *The West and China Since 1500* (New York: Palgrave Macmillan, 2003), 89.

125. Stokes and Hoover, *City on Fire*, 94.

126. "Interview with Director Louis Leterrier," *Unleashed*, DVD, directed by Louis Leterrier (Los Angeles: Universal, 2003).

127. "Serve No Master," *Unleashed*, DVD, directed by Louis Leterrier (Los Angeles: Universal, 2003).

128. Robert L. Irick, *Ch'ing Policy Toward the Coolie Trade, 1847–1878* (Chinese Materials Center, 1982), 5–6.

129. *Ibid.*, 6–7.

130. *Ibid.*, 209.

131. Chan, *Asian Americans*, 48.

132. Resat Kasaba, "Treaties and Friendships: British Imperialism, the Ottoman Empire, and China in the Nineteenth Century," *Journal of World History* 4.2 (1993): 233–34.

133. Christopher Munn, *Anglo-China: Chinese People and British Rule in Hong Kong, 1841–1880* (Hong Kong: Hong Kong University Press, 2009), 66.

134. Kasaba, "Treaties and Friendships," 240.

135. Dong Wang, "The Discourse of Unequal Treaties in Modern China," *Pacific Affairs* 76.3 (2003): 414.

136. *Ibid.*, 408.

137. "Interview with Leterrier."

138. *Unleashed.*

139. *Ibid.*

140. Peter Gries, "Narratives to Live By: The 'Century of Humiliation' and Chinese National Identity Today," paper presented at the annual meeting of the American Political Science Association, Chicago, September 2, 2004), 4, accessed May 26, 2009 www.allacademic.com/meta/p59334_index.html.

141. Franklin and Moss, *From Slavery to Freedom*, 43, 44–45.

142. Ronald Takaki, *A Different Mirror: A History of Multicultural America* (New York: Little, Brown, 1994), 61.

143. Franklin and Moss, *From Slavery to Freedom*, 36.

144. Takaki, *A Different Mirror*, 111.

145. *Ibid.*, 32, 52.

146. "Interview with Leterrier."

147. *Unleashed.*

148. *Ibid.*

149. *Ibid.*

150. *Ibid.*

151. *Ibid.*

CHAPTER 3

1. *Fist of Fury (The Chinese Connection)*, DVD, directed by Lo Wei (Hong Kong: Fortune Star, 1993).

2. Robert Bickers and Jeffrey Wasserstrom, "Shanghai's 'Dogs and Chinese Not Admitted' Sign: Legend, History and Contemporary Symbol," *China Quarterly* 142 (1995): 446.

3. *Ibid.*, 444, 449.

4. Teo, *Hong Kong Cinema*, 115.

5. Ishmael Reed, "Airing Dirty Laundry," in *The Reed Reader*, ed. Ishmael Reed (New York: Basic, 2000), 179.

6. Chin, "Confessions of a Chinatown Cowboy," 64.

7. Bruce Dick, "Ishmael Reed: An Interview," in *Conversations with Ishmael Reed*, ed. Bruce Dick and Amritjit Singh (Jackson: University Press of Mississippi, 1995), 349.

8. John O'Brien, "Ishmael Reed," in *Conversations with Ishmael Reed*, ed. Bruce Dick and Amritjit Singh (Jackson: University Press of Mississippi, 1995), 23.

9. Amritjit Singh and Bruce Dick, Introduction, *Conversations with Ishmael Reed*, ed. Bruce Dick and Amritjit Singh (Jackson: University Press of Mississippi, 1995), xii.

10. Sharon Jessee, "Ishmael Reed's Multi-Culture: The Production of Cultural Perspective," *MELUS* 13.3/4 (1986): 5.

11. Ishmael Reed, *The Free-lance Pallbearers* (Normal: Dalkey Archive, 1967), 8.

12. *Ibid.*, 155.

13. Ishmael Reed, *The Terrible Twos* (New York: Atheneum, 1988), 9.

14. Kan Ito, "Trans-Pacific Anger," *Foreign Policy* 78 (1990): 135.

15. Robert Eliot Fox, *Conscientious Sorcerers: The Black Postmodernist Fiction of LeRoi Jones/Amiri Baraka, Ishmael Reed and Samuel R. Delany* (New York: Greenwood Press, 1987), 6.

16. Chester J. Fontenot, "Ishmael Reed and the Politics of Aesthetics, or Shake Hands and Come Out Conjuring," *Black American Literature Forum* 12.1 (1978): 20.

17. Ishmael Reed, *Japanese by Spring* (New York: Penguin, 1993), 83.

18. *Ibid.*, 48–49.

19. *Ibid.*, 10.

20. *Ibid.*

21. *Ibid.*, 17.

22. *Ibid.*, 112.

23. *Ibid.*, 14.

24. *Ibid.*, 4.

25. *Ibid.*, 18.

26. *Ibid.*, 21.

27. Kenneth Womack, "Campus Xenophobia and the Multicultural Project: Ethical Criticism and Ishmael Reed's *Japanese By Spring*," *MELUS* 26.4 (2001): 232.

28. Reed, *Japanese by Spring*, 47, 49.

29. Quoted in Takaki, *Strangers from a Different Shore*, 387.

30. Herbert Norman, "The Genyosha: A Study in the Origins of Japanese Imperialism," *Pacific Affairs* 17.3 (1944): 267.

31. Marc Gallicchio, *The African American Encounter with Japan and China: Black Internationalism in Asia, 1895–1945* (Chapel Hill: University of North Carolina Press, 2000), 96.

32. Reed, *Japanese by Spring*, 178.

33. *Ibid.*, 40.

34. *Ibid.*, 62-63.

35. *Ibid.*, 121.

36. *Ibid.*, 62.

37. *Ibid.*

38. Reginald Kearney, *African American Views of the Japanese: Solidarity or Sedition?* (Albany: State University of New York Press, 1998), 72.

39. Gallicchio, *African American Encounter*, 71.

40. Kearney, *African American Views*, 74.

41. *Ibid.*, 75.

42. *Ibid.*, 77.

43. *Ibid.*, 42.

44. *Ibid.*, 16.

45. *Ibid.*, 19.

46. Reed, *Japanese by Spring*, 63.

47. *Ibid.*, 158.

48. Wu, *Yellow*, 58.

49. Vijay Prashad, *The Karma of Brown Folk* (Minneapolis: University of Minnesota Press, 2000), 6–7.

50. Reed, *Japanese by Spring*, 85.

51. *Ibid.*, 89.

52. *Ibid.*, 90.

53. *Ibid.*, 143.

54. *Ibid.*, 96.

55. *Ibid.*, 99.

56. *Ibid.*

57. *Ibid.*, 106.

58. *Ibid.*, 107.

59. *Ibid.*, 108.

60. *Ibid.*, 208.

61. *Ibid.*, 176–77.

62. Norman, "The Genyosha," 266.

63. *Ibid.*, 278.

64. Reed, *Japanese by Spring*, 103.

65. *Ibid.*, 135.

66. Hilary Conroy, "Lessons from Japanese Imperialism," *Monumenta Nipponica* 21.3/4 (1966): 344–45.

67. Norman, "The Genyosha," 278, 281.

68. Reed, *Japanese by Spring*, 104.

69. *Ibid.*, 138, 139.

70. *Ibid.*, 147.

71. *Ibid.*, 148.

72. Kearney, *African American Views*, 10.

73. *Ibid.*, 95.

74. *Ibid.*, 95.

75. Gallicchio, *African American Encounter*, 103–4.

76. *Ibid.*, 103.

77. *Ibid.*, 105.

78. *Samurai Champloo Roman*, trans. by Matthew Johnson (Milwaukie: Dark Horse Manga, 2006), 48.

79. Susan J. Napier, *Anime from Akira to Princess Mononoke: Experiencing Contemporary Japanese Animation* (New York: Palgrave, 2001), 6–7.

80. *Ibid.*, 21.

81. *Ibid.*, xii.

82. *Ibid.*, 22–23.

83. *Ibid.*, 27.

84. *Ibid.*, 135.

85. "Tempestuous Temperaments," *Samurai Champloo.*

86. *Ibid.*

87. *Samurai Champloo Roman*, 43.

88. L. M. Cullen, *A History of Japan, 1582–1941: Internal and External Worlds* (Cambridge: Cambridge University Press, 2003), 1, 7–8.

89. Katsuhisa Moriya, "Urban Networks and Information Networks," in *Tokugawa Japan: The Social and Economic Antecedents of Modern Japan*, ed. Chie Nakane and Shinzaburo Oishi (Tokyo: University of Tokyo Press, 1992), 102.

90. *Samurai Champloo Roman*, 86.

91. "Stranger Searching," *Samurai Champloo.*

92. Shinzaburo Oishi, "The Bakuhan System," in *Tokugawa Japan*, 26.

93. Oishi, "The Bakuhan System," 26.

94. "Baseball Blues," *Samurai Champloo.*

95. *Ibid.*

96. Cullen, *A History of Japan*, 178.

97. Gilles Poitras, *Anime Essentials: Everything a Fan Needs to Know* (Berkeley: Stone Bridge Press, 2000), 60.

98. *Ibid.*, 36.

99. *Samurai Champloo Roman*, 86.

100. Imani Perry, *Prophets of the Hood: Politics and Poetics in Hip-hop* (Durham: Duke University Press, 2004), 130.

101. Eric K. Watts, "An Exploration of Spectacular Consumption: Gangsta Rap as Cultural Commodity," in *That's the Joint: The Hip-Hop Studies Reader*, ed. Murray Forman and Mark Anthony Neal (New York: Routledge, 2004), 603.

102. "Hellhounds for Hire, Parts 1 and 2," *Samurai Champloo.*

103. Watts, "Spectacular Consumption," 604.

104. *Samurai Champloo Roman*, 78.

105. "Hellhounds for Hire," *Samurai Champloo.*

106. Andrea D. Barnwell, "Guilty (Blackfaced) Pleasures," in *iona rozeal brown: a3 . . . black on both sides*, ed. Andrea D. Barnwell (Atlanta: Spelman College Museum of Fine Art, 2004), 11.

107. Dick Hebdige, "Rap and Hip-Hop: The New York Connection," in *That's the Joint: The Hip-Hop Studies Reader*, 224.

108. Robert Farris Thompson, "Hip Hop 101", in *Dropping Science*, 215.

109. *Samurai Champloo Roman*, 43.

110. *Ibid.*

111. Hebdidge, "Rap and Hip Hop," 226.

112. "War of the Words," *Samurai Champloo*.

113. *Ibid.*

114. *Ibid.*

115. *Ibid.*

116. *Samurai Champloo Roman*, 1.

117. *Ibid.*, 44.

118. *Samurai Champloo Roman*, 2.

119. Sandy Kita, "From Shadow to Substance: Redefining Ukiyo-e," in *The Floating World of Ukiyo-e: Shadows, Dreams and Substance*, ed. Stanley Kita et al. (New York: Harry N. Abrams, 2001), 18, 19.

120. Alain Silver, *The Samurai Film* (Woodstock: Overlook Press, 2005), 16.

121. Kita, "Shadow to Substance," 18, 19.

122. Silver, *The Samurai Film*, 17.

123. *Samurai Champloo Roman*, 4.

124. David L. Howell, *Geographies of Identity in Nineteenth-Century Japan* (Berkeley: University of California Press, 2005), 133.

125. *Samurai Champloo Roman*, 45.

126. "Misguided Miscreants," *Samurai Champloo*.

127. "Tempestuous Temperaments," *Samurai Champloo*.

128. Silver, *The Samurai Film*, 16.

129. *Ibid.*, 13, 14.

130. *Ibid.*, 14.

131. Howell, *Geographies of Identity*, 57.

132. Chie Nakane, "Tokugawa Society," in *Tokugawa Japan: The Social and Economic Antecedents of Modern Japan*, 213–14.

133. Silver, *The Samurai Film*, 18.

134. *Ibid.*, 19.

135. *Ibid.*

136. "Disorder Diaries," *Samurai Champloo*.

137. Silver, *The Samurai Film*, 17.

138. *Ibid.*, 18.

139. "Tempestuous Temperaments," *Samurai Champloo*.

140. *Samurai Champloo Roman*, 2.

141. *Ibid.*

142. Sharon Kinsella, "Japanese Subculture in the 1990s: Otaku and the Amateur Manga Movement," *Journal of Japanese Studies* 24.2 (1998): 291.

143. *Ibid.*, 293.

144. *Samurai Champloo Roman*, 2.

145. *Ibid.*, 43.

CHAPTER 4

1. *The Big Boss*, DVD, directed by Lo Wei (Hong Kong: Fortune Star, 1993).

2. *Ibid.*

3. Teo, *Hong Kong Cinema*, 115.

4. Nancy Abelmann and John Lie, *Blue Dreams: Korean Americans and the Los Angeles Riots* (Cambridge: Harvard University Press, 1995), 149.

5. *Ibid.*, 152.

6. *Ibid.*, 7.

7. *Ibid.*, 158.

8. *Ibid.*, 150.

9. Eric Murphy Selinger, "Trash, Art, and Performance Poetry," *Parnassus: Poetry in Review* 23.2 (1998).

10. Paul Beatty, *Joker Joker Deuce* (New York: Penguin, 1994), 3–4.

11. *Ibid.*, 19.

12. Paul Beatty, *The White Boy Shuffle* (New York: Henry Holt, 1996).

13. *Ibid.*, 35.

14. *Ibid.*, 63.

15. *Ibid.*, 5.

16. *Ibid.*, 53.

17. *Ibid.*, 67.

18. Mark Anthony Neal, *Soul Babies: Black Popular Culture and the Post-Soul Aesthetic* (New York: Routledge, 2002), 140.

19. Beatty, *The White Boy Shuffle*, 35–36.

20. *Ibid.*, 37.

21. *Ibid.*, 153.

22. *Ibid.*, 155.

23. *Ibid.*, 79.

24. Shifu Nagaboshi Tomio, *The Bodhisattva Warriors: The Origin, Inner Philosophy, History and Symbolism of the Buddhist Martial Art within India and China* (York Beach: Samuel Weiser, 1994), 113.

25. Ming-Dao Deng, *Scholar Warrior: An Introduction to the Tao in Everyday Life* (San Francisco: Harper Collins, 1990), 14.

26. Beatty, *The White Boy Shuffle*, 5.

27. Kim, *Asian American Literature*, 18.

28. Chan, *Asian Americans*, 122–23.

29. *Ibid.*, 125.

30. Wu, *Yellow*, 98.

31. Takaki, *Strangers from a Different Shore*, 396.

32. Beatty, *The White Boy Shuffle*, 129.

33. *Ibid.*, 132.

34. Patricia Morton, *Disfigured Images: The Historical Assault on Afro-American Women* (Westport: Praeger, 1991), 3.

35. *Ibid.*, 4.

36. Vera Paster, "The Psychosocial Development and Coping of Black Male Adolescents," in *The American Black Male: His Present Status and Future*, ed. Richard C. Majors and Jacob U. Gordon (Chicago: Nelson-Hall, 1994), 222.

37. Clyde W. Franklin II, "Men's Studies, the Men's Movement, and the Study of Black Masculinities," in *The American Black Male: His Present Status and Future*, 13.

38. Abelmann and Lie, 165.

39. Beatty, *The White Boy Shuffle*, 21.

40. *Ibid.*, 22.

41. Prashad, *Everybody Was Kung Fu Fighting*, 130.

42. Beatty, *The White Boy Shuffle*, 22.

43. *Ibid.*, 137.

44. *Ibid.*, 21.

45. *Ibid.*, 114.

46. Donald Shively, *The Love Suicide at Amijima: A Study of a Japanese Domestic Tragedy*, ed. Donald Shively (Ann Arbor: Center for Japanese Studies, University of Michigan, 1991), 17.

47. *Ibid.*, 26–27.

48. *Ibid.*, 28.

49. Beatty, *The White Boy Shuffle*, 118–19.

50. *Ibid.*, 192.

51. *Ibid.*, 193.

52. *Ibid.*, 194.

53. Monzaemon Chikamatsu, "Love Suicide at Sonezaki," *Major Plays of Chikamatsu*, ed. Donald Keene (New York: Columbia University Press, 1961), 206.

54. *Ibid.*, 53.

55. Donald Keene, Introduction, *Major Plays of Chikamatsu*, 16.

56. Beatty, *The White Boy Shuffle*, 130.

57. *Ibid.*, 143.

58. *Ibid.*, 145–46.

59. *Ibid.*, 147.

60. *Ibid.*, 148.

61. Yukiko Koshiro, *Trans-Pacific Racisms and the U.S. Occupation of Japan* (New York: Columbia University Press, 1999), 16–17.

62. Roy Starrs, *Deadly Dialectics: Sex, Violence and Nihilism in the World of Yukio Mishima* (Honolulu: University of Hawaii Press, 1994), 161.

63. Shuichi Kato, *A History of Japanese Literature*, transl. Don Sanderson (Tokyo: Kodansha International, 1979), 289.

64. Starrs, *Deadly Dialectics*, 156.

65. *Ibid.*, 41.

66. *Ibid.*, 46.

67. John Nathan, *Mishima: A Biography* (Boston: Little, Brown, 1974), 189.

68. Beatty, *The White Boy Shuffle*, 200.

69. *Ibid.*, 202.

70. Sitkoff, *The Struggle for Black Equality*, 220.

71. Bakari Kitwana, *The Hip Hop Generation: Young Blacks and the Crisis of African American Culture* (New York: Basic, 2002), 23.

72. Cornel West, *Race Matters* (Boston: Beacon Press, 2001), 14–16.

73. Kitwana, *The Hip Hop Generation*, 14.

74. Neal, *Soul Babies*, 3.

75. Kitwana, *The Hip Hop Generation*, 13.

76. *Ibid.*, 148–49.

77. Beatty, *The White Boy Shuffle*, 118–19.

78. *Ibid.*, 119.

79. Kitwana, *The Hip Hop Generation*, 148.

80. Beatty, *The White Boy Shuffle*, 177.

81. *Ibid.*, 178.

82. *Ibid.*, 177, 178.

83. *Ibid.*, 187.

84. *Ibid.*, 186.

85. Angela Y. Davis, "Gender, Class and Multiculturalism: Rethinking 'Race' Politics," in *Mapping Multiculturalism*, ed. Avery F. Gordon and Christopher Newfield (Minneapolis: University of Minnesota Press, 1996), 45, 46.

86. Neal, *Soul Babies*, 177–78.

87. Beatty, *The White Boy Shuffle*, 183.

88. *Ibid.*

89. *Ibid.*, 185.

90. Neal, *Soul Babies*, 179, 180.

91. Beatty, *The White Boy Shuffle*, 2.

92. Abelmann and Lie, *Blue Dreams*, 9.

93. *Ibid.*, 177.

94. "Success Story of One Minority Group in U.S.," *U.S. News and World Report* (1966), in *Asian American Studies: A Reader*, ed. Jean Yu-wen Shen Wu and Min Song (New Brunswick: Rutgers University Press, 2000), 158.

95. *Ibid.*, 160.

96. John Higham, *Strangers in the Land: Patterns of Nativism, 1860–1925* (New Brunswick: Rutgers University Press, 1992), 247.

97. Beatty, *The White Boy Shuffle*, 28.

98. *Ibid.*, 29.

99. Christopher Newfield and Avery Gordon, "Multiculturalism's Unfinished Business," in *Mapping Multiculturalism*, ed. Christopher Newfield and Avery Gordon (Minneapolis: University of Minnesota Press, 1996), 91.

100. Beatty, *The White Boy Shuffle*, 30.

101. *Ibid.*, 30.

102. Wu, *Yellow*, 67.

103. *Ibid.*, 95.

104. Newfield and Gordon, "Multiculturalism's Unfinished Business," 80, 87.

105. Edward T. Chang, "Jewish and Korean Merchants in African American Neighborhoods: A Comparative Perspective," in *Los Angeles—Struggles toward Multiethnic Community: Asian American, African American and Latino Perspectives*, ed. Edward T. Chang and Russell C. Leong (Seattle: University of Washington Press, 1994), 11.

106. *Ibid.*

107. Beatty, *The White Boy Shuffle*, 99.

108. *Ibid.*

109. *Ibid.*, 106.

110. *Ibid.*, 133.

111. *Ibid.*, 165.

112. *Ibid.*, 166.

113. *Ibid.*, 170.

114. *Ibid.*, 167.

115. *Ibid.*, 211.

116. Daniel Leonard Bernardi, *Star Trek and History: Race-ing Toward a White Future* (New Brunswick: Rutgers University Press, 1998), 79.

117. Paul Gilroy, *The Black Atlantic: Modernity and Double Consciousness* (Cambridge: Harvard University Press, 1993), 44.

118. De Witt Douglas Kilgore, *Astrofuturism: Science, Race and Visions of Utopia in Space* (Philadelphia: University of Pennsylvania Press, 2003), 3.

119. Avery F. Gordon and Christopher Newfield, Introduction, *Mapping Multiculturalism*, 1–16.

120. Gordon and Newfield, "Multiculturalism's Unfinished Business," 91.

121. Bernardi, *Star Trek*, 34–35.

122. *Ibid.*, 35.

123. Eric Greene, *Planet of the Apes as American Myth: Race and Politics in the Films and Television Series* (Jefferson: McFarland, 1996), 32.

124. *Ibid.*, 5.

125. Ron Eglash, "Race, Sex and Nerds: From Black Geeks to Asian-American Hipsters," *Social Text* 20 (2): 52.

126. C. Richard King and David Leonard, "Is Neo White? Reading Race, Watching the *Matrix* Trilogy," in *Jacking in to the Matrix Franchise: Cultural Reception and*

Interpretation, ed. Matthew Kapell and William G. Doty (New York: Continuum, 2004), 36.

127. "Final Flight of the Osiris," *The Animatrix*, DVD, directed by Andy Jones (Burbank: Warner Brothers, 2004).

128. Andy Jones, "Documentary," *The Animatrix*. DVD, directed by Andy Jones (Burbank: Warner Brothers, 2004).

129. King and Leonard, "Is Neo White?" 44.

130. *The Matrix Reloaded*, DVD, directed by the Wachowski Brothers (Burbank: Warner Brothers, 2004).

131. *The Matrix*, DVD, directed by the Wachowski Brothers (Burbank: Warner Brothers, 2004).

132. Peter X Feng, "False Double Consciousness: Race, Virtual Reality and the Assimilation of Hong Kong Action Cinema in *The Matrix*," in *Aliens R Us: The Other in Science Fiction Cinema*, ed. Ziauddin Sardar and Sean Cubitt (London: Pluto Press, 2002), 155.

133. Quoted in Lisa Nakamura, *Cybertypes: Race Ethnicity and Identity on the Internet* (New York: Routledge, 2002).

134. *Ibid.*, 66.

135. Jason Haslam, "Coded Discourse: Romancing the (Electronic) Shadow in *The Matrix*," *College Literature* 32.3 (2005): 99.

136. *The Matrix*.

137. Yen Le Espiritu, *Asian American Panethnicity: Bridging Institutions and Identities* (Philadelphia: Temple University Press, 1992), 162.

138. Alice Walker, "Definition of Womanist," in *Making Face, Making Soul/ Haciendo Caras: Creative and Critical Perspectives by Feminists of Color*, ed. Gloria Anzaldùa (San Francisco: Aunt Lute, 1990), 370.

139. Stacy M. Floyd-Thomas, Introduction, *Deeper Shades of Purple: Womanism in Religion and Society*, ed. Stacey M. Floyd-Thomas (New York: New York University Press, 2006), 6.

140. Karen Baker-Fletcher, "A Womanist Journey," in *Deeper Shades of Purple: Womanism in Religion and Society*, 162.

141. Pui-Lan Kwok, "Womanist Visions, Womanist Spirit: An Asian Feminist's Response," in *Deeper Shades of Purple: Womanism in Religion and Society*, 257–58.

142. Walker, "Womanism," 370.

143. Floyd-Thomas, Introduction, 78.

144. Valerie Smith, "Black Feminist Theory and the Representation of the 'Other,'" in *African American Literary Theory: A Reader*, ed. Winston Napier (New York: New York University Press, 2000), 370.

145. Nakamura, *Cybertypes*, 82.

146. Patricia Hill Collins, *Black Feminist Thought: Knowledge, Consciousness and the Politics of Empowerment* (New York: Routledge, 1991), 71.

147. Isiah Lavender III, "Technicity: AI and Cyborg Ethnicity in *The Matrix*," *Extrapolation* 45.4 (2004): 446.

148. Morton, *Disfigured Images*, 7.

149. *Ibid.*, 72.

150. Haslam, "Coded Discourse," 104.

151. *Ibid.*, 103.

152. *The Matrix*.

153. *The Matrix Reloaded*.

154. Idris Samawi Hamid, "The Cosmological Journey of Neo: An Islamic Matrix," in *More Matrix and Philosophy: Revolutions and Reloaded Decoded*, ed. William Irwin (Chicago: Open Court, 2005), 143.

155. *The Matrix Reloaded*.

156. *Ibid.*

157. *The Matrix Revolutions*.

158. *The Matrix Reloaded*.

159. *Ibid.*

160. *The Matrix*.

161. *The Matrix Reloaded*.

162. *Ibid.*

163. *The Matrix Revolutions*.

164. *Ibid.*

165. Sandra Kumamoto Stanley, Introduction, *Other Sisterhoods: Literary Theory and U.S. Women of Color*, ed. Sandra Kumamoto Stanley (Urbana: University of Illinois Press, 1998), 5.

Bibliography

Aarim-Heriot, Najia. *Chinese Immigrants, African Americans, and Racial Anxiety in the United States, 1848–82*. Urbana: University of Illinois Press, 2003.

Abelmann, Nancy, and John Lie. *Blue Dreams: Korean Americans and the Los Angeles Riots*. Cambridge: Harvard University Press, 1995.

The Animatrix. DVD. Burbank: Warner Brothers, 2004.

Baker-Fletcher, Karen. "A Womanist Journey." In *Deeper Shades of Purple: Womanism in Religion and Society*, ed. Stacey M. Floyd-Thomas, 158–75. New York: New York University Press, 2006.

Baraka, Amiri. "The Revolutionary Theater." In *Home: Social Essays*. New York: William Morrow, 1966.

Barnwell, Andrea D. "Guilty (Blackfaced) Pleasures." *iona rozeal brown: a3 . . . black on both sides*, edited by Andrea D. Barnwell, 10–25. Atlanta: Spelman College Museum of Fine Art, 2004.

"Baseball Blues." *Samurai Champloo*. 6 vols. DVD. Directed by Shinichiro Watanabe. NP: Geneon Entertainment, 2004.

Beatty, Paul. *Joker Joker Deuce*. New York: Penguin, 1994.

———. *The White Boy Shuffle*. New York: Henry Holt and Co., 1996.

Bernardi, Daniel Leonard. *Star Trek and History: Race-ing Toward a White Future*. New Brunswick: Rutgers University Press, 1998.

Bhabha, Homi. *Location of Culture*. London: Routledge, 1994.

Bickers, Robert, and Jeffrey Wasserstrom. "Shanghai's 'Dogs and Chinese Not Admitted' Sign: Legend, History and Contemporary Symbol." *China Quarterly* 142 (1995): 444–66.

The Big Boss. DVD. Directed by Lo Wei. Hong Kong: Fortune Star, 1993.

Bordwell, David. *Planet Hong Kong: Popular Cinema and the Art of Entertainment*. Cambridge: Harvard University Press, 2000.

Bradford, Blake, Deborah Grant, Glenn Kaino, Peter Kang, Christine Y. Kim, and Dominic Molon. "Roundtable Conversation." In *Black Belt*, ed. Christine Y. Kim, 11–26. New York: Studio Museum of Harlem, 2003.

"Bruce Lee: In His Own Words." *Enter the Dragon*. DVD. Directed by Robert Clouse. Los Angeles: Warner Brother, 1998.

Carby, Hazel. Introduction to *Race Men: The W. E. B. Du Bois Lectures*. In *African American Literary Theory: A Reader*, ed. Winston Napier, 660–64. New York: New York University Press, 2000.

Chan, Jackie, with Jeff Yang. *I Am Jackie Chan: My Life in Action*. New York: Ballantine, 1998.

Chan, Jachinson. *Chinese American Masculinities: From Fu Manchu to Bruce Lee*. New York and London: Routledge, 2001.

Chan, Sucheng. *Asian Americans: An Interpretative History*. New York: Twayne, 1991.

Chang, Edward T. "Jewish and Korean Merchants in African American Neighborhoods: A Comparative Perspective." In *Los Angeles—Struggles toward Multiethnic Community: Asian American, African American and Latino Perspectives*, ed. Edward T. Chang and Russell C. Leong, 5–21. Seattle: University of Washington Press, 1994.

Chapman, James. *Licence to Thrill: A Cultural History of the James Bond Films*. New York: Columbia University Press, 2000.

Cheung, King-kok. "Warrior Woman Versus the Chinaman Pacific: Must a Chinese American Critic Choose Between Feminism and Heroism?" In *Asian American Studies: A Reader*, ed. Jean Yu-Wen Shen Wu and Min Song, 307–23. New Brunswick: Rutgers University Press, 2000.

Chikamatsu, Monzaemon. "Love Suicide at Sonezaki." In *Major Plays of Chikamatsu*, ed. Donald Keene, 39–56. New York: Columbia University Press, 1961.

Chin, Frank. "A Chinaman Meets His Chinese Critics: Frank Chin Responds to Detractors in Asia." *Kui Xing: The Journal of Asian/Diasporic and Aboriginal Literature* 1.2 (2005): 1–32.

———. "Come All Ye Asian American Writers of the Real and the Fake." In *The Big Aiiieeeee!: An Anthology of Chinese American and Japanese American Literature*, ed. Jefferey Paul Chan, Frank Chin, Lawson Fusao Inada, and Shawn Wong, 1–92. New York: Meridian, 1991.

———. "Confessions of a Chinatown Cowboy." *Bulletin of Concerned Asian Scholars* 4 (1972): 58–70.

———. *Gunga Din Highway*. Minneapolis: Coffee House Press, 1994.

Chu, Patricia. *Assimilating Asians: Gendered Strategies of Authorship in Asian America*. Durham: Duke University Press, 2000.

Collins, Patricia Hill. *Black Feminist Thought: Knowledge, Consciousness and the Politics of Empowerment*. New York: Routledge, 1991.

Conceison, Claire. *Significant Other: Staging the American in China*. Honolulu: University of Hawaii Press, 2004.

Condry, Ian. "A History of Japanese Hip Hop." In *Global Noise: Rap and Hip-Hop Outside the USA*, ed. Tony Mitchell, 222–47. Middletown: Wesleyan University Press, 2001.

Conroy, Hilary. "Lessons from Japanese Imperialism." *Monumenta Nipponica* 21.3/4 (1966): 334–45.

Crothers, Lane. *Globalization and American Popular Culture*. Plymouth: Rowan and Littlefield, 2007.

Cullen, L. M. *A History of Japan, 1582–1941: Internal and External Worlds*. Cambridge: Cambridge University Press, 2003.

Davidson, Jiton Sharmayne. "Sometimes Funny, But Most Times Deadly Serious: Amiri Baraka as Political Satirist." *African American Review* 37 (2003): 399–405.

Davis, Angela Y. "Gender, Class and Multiculturalism: Rethinking 'Race' Politics." In *Mapping Multiculturalism*, ed. Avery F. Gordon and Christopher Newfield, 40–48. Minneapolis: University of Minnesota Press, 1996.

Deng, Ming-Dao. *Scholar Warrior: An Introduction to the Tao in Everyday Life*. San Francisco: Harper Collins, 1990.

Dick, Bruce. "Ishmael Reed: An Interview." In *Conversations with Ishmael Reed*, ed. Bruce Dick and Amritjit Singh, 344–56. Jackson: University Press of Mississippi, 1995.

"Disorder Diaries." *Samurai Champloo*. 6 vols. DVD. Directed by Shinichiro Watanabe. Geneon Entertainment, 2004.

Donalson, Melvin. *Masculinity in the Interracial Buddy Film*. Jefferson: McFarland, 2006.

Eglash, Ron. "Race, Sex and Nerds: From Black Geeks to Asian-American Hipsters." *Social Text* 20 (2): 49–64.

Enter the Dragon. DVD. Directed by Robert Clouse. Los Angeles: Warner Brothers, 1998.

Espiritu Yen Le. *Asian American Panethnicity: Bridging Institutions and Identities*. Philadelphia: Temple University Press, 1992.

Feng, Peter X. "False Double Consciousness: Race, Virtual Reality and the Assimilation of Hong Kong Action Cinema in *The Matrix*." In *Aliens R Us: The Other in Science Fiction Cinema*, ed. Ziauddin Sardar and Sean Cubitt, 149–63. London: Pluto Press, 2002.

"Final Flight of the Osiris." *The Animatrix*. DVD. Directed by Andy Jones. Burbank: Warner Brothers, 2004.

Fist of Fury (The Chinese Connection). DVD. Directed by Lo Wei. Hong Kong: Fortune Star, 1993.

Floyd-Thomas, Stacy M. Introduction to *Deeper Shades of Purple: Womanism in Religion and Society*, ed. Stacey M. Floyd-Thomas, 1–14. New York: New York University Press, 2006.

Foeller-Pituch, Lizbieta. "Henry James's Cosmopolitan Spaces: Rome as Global City." *Henry James Review* 24.3 (2003): 291–97.

Fontenot, Chester J. "Ishmael Reed and the Politics of Aesthetics, or Shake Hands and Come Out Conjuring." *Black American Literature Forum* 12.1 (1978): 20–23.

Fox, Robert Eliot. *Conscientious Sorcerers: The Black Postmodernist Fiction of LeRoi Jones/Amiri Baraka, Ishmael Reed and Samuel R. Delany*. New York: Greenwood Press, 1987.

Franklin, John Hope, and Alfred A. Moss Jr. *From Slavery to Freedom: A History of Negro Americans*. 6th ed. New York: Alfred A. Knopf, 1988.

Franklin II, Clyde W. "Men's Studies, the Men's Movement, and the Study of Black Masculinities." In *The American Black Male: His Present Status and Future*, ed. Richard C. Majors and Jacob U. Gordon, 3–20. Chicago: Nelson-Hall, 1994.

Frankenberg, Ruth. "Local Whitenesses, Localizing Whiteness." In *Displacing Whiteness: Essays in Social and Cultural Criticism*, ed. Ruth Frankenberg, 1–33. Durham and London: Duke University Press, 1997.

Fuller, Hoyt. "Towards a Black Aesthetic." In *Within the Circle: An Anthology of African American Literary Criticism from the Harlem Renaissance to the Present*, ed. Angelyn Mitchell, 199–206. Durham: Duke University Press, 1994.

Gallicchio, Marc. *The African American Encounter with Japan and China: Black Internationalism in Asia, 1895–1945*. Chapel Hill: University of North Carolina Press, 2000.

Gilroy, Paul. *The Black Atlantic: Modernity and Double Consciousness*. Cambridge: Harvard University Press, 1993.

Goldfinger. DVD. Directed by Guy Hamilton. Los Angeles. MGM. 2007.

Gordon, Avery, and Christopher Newfield. Introduction to *Mapping Multiculturalism*, ed. Avery Gordon and Christopher Newfield, 1–16. Minneapolis: University of Minnesota Press, 1997.

Greene, Eric. *Planet of the Apes as American Myth: Race and Politics in the Films and Television Series*. Jefferson: McFarland, 1996.

Gregory, John S. *The West and China Since 1500*. New York: Palgrave Macmillan, 2003.

Grewal, Inderpal. *Transnational America: Feminisms, Diasporas, Neoliberalisms*. Durham: Duke University Press, 2005.

Gries, Peter. "Narratives to Live By: The 'Century of Humiliation' and Chinese National Identity Today." Presented at the annual meeting of the American Political Science Association, Chicago, September 2, 2004. Accessed May 26, 2009. www.allacademic.com/meta/p59334_index.html.

Griffin, Farah. *Who Set You Flowin'? The African-American Migration Narrative*. Oxford: Oxford University Press, 1996.

Guanzhong, Luo. *Three Kingdoms*. Transl. Moss Roberts. Beijing: Foreign Language Press, 2007.

Hall, Stuart. "Cultural Identity and Diaspora." In *Everyday Theory: A Contemporary Reader*, ed. Becky McLaughlin and Bob Coleman, 295–306. New York: Pearson Longman, 2005.

Hamid, Idris Samwai. "The Cosmological Journey of Neo: An Islamic Matrix." In *More Matrix and Philosophy: Revolutions and Reloaded Decoded*, ed. William Irwin, 136–53. Chicago: Open Court, 2005.

Haslam, Jason. "Coded Discourse: Romancing the (Electronic) Shadow in *The Matrix*." *College Literature* 32.3 (2005): 92–115.

Hazzard-Donald, Katrina. "Dance in Hip Hop Culture." In *Dropping Science: Critical Essays on Rap and Music and Hip Hop Culture*, ed. William Eric Perkins, 220–35. Philadelphia: Temple University Press, 1996.

Hebdige, Dick. "Rap and Hip-Hop: The New York Connection." In *That's the Joint: The Hip-Hop Studies Reader*, ed. Murray Forman and Mark Anthony Neal, 223–32. New York: Routledge, 2004.

"Hellhounds for Hire, Parts 1 and 2." *Samurai Champloo*. 6 vols. DVD. Directed by Shinichiro Watanabe. NP: Geneon Entertainment, 2004.

Higham, John. *Strangers in the Land: Patterns of Nativism, 1860–1925*. New Brunswick: Rutgers University Press, 1992.

Ho, Fred. "Kickin' the White Man's Ass: Black Power, Aesthetics and the Asian Martial Arts." In *AfroAsian Encounters: Culture, Politics, History*, ed. Heike Raphael-Hernandez and Shannon Steen, 295–312. New York: New York University Press, 2006.

Howell, David L. *Geographies of Identity in Nineteenth-Century Japan*. Berkeley: University of California Press, 2005.

Hughes, R. H. "Hong Kong: An Urban Study." *Geographical Journal* 117.1 (1951): 1–23.

———. "Hong Kong-Far East Meeting Point." *Geographical Journal* 129.4 (1963): 450–62.

"Interview with Director Louis Leterrier." *Unleashed*. DVD. Directed by Louis Leterrier. Los Angeles: Universal, 2003.

Irick, Robert L. *Ch'ing Policy Toward the Coolie Trade, 1847–1878*. Chinese Materials Center, 1982.

Ito, Kan. "Trans-Pacific Anger." *Foreign Policy* 78 (1990): 131–52.

Jessee, Sharon. "Ishmael Reed's Multi-Culture: The Production of Cultural Perspective." *MELUS* 13.3/4 (1986): 5–14.

Jones, Andy. "Documentary." *The Animatrix*. DVD. Directed by Andy Jones. Burbank: Warner Brothers, 2004.

Jones, Charles E., and Judson L. Jeffries. "'Don't Believe the Hype': Debunking the Panther Mythology." In *Black Panther Party Reconsidered*, ed. Charles E. Jones, 25–55. Baltimore: Black Classic Press, 1998.

Kaplan, Michael. "New York City Tavern Violence and the Creation of a Working-Class Male Identity." *Journal of the Early Republic* 15.4 (1995): 591–617.

Kasaba, Resat. "Treaties and Friendships: British Imperialism, the Ottoman Empire, and China in the Nineteenth Century." *Journal of World History* 4.2 (1993): 215–44.

Kato, Shuichi. *A History of Japanese Literature*. Transl. Don Sanderson. Tokyo: Kodansha International, 1979.

Kearney, Reginald. *African American Views of the Japanese: Solidarity or Sedition?* Albany: State University of New York Press, 1998.

Keene, Donald. Introduction to *Major Plays of Chikamatsu*, ed. Donald Keene, 1–38. New York: Columbia University Press, 1961.

Kelley, Robin D. G. *Freedom Dreams: The Black Radical Imagination*. Boston: Beacon Press, 2003.

———. *Yo' Mama's Disfunktional!: Fighting the Culture Wars in Urban America*. Boston: Beacon Press, 1997.

Kilgore, De Witt Douglas. *Astrofuturism: Science, Race and Visions of Utopia in Space*. Philadelphia: University of Pennsylvania Press, 2003.

Kim, Christine Y. "Artists." In *Black Belt*, ed. Christine Y. Kim, 28–67. New York: Studio Museum of Harlem, 2003.

Kim, Elaine. *Asian American Literature: An Introduction to the Writings and their Social Context*. Philadelphia: Temple University Press, 1982.

King, C. Richard, and David Leonard. "Is Neo White? Reading Race, Watching the *Matrix* Trilogy." In *Jacking in to the Matrix Franchise: Cultural Reception and Interpretation*, ed. Matthew Kapell and William G. Doty, 32–47. New York: Continuum, 2004.

Kinsella, Sharon. "Japanese Subculture in the 1990s: Otaku and the Amateur Manga Movement." *Journal of Japanese Studies* 24.2 (1998): 289–316.

Kita, Stanley. "From Shadow to Substance: Redefining Ukiyo-e." *The Floating World of Ukiyo-e: Shadows, Dreams and Substance*, ed. Stanley Kita, Lawrence E. Marceau, Katherine L. Blood, and James Douglas Farquhar, 27–80. New York: Harry N. Abrams, 2001.

Kitwana, Bakari. *The Hip Hop Generation: Young Blacks and the Crisis of African American Culture*. New York: Basic, 2002.

Koshiro, Yukiko. *Trans-Pacific Racisms and the U.S. Occupation of Japan*. New York: Columbia University Press, 1999.

Kwok, Pui-Lan. "Womanist Visions, Womanist Spirit: An Asian Feminist's Response." In *Deeper Shades of Purple: Womanism in Religion and Society*, ed. Stacey M. Floyd-Thomas, 252–59. New York: New York University Press, 2006.

Lavender III, Isiah. "Technicity: AI and Cyborg Ethnicity in *The Matrix*." *Extrapolation* 45.4 (2004): 437–79.

Lee, Robert G. *Orientals: Asian Americans in Popular Culture*. Philadelphia: Temple University Press, 1999.

Lo, Kwai-Cheung. *Chinese Face/Off: The Transnational Popular Culture of Hong Kong*. Urbana and Chicago: University of Illinois Press, 2005.

Lott, Eric. *Love and Theft: Blackface Minstrelsy and the American Working Class*. New York and Oxford: Oxford University Press, 1995.

Lowe, Lisa. *Immigrant Acts: On Asian American Cultural Politics*. Durham and London: Duke University Press, 1996.

Luo, Guanzhong. *Three Kingdoms*. Transl. by Moss Roberts. Beijing: Foreign Language Press, 2007.

The Matrix. DVD. Directed by the Wachowski Brothers. Burbank: Warner Brothers, 2004.

The Matrix Reloaded. DVD. Directed by the Wachowski Brothers. Burbank: Warner Brothers, 2004.

The Matrix Revolutions. DVD. Directed by the Wachowski Brothers. Burbank: Warner Brothers, 2004.

Majors, Richard, and Janet Mancini Billson. *Cool Pose: The Dilemmas of Black Manhood in America*. New York: Lexington, 1992.

Mathews, Gordon, Eric Kit Wai Ma, and Tai-Lok Lui. *Hong Kong, China: Learning to Belong to a Nation*. London: Routledge, 2008.

Matthews, Tracye. "'No One Ever Asks, What a Man's Role in the Revolution Is': Gender and the Politics of the Black Panther Party, 1966–1971." In *Black Panther Party Reconsidered*, ed. Charles E. Jones, 267–304. Baltimore: Black Classic Press, 1998.

McDonogh, Gary, and Cindy Wong. *Global Hong Kong*. New York: Routledge, 2005.

"Misguided Miscreants." *Samurai Champloo*. 6 vols. DVD. Directed by Shinichiro Watanabe. Geneon Entertainment, 2004.

Moriya, Katsuhisa. "Urban Networks and Information Networks." In *Tokugawa Japan: The Social and Economic Antecedents of Modern Japan*, ed. Chie Nakane and Shinzabur Oishi, 97–123. Tokyo: University of Tokyo Press, 1992.

Morton, Patricia. *Disfigured Images: The Historical Assault on Afro-American Women*. Westport: Praeger, 1991.

Mullen, Bill. *Orientalism*. Minneapolis: University of Minnesota Press, 2004.

Munn, Christopher. *Anglo-China: Chinese People and British Rule in Hong Kong, 1841–1880*. Hong Kong: Hong Kong University Press, 2009.

Nakamura, Lisa. *Cybertypes: Race Ethnicity and Identity on the Internet*. New York: Routledge, 2002.

Nakane, Chie. "Tokugawa Society." In *Tokugawa Japan: The Social and Economic Antecedents of Modern Japan*, ed. Chie Nakane and Shinzaburo Oishi, 213–31. Tokyo: University of Tokyo Press, 1992.

Napier, Susan J. *Anime from Akira to Princess Mononoke: Experiencing Contemporary Japanese Animation*. New York: Palgrave, 2001.

Nathan, John. *Mishima: A Biography*. Boston: Little, Brown, 1974.

Neal, Larry. "The Black Arts Movement." In *Within the Circle: An Anthology of African American Literary Criticism from the Harlem Renaissance to the Present*, ed. Angelyn Mitchell, 184–98. Durham: Duke University Press, 1994.

———. "Black Writers Role I." In *Visions of a Liberated Future: Black Arts Movement Writings*. New York: Thunder's Mouth Press, 1989.

Neal, Mark Anthony. *Soul Babies: Black Popular Culture and the Post-Soul Aesthetic*. New York: Routledge, 2002.

Newfield, Christopher, and Avery Gordon. "Multiculturalism's Unfinished Business." In *Mapping Multiculturalism*, ed. Christopher Newfield and Avery Gordon, 76–115. Minneapolis: University of Minnesota Press, 1996.

Norman, E. Herbert. "The Genyosha: A Study in the Origins of Japanese Imperialism." *Pacific Affairs* 17.3 (1944): 261–84.

Nguyen, Mimi Thi, and Thuy Linh Nguyen. Introduction to *Alien Encounters: Popular Culture in Asian America*, ed. Mimi Thi Nguyen and Thuy Linh Nguyen, 1–32. Durham: Duke University Press, 2007.

O'Brien, John. "Ishmael Reed." In *Conversations with Ishmael Reed*, ed. Bruce Dick and Amritjit Singh, 14–24. Jackson: University Press of Mississippi, 1995.

Oishi, Shinzaburo. "The Bakuhan System." In *Tokugawa Japan: The Social and Economic Antecedents of Modern Japan*, ed. Chie Nakane and Shinzaburo Oishi, 11–36. Tokyo: University of Tokyo Press, 1992.

Omi, Michael, and Howard Winant. "Racial Formations." In *Race, Class, Gender: An Integrated Study*, 6th ed., ed. Paula S. Rothberg, 13–22. New York: Worth Publishers, 2001.

Osumare, Halifu. "Global Hip-Hop and the African Diaspora." In *Black Cultural Traffic: Crossroads in Global Performance and Popular Culture*, ed. Harry J. Elam Jr. and Kennell Jackson. Ann Arbor: University of Michigan Press, 2005.

Palumbo-Liu, David. *Asian/American: Historical Crossings of a Racial Frontier*. Stanford: Stanford University Press, 1999.

Park, Ji Hoon, Nadine G. Gabbadon, and Ariel R. Chernin. "Naturalizing Racial Differences Through Comedy: Asian, Black and White Views on Racial Stereotypes in *Rush Hour 2*." *Journal of Communication* 56 (2006): 157–77.

Paster, Vera. "The Psychosocial Development and Coping of Black Male Adolescents." *The American Black Male: His Present Status and Future*, ed. Richard C. Majors and Jacob U. Gordon, 215–29. Chicago: Nelson-Hall, 1994.

Perry, Imani. *Prophets of the Hood: Politics and Poetics in Hip Hop*. Durham: Duke University Press, 2004.

Pham, Min-Ha T. "The Asian Invasion (of Multiculturalism) in Hollywood." *Journal of Popular Film and Television* 32.3 (2004): 121–31.

Poitras, Gilles. *Anime Essentials: Everything a Fan Needs to Know*. Berkeley: Stone Bridge Press, 2000.

Prashad, Vijay. *Everybody Was Kung Fu Fighting: The Myth of Cultural Purity*. Boston: Beacon Press, 2002.

——. *The Karma of Brown Folk*. Minneapolis: University of Minnesota Press, 2000.

Raphael-Hernandez, Heike, and Shannon Steen. Introduction to *AfroAsian Encounters: Culture, History, Politics*, ed. Heike Raphael-Hernandez and Shannon Steen, 1–14. New York: New York University Press, 2006.

Reed, Ishmael. "Airing Dirty Laundry." In *The Reed Reader*, ed. Ishmael Reed, 179–202. New York: Basic, 2000.

——. *The Free-lance Pallbearers*. Normal: Dalkey Archive, 1967.

——. *Japanese by Spring*. New York: Penguin, 1993.

——. *The Terrible Twos*. New York: Atheneum, 1988.

Rising Sun. DVD. Directed by Philip Kaufman. Los Angeles: Twentieth Century-Fox, 2002.

Rush Hour 2. DVD. Directed by Brett Ratner. New Line Productions, 2001.

Samurai Champloo. 6 vols. DVD. Directed by Shinichiro Watanabe. Geneon Entertainment, 2004.

Samurai Champloo Roman. Transl. Matthew Johnson. Milwaukie: Dark Horse Manga, 2006.

Selinger, Eric Murphy. "Trash, Art, and Performance Poetry." *Parnassus: Poetry in Review* 23.2 (1998).

"Serve No Master." *Unleashed*. DVD. Directed by Louis Leterrier. Los Angeles: Universal, 2003.

Shively, Donald. *The Love Suicide at Amijima: A Study of a Japanese Domestic Tragedy*, ed. Donald Shively. Ann Arbor: Center for Japanese Studies, University of Michigan, 1991.

Silver, Alain. *The Samurai Film*. Woodstock: Overlook Press, 2005.

Singh, Amritjit, and Bruce Dick. Introduction to *Conversations with Ishmael Reed*, ed. Bruce Dick and Amritjit Singh, ix–xx. Jackson: University Press of Mississippi, 1995.

Sitkoff, Harvard. *The Struggle for Black Equality, 1954–1992*. Rev. ed. New York: Hill and Wang, 1994.

Smith, Valerie. "Black Feminist Theory and the Representation of the 'Other.'" In *African American Literary Theory: A Reader*, ed. Winston Napier, 369–84. New York: New York University Press, 2000.

Stanley, Sandra Kumamoto. Introduction to *Other Sisterhoods: Literary Theory and U.S. Women of Color*, ed. Sandra Kumamoto Stanley, 1–21. Urbana: University of Illinois Press, 1998.

Starrs, Roy. *Deadly Dialectics: Sex, Violence and Nihilism in the World of Yukio Mishima*. Honolulu: University of Hawaii Press, 1994.

Stokes, Lisa Oldham, and Michael Hoover. *City on Fire: Hong Kong Cinema*. London: Verso, 1999.

"Stranger Searching." *Samurai Champloo*. 6 vols. DVD. Directed by Shinichiro Watanabe. Geneon Entertainment, 2004.

"Success Story of One Minority Group in U.S." *U.S. News and World Report* (1966). In *Asian American Studies: A Reader*, ed. Jean Yu-wen Shen Wu and Min Song, 158–63. New Brunswick: Rutgers University Press, 2000.

"Tempestuous Temperaments." *Samurai Champloo*. 6 vols. DVD. Directed by Shinichiro Watanabe. Geneon Entertainment, 2004.

Taeuber, Irene. "Hong Kong: Migrants and Metropolis." *Population Index* 29.1 (1963): 3–25.

Takaki, Ronald. *A Different Mirror: A History of Multicultural America*. New York: Little, Brown, 1994.

———. *Strangers from a Different Shore*. New York: Penguin, 1990.

Teo, Stephen. *Hong Kong Cinema: The Extra Dimension*. New York: BFI, 1998.

Thompson, Robert Farris. "Hip Hop 101." In *Dropping Science: Critical Essays on Rap Music and Hip Hop Culture*, ed. William Eric Perkins, 211–19. Philadelphia: Temple University Press, 1996.

Tomio, Shifu Nagaboshi. *The Bodhisattva Warriors: The Origin, Inner Philosophy, History and Symbolism of the Buddhist Martial Art within India and China*. York Beach: Samuel Weiser, 1994.

Uba, Laura. *Asian Americans: Personality Patterns, Identity and Mental Health*. New York: Guilford Press, 1994.

Walker, Alice. "Definition of Womanist." In *Making Face, Making Soul/Haciendo Caras: Creative and Critical Perspectives by Feminists of Color*, ed. Gloria Anzaldùa, 370. San Francisco: Aunt Lute, 1990.

Wang, Dong. "The Discourse of Unequal Treaties in Modern China." *Pacific Affairs* 76.3 (2003): 399–425.

"War of the Words." *Samurai Champloo*. 6 vols. DVD. Directed by Shinichiro Watanabe. Geneon Entertainment, 2004.

Way of the Dragon (Return of the Dragon). DVD. Directed by Bruce Lee. Hong Kong: Fortune Star, 1993.

Warf, Barney, and Brian Holly. "The Rise and Fall and Rise of Cleveland." *Annals of the American Academy of Political and Social Science* 55.1 (1997): 208–21.

Watts, Eric K. "An Exploration of Spectacular Consumption: Gangsta Rap as Cultural Commodity." In *That's the Joint: The Hip-Hop Studies Reader*, ed. Murray Forman and Mark Anthony Neal, 593–609. New York: Routledge, 2004.

Wei, William. *The Asian American Movement*. Philadelphia: Temple University Press, 1993.

West, Cornel. *Race Matters*. Boston: Beacon Press, 2001.

Wilson, David. *Cities and Race: America's New Black Ghetto*. London and New York: Routledge, 2007.

Winder, Simon. *The Man Who Saved Britain: A Personal Journey into the Disturbing World of James Bond*. New York: Farrar, Straus and Giroux, 2006.

Womack, Kenneth. "Campus Xenophobia and the Multicultural Project: Ethical Criticism and Ishmael Reed's *Japanese By Spring*." *MELUS* 26.4 (2001): 223–44.

Wonder, Stevie. "Living for the City." *At the Close of the Century*. CD. New York: Motown Record Company, 1999.

Wong, Sau-ling. "Denationalization Reconsidered: Asian American Cultural Criticism at a Theoretical Crossroads." *Amerasia* 21.1-2 (1995): 1–27.

Wong, Siu-lun. "Modernization and Chinese Culture in Hong Kong." *China Quarterly* 106 (1986): 306–25.

Wu, Frank H. *Yellow: Race in America Beyond Black and White*. New York: Basic, 2002.

Index

CPSIA information can be obtained at www.ICGtesting.com
Printed in the USA
LVOW08*2253110714

394008LV00006B/23/P